D0948441

ḤURBAN

RESPONSES TO CATASTROPHE
IN HEBREW LITERATURE

ḤURBAN

RESPONSES TO CATASTROPHE
IN HEBREW LITERATURE

ALAN MINTZ

COLUMBIA UNIVERSITY PRESS
NEW YORK
1984

Columbia University Press gratefully acknowledges the following sources for permission to reprint materials for this book:

Sandor Klein and Colman Klein for A. M. Klein's translation of Ch. N. Bialik's "In the City of Slaughter,"

The Jewish Publication Society of America for translations by Stephen Mitchell of poems by Dan Pagis in *Points of Departure,* copyright © The Jewish Publication Society of America, 1982: "Autobiography," "The Roll Call," "Testimony," and "Instructions for Crossing the Border,"

Penguin Books Ltd. for "The Sacrifices" (David bar Meshullam of Speyer) and "At the Rim of the Heavens" (Uri Zvi Greenberg) from *The Penguin Book of Hebrew Verse,* edited and translated by T. Carmi (Allen Lane 1981), copyright © T. Carmi, 1981.

LIBRARY OF CONGRESS CATALOGING IN PUBLICATION DATA

Mintz, Alan L.
Ḥurban: responses to catastrophe in Hebrew
literature.

Bibliography: p.
Includes index.
1. Hebrew literature—History and criticism.
2. Jews—Persecutions.   3. Holocaust, Jewish
(1939–1945), in literature.   4. Bible. O.T.
Lamentations—Criticism, interpetation, etc.
5. Piyutim—History and criticism.   6. Holocaust
survivors in literature.   I. Title
PJ5012.H65M5   1984   892.4'09'358   83-23979
ISBN 0-231-05634-6 (alk. paper)

Columbia University Press
New York   Guildford, Surrey
Copyright © 1984 Columbia University Press
All rights reserved

Printed in the United States of America

Clothbound editions of Columbia University Press books
are Smyth-sewn and printed on permanent and
durable acid-free paper

Book Design by Ken Venezio

To the memory of
my teacher

HARRY (ZVI) PLICH
(1893–1982)

CONTENTS

PREFACE

The impetus for this study was a dissatisfaction with the conception in literary studies of Holocaust literature as a distinct genre or body of works existing in several languages and characterized by a common set of techniques and concerns. Imaginative literature in Hebrew and Yiddish did not seem well illumined by this autonomous, horizontal classification; as works of art, they owed more to a vertical axis of literary tradition, which extended back to the Middle Ages and the Bible. The importance of this vertical axis strongly suggested that the Holocaust, like any historical event, has no "meaning" of its own to divulge. Its meaning, instead of being a discoverable essence, depends upon the interpretive traditions of the community or culture seeking that meaning. I therefore endeavored to take the Holocaust literature of one interpretive community, Israeli culture and Hebrew literature, and read it against the background of its traditions: the goal was to investigate the interplay of catastrophic contemporary events upon longstanding literary traditions.

In the course of the study, background became foreground. The pre-Holocaust literature of catastrophe in Hebrew proved to be so rich and elaborate that it claimed equal footing with the contem-

porary materials. Jewish society is unique in this respect. It has had
many massive national catastrophes visited upon it and still survived; and in each case the reconstruction was undertaken in significant measure by the exertions of the Hebrew literary imagination, as expressed in prophecy, liturgy, exegesis, and poetry. It
is the story of the transcendence of catastrophe rather than of the
catastrophe itself which is compelling. Indeed, Salo W. Baron is
right to deride the "lachrymose view of Jewish history," which
presents Jewish civilization as a series of persecutions, expulsions,
and martyrdoms. This intense interest in how Jews have died, the
passion of the Jews, as it were, is surely one of the forces behind
the preoccupation with Holocaust literature. In this study the emphasis is not on destruction but on creative survival. In fact, the
definition of catastrophe in these pages does not relate directly to
the quantum of pain and suffering caused by historical events. The
catastrophic element in events is defined as the power to shatter
the existing paradigms of meaning, especially as regards the bonds
between God and the people of Israel. Crucial to creative survival
was the reconstruction of these paradigms through interpretation,
and in this enterprise the literary imagination was paramount.

In choosing what to include and exclude from a vast body of
literature ranging over many periods I have been governed by a
principle of discontinuity. I have concentrated on the points of
pressure in the tradition. These moments of paradigm shift are
embodied in texts which cannot easily accommodate the received
explanations and must mobilize new means to recover meaning.
History and literature sometimes come out at odds in this scheme.
The Ukraine massacres of 1648, for example, had a far greater
material and political impact on Jewry than the Crusade massacres of 1096; however, at the level of the literary-iconographic
imagination, 1096 established a set of strong, unprecedent norms
which were not challenged by the later, more terrible disaster.

The dynamics of literary history is the justification for a rather
large exclusion: medieval Sepharad. Maimonides' epistle on the
Almohade persecutions and, later, Abravanel's messianism, Ibn
Verga's historical consolations, and other responses to the Spanish
Expulsion are all germane to the question of catastrophe. I have

left these writers out in part because they open onto large and separate fields of inquiry in which the documents are less narrowly literary than others in this study. The main reason has to do with issues of continuity and discontinuity. In contrast to the radical departure embodied in the Ashkenazic piyyutim, the Sephardic writings represent accentuations of tendencies explicit already within the earlier rabbinic paradigm of explanation. Conversely, from the retrospective vantage point of modern Hebrew literature, it was the vivid images of martyrdom on the Ashkenazic model which summed up the past to be espoused or rejected. The traditions of consolation in Sepharad were picked up more conspicuously in the historiography and philosophy of the modern period—Krochmal, for example—than in its belles lettres.

The arrangement of the sections of this book represent a conception of how these norm-setting moments can be organized. The three chapters of part one examine distinct stages in the formation of a premodern tradition in Bible, midrash, and the separate literary spheres of Ashkenaz and Sepharad. Part two deals with the responses in the new secular Hebrew literature to the pogroms of 1881–1882 and 1903–1905. The introduction and three chapters of part three treat the problematic place of the Holocaust in Israeli literature and give special attention to the works of Uri Zvi Greenberg and Aharon Appelfeld.

Several other considerations guided the selection of materials. To begin with, this is not a study of the problem of evil in literature. Collective, national catastrophe is the subject and not the plight of the individual. Theodicy enters only in its historical dimension. A central criterion has been a narrow construction of what qualifies as literature of catastrophe altogether. Included have been only those texts which make explicit reference to specific historical events. So, for example, Lurianic Kabbalah, whose doctrine of primal catastrophe is speculatively linked by many to the Spanish Expulsion, is excluded from discussion because the link, if it exists, remains rendered in mythic terms only. On an even larger scale, one may well take the theology of Deuteronomy and its traditions as an anticipatory explanation for catastrophe, or the consolidation of Pharisaic Judaism after the Second Destruction as an explanatory system after the fact. These developments are undoubtedly embroiled in the question of catastrophe, and they naturally become the background to the discussion of specific texts, but to take them on their own terms would mean to write a full-scale history of Judaism rather than the more focused inquiry at hand.

Finally, this is a study of *Hebrew* literature. In reconstructing the classical tradition, I have stayed close to the texts that an educated Jew would have been familiar with from earlier periods, and these were limited by and large to Hebrew texts, with the exception of Aramaic. While a historical study of Late Antiquity would make central use of Josephus and the postbiblical apocalypticists, because they wrote in Greek they were unread by the Rabbis and by their medieval successors, and thus they do not form a link in the vertical tradition. Josephus' now-familiar account of the suicides of Massada, for example, was not known in its original form until the Renaissance. Similarly, the case of Usque's beautiful *Consolaçam as Tribulocuens di Israel* (1553), whose Portuguese could be read only by Jewish refugees for a generation or two after their banishment from Iberia. Even in the case of such Hebrew documents as the Crusade chronicles, I have concentrated on the liturgical poems rather than the chronicles because they were much more widely disseminated in the tradition.

In the modern period I have excluded Yiddish literature. My sole concern has been the point of view of the literary culture of the Yishuv and the state of Israel. Because this was a bystander community which had rejected European Jewish life and adhered exclusively to the Hebrew language, its problematic stands alone. Yiddish literature is no less important and its works are no less interesting, but they are different. I am sanguine about this exclusion because the story will be told elsewhere. The coordinated work of my colleague David G. Roskies stresses the role of Yiddish texts in his own approach to the literature of destruction. I hope that together our work will form a comprehensive introduction to the problem.

ACKNOWLEDGMENTS

A volume which covers so much ground incurs many debts. The courage to undertake the journey was provided by my colleagues Paula Hyman and Arnold Eisen and the spirit of intellectual adventure at Columbia, where the project was begun; the encouragement to bring the work to completion was warmly supplied by my new colleagues at the University of Maryland. Many friends labored to save me from egregious embarrassment when writing about areas of their specialties: Edward Greenstein, Yehoshua Gitay, George Savran, Adele Berlin, Shaye Cohen, Ivan Marcus, David Ruderman, Michael Stanislawski, Shira Wolosky, and Jacqueline Gutwirth. Barry Holtz and David Stern read each of the chapters and provided a flow of invaluable criticisms and suggestions. David Roskies, a close associate working on similar materials, showed a perfect balance of sharing and tact. I am particularly grateful to Chaim Henoch for help in understanding the issues underlying the writing. Arnold Band was always available for guidance; Robert Alter made suggestions that significantly affected the final shape of the book.

Valuable time for writing during the summer was made possible by grants from Columbia's Council for Research in the Humanities and the General Research Board of the University of Maryland. Without a year's leave in 1980–1981 provided by a senior fellowship of the American Council of Learned Societies the work could never have been done. I am further grateful to *PROOFTEXTS: A Journal of Jewish Literary History* and the *Association for Jewish Studies Review* for permission to reprint articles which appear here as portions of chapters 1 and 4, respectively.

Finally, I extend my thanks to the staffs of the library of the Jewish Theological Seminary of America and the National and University Library of Jerusalem, and especially to my friends at the Hebraic Section of the Library of Congress, whose kindness is without end.

HURBAN

RESPONSES TO CATASTROPHE
IN HEBREW LITERATURE

THE LITERARY HISTORY

OF CATASTROPHE

 The responses to catastrophe in Hebrew literature form part of a larger question: to what degree is the new Hebrew literature that arose in the nineteenth and twentieth centuries continuous or discontinuous with the millennia of Hebrew writing that preceded it? How does Hebrew literature generate, embody, and mediate the dynamics of tradition and modernity in Jewish society? Regarding the modern period, the question has been posed with polemical brilliance, though not answered, in the works of Baruch Kurzweil. There is room and warrant for extending the question backward as well, that is, for probing the question of continuity not just in the relationship between the modern and the classical but *within* the classical tradition, in the tensions and displacements among its many periods and genres. The response to catastrophe is a specific problem which, sadly, is present in several phases of the tradition as well as in the modern period, and it draws upon a particular set of resources from within the larger repertoire of the literature. Beyond its intrinsic thematic interest, then, the study of responses to catastrophe is a test case for exploring this larger issue in the history of Hebrew literature.

The particular set of critical issues relating to catastrophe derives from the effort to reconstruct paradigms of explanation in the aftermath of national destruction. Catastrophe in Jewish tradition is best understood not in terms of physical and material devastation; a destructive event becomes a catastrophe when it convulses or vitiates shared assumptions about the destiny of the Jewish people in the world. In premodern times this means specifically the terms of the covenant between God and Israel. The responses to catastrophe in Hebrew literature involve attempts first to represent the catastrophe and then to reconstruct, replace, or redraw the threatened paradigm of meaning, and thereby make creative survival possible. In this undertaking there is a set of critical issues that recurs with different solutions and in different configurations: (1) the distance in time between the catastrophic event and the response to it; (2) the relationship of the writer to the event: survivor, bystander-witness, or descendent; (3) the reflexive focus of the writer on his own ordeal in writing about the catastrophe, and thus the balance of attention between his drama and the event itself; (4) the role of figurative language in representing this subject, especially metaphor, analogy, and parable; (5) attitudes to the enemy: the presence or absence of the enemy in the text as a function of the catastrophe's being understood as an internal Jewish drama or an antagonism with the gentile world; (6) the resort to forms of personhood, such as personification and individual vignette, as a means of representing the collective nature of national catastrophe; (7) the image of the world lost in the catastrophe and how its valence changes before and after the event; and (8) the burden or opportunity presented by the texts of the past in the accumulating traditions of catastrophe.

The play of these factors in the literature of selected periods and authors forms the subject of the individual studies in this volume. Before beginning this undertaking, and the distinctions and qualifications appropriate to the study of each body of texts in its own terms, it will be useful to step back and survey the canvas as a whole. The following overview endeavors to abstract some of the principles of continuity and discontinuity immanent in the individual analyses, with the purpose of putting the relationship between old and new into sharp relief. These pages are introductory in intent, yet because they refer to concepts developed later on, some readers may find profit in using this section as a summary conclusion.

The Deuteronomic traditions, refined by the classical prophets in anticipation of a national catastrophe, established a basic paradigm of explanation at whose core was the covenant between God and Israel. Destruction, according to the covenant, is a sign neither of God's abandonment of Israel and the cancellation of His obligations to the people, nor of God's eclipse by competing powers in the cosmos. The Destruction is to be taken, rather, as a deserved and necessary punishment for sin, a punishment whose magnitude is in proportion to the transgressions committed. As a chastisement, the Destruction becomes an expression of God's continuing concern for Israel, since the suffering of the Destruction expiates the sins that provoked it and allows a penitent remnant to survive in a rehabilitated and restored relationship with God. In the drama of Israel's downfall, the enemy plays the role of merely an instrument of God's purpose which has been chosen for its own iniquities and which will be destroyed as soon as it has served its function.

Written in the immediate aftermath of the fall of Jerusalem in 587, the Book of Lamentations reveals that, despite this theological preparation, the trauma to the covenantal paradigm caused by the Destruction was massive. While professing allegiance to the conditional terms of the covenant, the poets of Lamentations represent traditions more popular in nature than classical prophecy: the belief that no matter how much Israel should be found wanting, the Temple Sanctuary and the Davidic monarchy would remain inviolable. The awareness of sin in Lamentations is therefore secondary to the experience of abandonment and the horror of destruction. The first task of the poets of Lamentations is to find adequate language for the horror. They employ two principal strategies. Individual dramatic figures are deployed in order to make the mass, collective situation of the people graspable and affecting. First there is a female figure, Fair Zion, used to emblemize the experience of victimization, and then a male figure, who is used to represent the struggle for theological reconciliation. The second strategy is the employment of the rhetorical arrangements of dramatic speech (person and point of view, especially) to reflect the traumatized and alienated relations of the covenant. The very enterprise of writing about catastrophe is put in jeopardy when the poet-witness to the Destruction sustains a breakdown; he despairs of his capacity to console the victims through the use of language. At issue is the possibility of fashioning adequate metaphors for the catastrophe, that is, metaphors which, in comparing the calamity to familiar things, serve to mitigate that which is most frightening in the Destruction: its unprecedentedness and its incomensurability. Alleviation of the pain comes only when, by asserting a willed recollection of past truths, the sufferer makes the connection between suffering and sin. This realization releases him from his isolated victimization and allows him to join in a communal appeal to God. God remains silent in Lamentations, but the sufferer's emergence from soliloquy to prayer enables him at least to recover God as an addressable other. Further, the brutal antagonism between God and the sufferer is eventually mediated by the presence of the enemy. The enemy, who until this point has been confused with God, now enters as a separate figure onto whom the burden of calumny can be transferred.

After the destruction of the Second Temple, the paradigm put forward by the Rabbis of the midrash was largely continuous with the Bible's: the Destruction was viewed as a corrective moment in the ongoing relationship between God and His people rather than as its end. To the biblical view the Rabbis added the study of Torah and the observance of the mitsvah system as principal means of reconciliation with God, as well as the idea of a final redemption—certain of execution yet indefinitely deferred—to take place at the end of historical time rather than within it. The great task that faced the Rabbis was to validate this paradigm through the revealed text of Scripture. The main locus of statements about the Destruction, the Book of Lamentations, was in fact the most problematic and resistant to this purpose. God's silence, the absence of specifically enumerated sins, and the shame before the triumph of the Nations in Lamentations were obstacles which had to be overcome through a concerted project of textual interpretation. Unlike Lamentations itself, which embodies an immediate response to catastrophe, the interpretive enterprise of the Rabbis was undertaken in the centuries after the event. This distance allowed for the application of virtuoso techniques of exegesis to the "difficulties" of Lamentations, with a number of results: ways were found to introduce extravagant sins into the text, which would then justify the Destruction as a punishment; God's pathos for Israel was established by assigning God as the speaker of certain verses in Lamentations and by picturing Him as a mourner who suffers along with His exiled subjects. In depicting the expiative suffering of the victims of the Destruction, the midrash draws on what is already a strength in the biblical text and employs a similar individualizing and personifying strategy in rendering the extremity of the afflictions.

If in Lamentations the basis for hope is the willed recollection of God's past goodness, in the midrash it is the willed recollection of God's revealed texts. Although as an isolated text Lamentations is problematic, its belonging to a larger canonical system of texts— the Hebrew Bible—provides a firm ground for resistance to despair. The unrelieved severity of Lamentations' outlook can be balanced and counteracted by the Rabbis through mobilizing other verses of Scripture—of equally revealed authority—which assure Israel that destruction will ineluctably lead to redemption. There remains one area, however, in which the Rabbis fail to reconcile God's ways to His people: Israel's humiliation in the eyes of the corrupt yet prospering Nations. The emotion of shame, so strongly felt in Lamentations, is never neutralized by the Rabbis. To the contrary: they amplify the accusation and its implicit suggestion of divine neglect and injustice. Rather than expressing this vulnerability directly, it was voiced through the coded medium of the *mashal,* the rabbinic parable. The allegorical narrative and discursive solution of the mashal allowed sufficient ambiguity for these doubts to be expressed but not vaunted.

This margin of shame is carried over in the Middle Ages in the literature of Sephardic Jewry, especially in the historiography of the sixteenth-century Spanish exiles. Responses to the Almohade persecutions and the Spanish Expulsion strove tc explicate the

fluctuations of Jewish history in ways that could account for recent distresses and thereby offer consolation for these tribula-
tions. To be sure, their explications differed from those of the
Rabbis and their confidence in their explanatory powers was not
serene. Yet in their experience of the crisis and their attempt to
contain its trauma, these medieval Sephardic writers were in a line
with the Rabbis of the midrash.

In the sphere of Ashkenazic Jewry, however, the received paradigm was transformed altogether. Catastrophe as punishment, the
central component of the biblical-rabbinic view, was no longer experienced as applicable to explaining what took place in the
Rhineland Jewish communities during the Crusader massacres in
the eleventh and twelfth centuries. The correlation between the
massive visitation of destruction and the massive commission of
transgression was an admission that the self-perception of the Jews
of Mainz, Speyer, and Worms could not authorize. Their confidence in the righteousness and strength of their scholarship and
piety was so secure that an alternative means of explanation had
to be found. The solution was to adopt the concept of "afflictions
from love," a minor rabbinic explanation for suffering, akin to the
idea of the trial in the Bible, which had hitherto been applied to
cases of anomalous individual misfortune but not to collective destruction. Rehabilitated and reinforced, this conception held that
suffering is an opportunity awarded by God to the most worthy
for the display of righteousness and for the garnering of the otherworldly rewards. Destruction was thus divorced from sin; the
singling out of the generation's leaders for suffering became a
spiritual compliment.

The ritual suicides and homicides with which some Jews met the
Crusader demands for conversion were unprecedented acts, and
indeed ones unmandated by Jewish law. In the treatment given
these events in the liturgical poetry of the next generation, the
historical circumstances recede before the symbolic concentration
on the sacrificial acts themselves. In the payyetanic imagination these
contemporary martyrdoms become assimilated to the drama of the
sacrificial cult of the ancient Jerusalem Temple. The self-willed,
ritually perfect *human* offering of the martyr not only collapsed

the exilic distance between himself and the lost Temple but also transcended the ancient cult's restriction to animal sacrifice.

The act of martyrdom now moves to the center of the literary responses to catastrophe. In the midrash, the portrayal of individual suffering functioned merely to underscore the pathos of the Destruction and to convey the convenantal meaning of the event. Nowhere is the moment and manner of dying dilated upon as it is in medieval Ashkenaz. There, martyrdom became interpreted as a spiritual arrival which conferred distinction not only upon the martyr but upon his descendents, who could use his example as an argument to God for averting future persecutions, or, if it came to that, as a model for doing their duty. The sense of shame before the Nations, which is prominent in the midrashic and Sephardic responses, is absent in Ashkenaz. Feelings about the gentiles are projected outward in the form of contempt and malediction; the role played by the victimizer is secondary to the inner Jewish drama of the martyr's consummation.

The persecutions and depredations that followed the Crusader period—especially at the time of the Black Death in 1348 and the Chmielnicki uprising in 1648—took place under varying constellations of religious and political forces. Each crisis confronted the Jews with a different set of demands and choices, and the actions taken in response were not uniform. In absolute terms of material destruction and loss of life, moreover, the Crusader massacres were less devastating than later misfortunes. Yet at the level of the iconographic imagination, especially as expressed in the traditions of synagogue poetry, the martyrological norm set in the Crusader period remained dominant.

Although piyyutim continue to be written throughout the modern period, there arose alongside them a new secular Hebrew literature in the nineteenth century. The poetry and social criticism of this new literature were the vehicles of an "enlightened" intellegentsia in Eastern Europe which, distinct from the traditional pietism of the masses, committed itself to ideas of progress, reform, and westernization. This program was already foundering on the resistance of Russian conservatism and antisemitism when waves of officially tolerated pogroms swept through the Pale of

Settlement in 1881–1882 and again in 1903–1905. The response
of the intellegentsia in the Hebrew press was to revert to the high
pathos of the lamentation literature and to rehabilitate the martyrological mystique which had not long before been rejected. In
contrast, the serious literary art of the time undertakes an anatomy and critique of this return to the medieval ethos. Abramowitsch's fiction parodies the eagerness to absorb particular historical
events into the lachrymose effusions of the tradition, and Tchernichowsky's poetry undermines the contemporary idealizations of self-
sacrifice by examining the ways in which madness and venality can
be confused with martyrdom.

Bialik's "In the City of Slaughter," an attack on the failure of
Jewish self-defense during the pogrom at Kishinev in 1903, is the
strongest text of the period. The poem simultaneously evokes and
transforms nearly the entire received body of literary motifs bearing on destruction. Bialik dismisses martyrology, especially the expectation of otherworldly reward, and reaches back to the reper-
toire of biblical gestures. The covenantal drama of the classical
prophets provides him with conventions which, once secularized
and displaced, serve for exploring the present dilemma of the national poet in the face of catastrophe. In the rhetorical arrangements of the poem, which is a monologue in which God is the
speaker and the poet-prophet the addressee, God remains a norm
of value positioned above the fallen reality of communal behavior,
and the poet-prophet constitutes the only uncompromised point
of human perception of the destruction. By evoking the covenantal paradigm, Bialik returns to the conception of destruction as
punishment for sin; however, through a great arrogation, he
transposed the definition of sin from the failure to be faithful to
Torah piety to the failure to undertake political action, even to
rebel against God.

In the progress of the poem, the indictment of the victims and
survivors becomes subordinated to the passion of the poet's role
in speaking of the catastrophe. The models provided by the persecution of Jeremiah and the breakdown of the poet in Lamentations are exploited, but in the end undercut. The biblical figures
abruptly shifted their discourse from reproach to consolation the

moment that the calamity became fact, and they went on to relieve the intimate antagonism between God and Israel by attaching hostlity to the external enemy. The belated poet-prophet of "In the City of Slaughter," by contrast, is enjoined from betraying the least expression of empathy or from introducing any mediation of the antagonism. The people, he is told, are beyond reaching. The proffered comfort would only become grist for the mills of delusion and denial. As for the poet, whose vocation is the word, the consequences are baleful. He must either be poisoned by stifling the condemnatory utterance within himself, or unleash it onanistically into the void.

Bialik's poem became an illustrative text in the construction of a new paradigm, both descriptive and predictive, for the explanation of catastrophe: Zionist ideology. Because of antisemitism and assimilation, according to the Zionist analysis, the entire enterprise of European Jewry had to be viewed as no longer viable and as already under the aspect of destruction. During World War I and the Russian Revolution and Civil War, the violence against Jews, on a much vaster scale than in the preceding decades, strengthened the power of this analysis, and, practically, caused the removal of almost all Hebrew writers and the institutions of Hebrew literary production to Palestine. In Hebrew literature between the wars, the works of Uri Zvi Greenberg, Yitshak Lamdan, Hayim Hazaz, and S. Y. Agnon, often written under the influence of Expressionism, established an apocalyptic mode replete with visions of destruction.

When the terrible events of the forties became known to the Yishuv in Palestine, a framework of explanation was, then, already in place. Although no one had foreseen its absolute, titanic proportions, nor the country from which it would issue, in Zionist thinking the Holocaust remained a tragic realization of an inevitable tendency. The paradigm was reinforced rather than questioned or destabilized. In the culture of the Yishuv and the early State the Holocaust was not experienced as a catastrophe in the narrow sense of an event which possesses the potential for unhinging meaning. Between World War II and the Eichmann trial in 1961 there is, with the exception of Greenberg's poetry, virtually no serious literary art on the subject of the Holocaust in Hebrew literature. This is in part the result, of course, of the fact of the Holocaust itself: the destruction of a Jewry from whose ranks new Hebrew writers would have emerged. This silence is also due to the young literary generation which took control of the Israeli cultural scene in the fifties. Called the Palmah generation (S. Yizhar, A. Meged, M. Shamir, N. Shaham, and others), these writers derived both their authority and their themes from their partcipation in the War of Independence in 1948. Unfamiliar with European Jewish life, the Palmah writers committed themselves to the creation of a new Jew on Palestinian soil who would take charge of Jewish destiny. The antithesis of this self-image was the death of European Jews, who were perceived at the time to have gone to their death "like sheep to the slaughter." This supposed spectacle of mass passivity induced a deep experience of shame; engagement, even contact, with the themes of the Holocaust became subject to deep denial.

The poetry of Uri Zvi Greenberg and the fiction of Aharon Appelfeld stand as two crucial exceptions to the silence of postwar Hebrew literature. The greatness of these two writers consists not in the production of isolated successful works but in the creation of sustained imaginative worlds of immense artistic power and originality. They are two different types. Greenberg is a bystander to the catastrophe; his education was traditionally Jewish and he wrote in Hebrew well before the war. Appelfeld is a survivor; he was raised in an assimilated home and experienced the war as a boy, and at its conclusion had no literary language of his own. Whereas Greenberg makes strong though disjunctive use of the motifs of the Hebrew traditions of catastrophe, Appelfeld employs a defamiliarizing style which owes more to the techniques of modernism.

The central moment in Greenberg's Holocaust poetry is the breakdown of the poet's prophetic persona. His efforts to persist after the war in his bardic posture, with its Bialik-like wrath, collapse when he is involuntarily visited by a vision of the unburied corpses of his murdered family in Galicia. This vision haunts him. Engulfed in guilt, the poet loses the sense of mastery attendant upon his self-assigned prophetic office, and is now forced to view existence from the aspect of loss rather than judgment. The poet's breakdown recalls the sudden shift in perspective from chastisement to pathos in the prophets, Lamentations, and the Rabbis. The catalyst is similarly familiar: the embodiment of the collective destruction in the figure of individual persons and the deep shame engendered by the spectacle of their victimization before the Nations. Greenberg's struggle to purge himself of his debilitation and reaccede to his vocation resembles nothing so much as the exegetical program of the Rabbis in the midrash. Like them, the poet searches for a source of strength and value recoverable from the destruction. He finds it in two places: in the wordless and wistful melody, the niggun, which unites him and his father, and in the endurance of Greenberg's own poetry, which is akin to the saving persistence of the scriptural text and its interpretation for the Rabbis. Furthermore, as Bialik secularized and appropriated the covenantal idea of sin, Greenberg did the same for the concept of redemption. Supernatural eschatology was translated into Revisionist-Zionist fantasies of political and military triumph and vindication; like Second Isaiah in the depths of exile, Greenberg willfully projects magnificent visions of restoration even from under the shadow of immediate destruction.

The great disjunction with the tradition in Greenberg's poetry lies in the poet's megalomania. Based on the complaints of the prophets, Bialik had taken the theme of the ordeal of the poet in the representation of catastrophe and amplified it into a major focus. Greenberg goes further: the poetic ego becomes the ground and substance of being, and its utterance the source of truth. Although this claim enlists the precedent of the prophets, it remains a distinctly Promethean rejection of external authority; it rests on a Romantic-Expressionist notion of the genius of the artist as electrified by violence. This overriding myth of the self is crucial in Greenberg's confrontation with the Holocaust. Only so global a poetic ego could have opened itself so deeply to an encounter with catastrophe and still recovered an identifiable identity.

Appelfeld's relationship to the elaborate traditions of catastrophe in Hebrew literature is emblemized by the paradox of his literary language. Although Appelfeld's chosen language is Hebrew, his style, in contrast to Bialik's and Greenberg's, is barren of allusions to previous Jewish texts. His Hebrew is spare, densely textured, and exceptionally beautiful, yet largely ahistorical. In his fiction, language is a parable for fate: no matter how extreme or thorough is a Jew's attempt to evade his identity, the conditions of historical reality return him to his Jewishness. The Jewishness of Appelfeld's fiction is expressed in its commitment to remain entirely within the world of the victim, and thereby to create an internal Jewish drama, one from which the sensational presence of the victimizer is kept out.

Appelfeld's art is founded on principles of obliqueness and metonomy. Atrocity itself is never represented but only suggested; it is understood as the point at which all lines of sight in the fiction eventually arrive. This fiction, made up of many short texts, constructs—and is already located within—a coherent and undisplacable imaginative world. Appelfeld's world is imagined at several temporal removes from the absent center of the war itself: the already condemned ancestral order, the parallel world of those Jews who transmuted themselves into gentiles, the time of the Liberation together with the first violent stirrings of memory, and, twenty years later, the precarious society of survivors who settled in Israel. No matter where they are located in this world, the lives of Appelfeld's characters are governed by the immutable law of the return of the past. What is brought back by the past is always the shame of some compromised but never specified behavior during the war years. Although the law is the same for all, the strategies of evading it are nuanced and various. At the center of the Appelfeld short story is the moment when the evasion founders and the carefully restored edifice of normalcy breaks down. There is a way out of this deterministic vice, but only for the very few. These are female figures whose memories have not been narcotized and who possess the strength to retain an emotional bond with the life lost in the war.

A breakthrough in Israeli literature in the sixties made Appelfeld's literary enterprise not quite so lonely and special. The trial of Adolf Eichmann was a collective communal drama which produced an unprecedented encounter between survivors and sabras. Although the facts had been on record since the war, the Holocaust had simply not figured as part of the artistic agenda of the Palmah writers; the trial transformed information into knowledge and pushed the event into consciousness. The systematic presentation of the complexity and proportions of the Final Solution eroded the summary judgment of the supposed passivity of European Jewry. As the survivors were given the chance for the first time to tell their stories publicly and in their own voices, the tainted stereotypes of them were similarly undercut. The Yishuv's own purity regarding its behavior during the war—did *it* do enough?— became an issue to be faced openly for the first time as well.

The imprint of these realizations on Israeli culture has been noticeable on the level of journalistic discussion and public consciousness; in serious literary art the record has been more tenuous. These equivocal efforts are nonetheless significant in what they reveal about future possibilities. During the sixties several important Palmah generation writers departed from the course of their customary themes to produce each a single novel devoted to the subject of the Holocaust. Taken together, these works describe a gradient of involvement in the thematics of the Holocaust: at one end, the Holocaust remains significant inasmuch as it figures in the lives of Israelis, and at the other, the Holocaust becomes a subject of representation in and for itself. Hanoch Bartov's novel about the Jewish Brigade in Italy at the close of the war, for example, anatomizes the passion for revenge on the part of these Palestinian Jewish soldiers and explores its basis in the impotence of the bystander. Bartov is the first Israeli writer to describe forthrightly the instinctive repulsion and shame felt by the Yishuv members in the presence of the survivors after the Liberation. Yehuda Amichai's *Not of This Time, Not of This Place* makes a correlation between the midlife crisis of his generation, whose youth was sacrificed in the War of Independence, and the absolute death of innocence in the Holocaust; this autobiographical novel suggests that the Holocaust must be confronted before Israelis of Amichai's generation can proceed creatively with the business of life. In *Adam Resurrected,* Yoram Kaniuk uses black humor to present the experience of survivors as a world of madness and psychic damage impervious to the supposed therapeutic rationality embodied in the modern state of Israel. Finally, in *The Chocolate Deal* Haim Gouri breaks with the Israeli reality altogether, both in theme and style, and attempts to enter the consciousness of refugees as they enact the dilemmas of survival.

The fiction of these native Israeli writers, the strong poetry of the survivor poets Abba Kovner and Dan Pagis, the immense achievement of Aharon Appelfeld—all this has had the effect of undoing the early treatment of the Holocaust in Israeli culture. The quick imposition of a Zionist paradigm of explanation on the Holocaust in the years after the war blocked a series of moments that had been central to the response to catastrophe in the past: the acknowledgment of loss, the experience of loss, and the mourning of loss. A more direct encounter with the Holocaust has been the contribution of recent Israeli writing. The larger framework of meaning into which the Holocaust will be drawn in the future—whether this will involve continuity with the past or a radical break from it—will in time emerge. But at least a proper groundwork for that project of interpretation has been laid.

PART
·I·

THE TRADITION

·I·

THE RHETORIC OF

LAMENTATIONS

 Fifteen hundred years before the destruction of the First Jerusalem Temple the great Sumerian city-state of Ur fell to Elamite invaders. The event is memorialized in a vivid five-hundred-line poem that pictures the titanic dislocations of an ancient civilization in dissolution. In affecting epic detail the "Lamentation over the Destruction of Sumer and Ur" reveals a world in havoc: the fields grow bitter weeds; the irrigation channels are flooded; the sheepfolds are wiped out; the husband no longer turns with affection to his wife and the child no longer grows sturdy on the knee; famine bends low the faces of the survivors and swells their sinews; the sacred altars are shattered and the evening offerings to the gods suppressed. "Like an ox thrown instantly by the nose rope," Ur has been brought down, her people expire "like fish caught by hand."[1] Moved by this mass of suffering, the city's deity Sin comes before his father Enlil to plead for the return of the city to divine protection. What has been Ur's offense, Sin entreats, that Enlil has turned against it? Replying on behalf of the assembly of the gods, Enlil pronounces:

> The verdict of the assembly cannot be turned back,
> The words commanded by Enlil know no overturning,
> Ur was granted kingship, it was not granted eternal reign,
> . . . .
> Its kingship, its reign has been cut off . . . ,
> . . . be not aggrieved, depart from your city.
>
> (ll. 365–367, 371–372)

With a heavy spirit Sin submits to Enlil's will and with his consort abandons Ur.

What we are least prepared for in the Sumerian lamentation is the stoniness of Enlil's reply. Against so vast a canvas of pathos, a calamitous suffering before which the poet could only cry "There are no words!"—to be given so little consolation! Ur's fall, we are instructed, is part of the nature of things. The city's fate is not governed by questions of sin or corruption; Ur is portrayed throughout the poem as a society faithful in its obligations to man and to the gods. It is rather that the sphere of divine intention turns on a different axis from the sphere of human action. Kingship passes from state to state; it is a trust which the gods do not grant in perpetuity, and no amount of intercession can now alter its removal. Simply, Ur's time has come.

Perhaps more remarkable than Enlil's decree is Sin's mute submission. We know of course that Sin's response could not be otherwise, that he is bound in obedience to his father Enlil, that the authority of the assembly of gods in Mesopotamian religion is paramount. It is difficult nevertheless to lend assent to the groundlessness of the city's devastation. The disjunction between Ur's worthiness and her fall is troubling. There is something in us that resists the spectacle of a destruction that is not in some sense a punishment.

This discomfort is the residue of a stronger feeling which I believe can be traced back through Western thought to the Hebrew Scriptures. The originating event of the Bible is God's covenant with Israel. Although it was modeled—in its Deuteronomic crystalization—on Hittite suzerain-vassal treaties, the biblical covenant represented the unprecedented notion that a treaty could be made not between temporal rulers but between a god and a people. The terms of the covenant stipulated that Israel pledge exclusive loy-

alty to the God YHWH and that this loyalty be expressed by obedience to a set of ethical and ritual obligations and interdictions
revealed at Sinai and recorded in the Torah. In return God pledged
to make Israel His special people, to establish Israel in the land,
and to protect Israel from harm. The consequences of betrayal are
set forth in Deuteronomy 28: famine and devastation, alienation
from the land, persecution in exile. Reduced in number and in
spirit, a wretched remnant will finally acknowledge that sin is the
cause of its fate and turn in contrition to God, who will repent of
His wrath and restore Israel to its original status as God's protec-
torate.

The establishment of the covenant had the simple but extraordinary effect of endowing history with meaning. History ceased
being a list of rises and falls, the removal of hegemony from one
nation to another. Instead, history became the record of the vicissitudes of a relationship acted over time. Since the course of events
now bore meaning, there could be a hermeneutic for reading the
graph of history. Independence and prosperity were seen as signs
that Israel had kept faith with the terms of the covenant;
wretchedness and depredation signs of sinful rebellion against the
Law. It was not just that national suffering became intelligible; in
the depths of suffering there was a further basis of hope: God in
His wrath would punish, but not destroy utterly. The relationship
was at bottom unconditional and contained an element of *hesed*,
"covenant love," which insured that there would always be a remnant and always a restoration.

It was for this last reason that the destruction of Jerusalem by
the Neo-Babylonian army of Nebuchadnezzar in 587 must be
counted as a true catastrophe. The physical devastation, it is true,
was enormous: the city was put to the torch and its walls leveled;
King Zedekiah was blinded and led off to Babylonia in chains;
military, civil, and ecclesiastical leaders were executed or deported; Judah as a state was crushed forever. The spiritual damage was no less devastating. For with the ravaging of the Jerusalem Temple the religious life of the nation had been broken. The
suppression of the sacred service and the sacrificial offerings meant
that all means of communication with God were terminated.

These despoliations were terrible in their own right; worse was their putative meaning. The events of 587 constituted no ordinary destruction explainable within the terms of the covenant and its periodic movements among sin, chastisement, and reconciliation. Many blows had been struck Israel in the past but never before had the two critical channels of hope and regeneration been cut off. Four centuries earlier God had promised David, "Your house and your kingship shall ever be secure, . . . your throne shall be established forever" (2 Samuel 7:16). It had become an unshaken conviction of the people that come what may the Davidic line would be maintained. Now, with Zedekiah blinded and deported, and not even a puppet king on the throne of Judah, it seemed to all that the Divine promise had been rescinded. Jerusalem and the Temple, though not the subjects of a formal promise, were similarly widely and passionately believed to be inviolable. "The kings of the earth did not believe, / Nor any of the inhabitants," the poet of Lamentations exclaims, "That foe or adversary could enter / The gates of Jerusalem" (4:12). Yet the inconceivable had indeed taken place. The alien armies had not only entered and contaminated the Temple but destroyed it for all eternity. The abrogation of the Temple service, moreover, meant that the apparatus for atonement was now beyond reach. The man who sought to be forgiven for his sins, to give thanks for his crops, to pray for children, to join the throng of pilgrims, had nowhere to turn. The very means of reconciliation with God had been taken away.

It was the despairing conclusion of the people that the fall of Jerusalem was more than an act of divine retribution. The fall, it was feared, was not a moment of strain in an eternal relationship between God and Israel but the end of that relationship. The abandonment of the Davidic line and the destruction of the Temple were taken as signs that God had indeed turned away, abdicated his protectorship, and returned Israel to the chaos of history. God, in sum, had unleashed a destruction that was *more* than a punishment.

The special nature of the crisis of 587 provides us with terms for a definition of catastrophe that differentiates it from "mere" horror and destruction. Just as the true force of the fall of Jerusalem lay in its being perceived as a cancellation of the covenant, so we may define catastrophe generally as a destructive event whose horror derives from its bursting of the available paradigms of explanation. The actual quantum of human misery is therefore not the only factor. The number of lives taken in the siege and sack of Jerusalem might fail to impress us today, nor in its own time did the scale of destruction dwarf the ruin of other great cities. It was the cognitive disorientation it provoked that made the fall of Jerusalem a catastrophe. It was a destruction that did not make sense.

But what of survival? Catastrophes are catastrophic because they most often signal an end. It was to be expected that, crushed and demoralized, the career of Israel as a people too would end: the exiled leaders would take up their lives on foreign ground and merge into Babylonian society; the broken masses that remained behind would return to the palpable solace of popular paganism. Yet the expected did not happen. Many of the exiles returned, the Temple was eventually rebuilt, a second Jewish commonwealth established. Now, many geopolitical factors can certainly be advanced to account for this regeneration, but they are not sufficient unless we introduce into our efforts to understand this phenomenon of creative survival, not miracles or mystification, but a factor of spirit. Something had to have answered to the disorientation of meaning that was inspiriting enough to make a new beginning possible. Somehow the religious myths were restored and the paradigm of explanation redrawn.

To trace the role of the verbal imagination in his regenerative process I have chosen texts from Lamentations, Second Isaiah, and Daniel because they represent different stages in the formation of a response to the Destruction and because they work through the main features of the generic structures that play the greatest role in the later literature of Israel: lamentation, consolation, and apocalypse. I have not used Jeremiah and Ezekiel, whose writings are more representative of biblical thought, because their fierce belief in the covenant paradigm was not seriously shaken by the Destruction. The authors of Lamentations write out of traditions more deeply attached to the monarchy and the sanctuary, and the sudden loss of those institutions was experienced in a more im-

mediately calámitous way. The response of Lamentations to the
fall of Jerusalem is therefore more interesting for the purposes of
this study; it has the most to tell us about the problems of language and catastrophe. Furthermore, I deal only with the first three
out of the five chapters of Lamentations. Chapter 4 is a sustained,
eye-witness account of the siege and fall of the city told in the third
person. Chapter 5 shifts entirely to the communal "we" to conclude the book in the mode of collective prayer. Together, the
concluding chapters represent a relaxing of the rhetorical tension
and complexity of the earlier chapters, consolidating their gains
and moving them toward a liturgical conclusion.

We brood much nowadays on such themes as atrocity and speech,
the Holocaust and silence, on the general insufficiency of language in the face of the horrors of the age. The infernal quality
of those horrors, their special nature and magnitude, seem to defeat every attempt at description and expression. The history of
literature seems to conspire in this defeat. Every century has done
its utmost to convey the evilness of evil and painfulness of pain,
and the accumulating weight of these efforts hardens into bodies
of received motifs and bears down heavily on the belated writer
bent on avoiding banality, denying him much more than it grants.
These claims may indeed be true, but their truth does not take
away from the fact that this same sense of impossibility is the experience of writers in every age. The Sumerian poet two millennia
before Christ cried "There are no words!" as, in the case at hand,
did the poets of Lamentations, fifteen hundred years later, who
stood before an unprecedented event equipped with and burdened by long-used traditions of communal laments and funereal
songs. Ancient writers, no more than their successors, were denied the possibility of directly and unaffectedly transcribing the
authentic cry of human pain in the purity of its original expression. If the Book of Lamentations does indeed exude a sense of
primal outrage, it is only because its authors labored and schemed
to exploit in new ways the devices of language available to them
in order to mount a successful literary representation of primal

outrage. The text of Lamentations, which is in fact deeply figured and deeply troped, instructs us in how lacking in innocence the representation of extreme events must necessarily be.

The theme of unexplained or undeserved individual suffering is dealt with in many places in biblical literature, but nowhere, except in Daniel at the very close of the biblical period, is the problem in the least related to the vicissitudes of history. Individual affliction may be a problem but never a historical problem. The ordeal of Job and the persecutions of the many unnamed supplicants in Psalms are fixed in reference to no time or place. History partakes only of the relations between God and the people of Israel as a whole. When the people sins it is the people as a corporate body, not selected individuals, that is punished, and it is likewise the people as a whole that is the subject of redemptive acts.

No event was more clearly experienced and understood in this way than the catastrophe of 587. And it is just this, the irreducibly collective nature of the event, that posed one of the great difficulties in writing of the Destruction. It is by individuals that pain and humiliation are experienced even if they are inflicted on a group for group reasons, and it is only by virtue of the knowledge born of our individual experience of these states that we are susceptible of being moved to pity or anger. If we assume that the goal of such a work as Lamentations is to achieve the maximum register of pain so that we might be so moved, then how difficult must have been the task of making the ordeal of a collective entity pathetic and to do so without betraying the integrity of the collective and thereby dissolving the fate of the nation into an anthology of separate vignettes.

The solution undertaken by the authors of Lamentations was to transfer to the collective the attributes of individual experience and to view the nation as a whole in the aspect of a single individual; simply put: personification.[2] The nation is represented as an abandoned woman or, in a more complex instance, as a persecuted man. Although this may seem like a simple move, the ways in which the personification are worked out in the text are not simple, nor are the uses to which it is put, and the fact of the nec-

essary resort to personhood in Lamentations is the first instance
and perhaps the most subtle in what amounts to a general principle in Hebrew literature of responses to catastrophe.

Jerusalem, personified as *bat tsion*, Fair Zion, is pictured as a once
beautiful woman who was ravaged and abandoned by the enemy.
Her friends betrayed her, and all her children have been torn from
her and sent into exile, and she has been left utterly alone with no
one to console her. Once a great beauty, bedecked with precious
jewels and ornaments, she had amused herself promiscuously
without giving heed to the consequences of her defilement. In a
moment all her glory was dragged down and soiled. "All who
honored her despise her, / For they have seen her nakedness" (1:8);
once an object of admiration, now she is an outcast.[3] Wretched
and forlorn, she sits by the side of the road, sighing for the loss
of her children and bewailing her afflictions.

The serviceableness of the image of Jerusalem as an abandoned
fallen woman lies in the precise register of pain it articulates. An
image of death would have purveyed the false comfort of finality;
the dead have finished with suffering and their agony can be evoked
only in retrospect. The raped and defiled woman who survives,
on the other hand, is a living witness to a pain that knows no release. It is similarly the perpetualness of her situation that comes
through most forcefully when Zion is pictured as a woman crying
bitterly alone in the night with tears wetting her face (1:2). The
cry seems to ullalate permanently in the night; the tear forever
falls to the cheek. It is a matter not just of lingering suffering but
of continuing exposure to victimization. *Almanah*, "widow," is the
term used to describe Zion in the opening verse of Lamentations,
and we know that in the ancient Near East *almanah* designated
not so much a woman who has lost her husband as the social status of a woman who has no legal protector and who may thus be
abused with impunity.[4] As an imaginative invention, furthermore,
the figure of the forlorn woman is precise in its correspondence
to the conditions of the historical moment. Nebuchadnezzar's army
had dealt Jerusalem a double blow: the city was razed and its leaders were led away into exile. The figure of the grieving woman
who remains forlornly in place while her sons are taken captive to

a far-off land mirrors the simultaneous stasis and dispersion that were Israel's fate.

It is in the illicit aspect of womanhood that the possibilities of the figure are best exploited. Even in the anguish of her victimage Zion is not held to be entirely innocent of complicity in her fate. (One of the great problems of Lamentations as a whole is its elusiveness on the score of the precise nature of the sin for which Israel has been made the subject of such massive retribution.) The text here implies that in her glory Fair Zion conducted herself with easy virtue and "gave no thought to her end" (1:8), so that what began as unwitting, voluntary promiscuity, suddenly turned into unwished for, forcible defilement. The force of this image of violation is founded on the correspondence body ‖ Temple and genitals ‖ Inner Sanctuary. So far have things gone that even in the secret place of intimacy to which only the single sacred partner may be admitted, the enemy has thrust himself and "spread his hands over everything dear to her" (1:10). Violated and desolate, Fair Zion's nakedness (the Hebrew ʿervah conveys both physical nakedness and sexual disgrace) lies exposed for the world to see.

Now once the substance of the figure has been laid down—that is, the identifying of the personification and the thing personified—there remains to be established the mode in which we see and hear the Zion figure. There remains the question of relationship. We are shaken into an awareness of this issue when precisely in the middle of the first chapter of Lamentations a voice begins to speak in the first person. This is a moment of importance in the text. It is then we realize that until this point Zion has been described in the third person and that now she begins to speak in her own voice. At first she speaks about her treatment by God and then she appeals to God directly; shortly afterwards God's actions are described by an unidentified voice, which is revealed as that of the poet, who in turn addresses Zion and exhorts her to cry out to God. And so the text continues to move through a series of manipulations of speakers and addressees in which sudden shifts are announced by no explicit notation and are often discoverable from grammatical markings alone.

Who speaks to whom about whom as seen from whose point of view? It is in the play of these questions, which defines the rhetorical situation of the text, that the deepest theological business of Lamentations gets transacted. If we can state the theme of Lamentations as an exploration of the traumatized relations between Israel and God in the immediate aftermath of the Destruction, and if we pause to realize that as a poem Lamentations has as its medium dramatized speech and not theological statement, then we must appreciate the significance of the poem's rhetoric. It is through transformations of the rhetorical situation that the fundamental categories of God, Israel, and adversary are brought into relationship, and thus, in this way, the drama of the covenant played out. The credibility of these rhetorical transactions, it should be kept in mind, is predicated upon the construct of individual personhood, which guarantees the possibility of a believable human speaker.

In chapter 1, for example, the shift to the first person emphasizes the difference between inside and outside. The poet's description of Zion in vss. 1–11 stresses the reversal of her fate relative to her enemies. Splendor and esteem, the qualities Zion has most conspicuously forfeited, take their value from the attitude of the other to the self, and even more other-directed are the experiences of nakedness and humiliation that have subsequently become Zion's fate. As affectingly as Zion's fallen situation is presented, the sympathy is cut with judgment, for we are aware that in her wantonness Zion has brought the inevitable upon herself. All this changes in v. 12. When Zion in her own words exclaims, "Is there any agony like mine?", it has the effect of a mute and distantly observed object suddenly springing to life and coming forward to speak. What has been a personification becomes more like a person. Endowed with speech, Zion gives articulation to the experience of physical pain in its lived immediacy without reference to the glories of the past or to her shame before the Nations.

It is in Zion's speech that God first enters the text of Lamentations. He enters not as a source of comfort or appeal.

> From above [the LORD] sent a fire
> Down into my bones.

> He spread a net for my feet,
> He hurled me backwards;
>
> (1:13)

In an image of unmitigated antagonism, God is pictured as a fierce hunter, stalking and ensnaring his prey. In the first half of chapter 1 it was the foreign conquerors who crushed and degraded Israel; in the second half the enemy is virtually absent. The sole source and agent of retribution is God Himself. It is significant, I believe, that his perception of catastrophe is disclosed through the articulation of the inner, first-person experience of the victim. The factor of shame before the Nations is subordinated here to the intimate, unmediated drama of Israel's relations with God. It is the massive dislocation of these relations and not the depredations of the enemy that is responsible for what is most deeply disturbing in Israel's situation. Exactly who is the destroying other who stands over and against Israel is a question asked continually and answered differently throughout the traditions of response to catastrophe in later literature. Whether it is the God of Israel or the nations of the world who are conceived as bearing responsibility has a great deal to do with the potential nature of the response. For the poets of Lamentations it is unhesitatingly God Himself; the Nations are a mere instrumentality of divine purpose. But this will not always be the case.

Although the reader may be dimly aware that behind the manipulations of point of view in the text there moves the hand of a manipulator, it is not until the second chapter of Lamentations that the poet draws attention to himself. How and why the intrusion comes about are important. When chapter 2 carries forward the theme of God's personal authorship of the Destruction, now in the third person, it is as if the poet has been compelled by the truth of Zion's perception of God as warrior. To be sure, the image of divine malevolence is modified: Rather than a figure engaged in single gladiatorial persecution, God is now pictured as the general of a ravaging army. The amplitude of the personification, too, is constricted: Zion is conceived less as an individualized woman than as the corporate embodiment of the Judean polity. Nonetheless, the fact of God's direct persecution remains not only unaltered but sweepingly elaborated. He strips, smashes, razes, cuts down, and lays waste (vss. 1–9). With premeditated and systematic antipathy, God dismantles Zion: her sacred objects (altar, sanctuary, temple), people (king and priest), and institutions (festival and sabbath). Zion's elders sit dumb on the ground, girt in sackcloth, heads sprinkled with dust, bemoaning the calamity.

Juxtaposed to the stunned silence of these conventional rituals of mourning we are given the abandoned, ungovernable grief of the poet, who undergoes a process of breakdown which prevents him from proceeding with the task of lamentation. "My eyes are spent with tears," he groans, "My heart is in tumult, / My being melts away" (2:11). It is significant, I believe, that what brings him to this state—and what finally forces his own voice into the text— is not the specter of state and temple destroyed but a domestic detail from the horrors of the siege: children expiring from hunger in the streets of the city. That it is the childrens' plight that triggers the poet's prostration becomes clear not only from the syntax but from an affecting verbal linkage. The use of the root sh-f-kh when the poet cries "My being *melts away*" (literally, "My liver spills on the ground," *nishpakh la'arets kevedi*) indicates that his condition is an empathetic vibration of the terminal fate of the children, whose "life *runs out* in their mothers' bosoms" (*behishtap-pekh nafsham*). The linkage is significant because it signals a reversion to the rhetoric of personhood. As long as the poet has been lamenting the ruin of the Judaean state and its institutions he has kept firm control over his voice. The breakdown comes only when the monumental height of the song is undercut by the sight of child suffering.

The crux of the breakdown is given in verse 13. In the intimate light it casts on the dilemma of the ancient writer in the face of catastrophe, this passage is one of the most important in biblical literature.

> What can I compare or liken to you
> O Fair Jerusalem?
> What can I match with you to console you,
> For your ruin is vast as the sea:
> Who can heal you?

The end of the verse explains the situation of Zion that has provoked the poet's crisis. In comparing the extent of Zion's ruin to
the vastness of the sea, the poet is indicating the horror of the loss
lies not in the absolute quantum of pain it has engendered but in
its seeming boundlessness. Because the destruction is unprecedented, its duration and severity have no foreseeable limits; the
Destruction is as unfathomable as the ocean's depths and as extensive as its unseen reaches. So when Zion cried in chapter 1, "Is
there any agony like mine?" we were meant to take this ejac-
ulation not as a hysterical hyperbole but as an accurate if frenzied
statement of the fundamental problem: the incommensurability of
Zion's pains. There *is* no agony like hers. She is adrift in a world
without analogue, threatened every moment with engulfment.

It is the fact of incommensurability that drives the poet to his
own desperation. He perceives his calling as requiring him not only
to document and memorialize the catastrophe but also to console
and heal its victims. And this he must do through the only means
available to him: the ministry of language. What this involves can
be inferred from the particular means the poet despairs of being
able to mobilize successfully. To console Zion and heal her, according to the beginning of verse 13, would mean to find something to which her ruin can be compared, likened, matched. "What
can I compare or liken to you?" the poet despairs, "What can I
match with you to console you?" What the poet searches for is what
we would call metaphors. For he believes that if he could find
metaphors adequate to Zion's condition then her anguish could be
relieved. The fact of incommensurability, however, stands squarely
against his intention. Unprecedented and therefore unimaginable, the Destruction admits of no comparisons. There can be no
"adequate" metaphors.

But there are at least inadequate metaphors. The highly figurative language of Lamentations as a whole as well as the present
simile comparing Zion's ruin to the sea are their own strong evidence. They indicate that this momentary despondency has not
become a paralysis of will and an abandonment of the vocation of
healing-through-language. There is an implicit recognition that
inadequate metaphors possess their own consoling powers. For if

comparisons could be made between Zion's unparalleled devastation and experiences that are finite and known then Zion might
be given some anchorage and orientation in the world as a protection against the oceanic swell of suffering.

There is an issue here concerning the function of figurative language that reverberates in the later writings on catastrophe. The
function and therefore the direction of a metaphor crucially depend on who is being addressed. When the recipient is the victim,
the purpose of the metaphor is to reduce the power of the catastrophe by comparing downscale with the known and the familiar;
the metaphor moves from major to minor. When the recipient of
the discourse is not the victim—this includes later generations, bystanders, and, as in the case of Lamentations, God Himself—the
purpose becomes to suggest the full horror of the event to those
who have no primary experience of it. Under these circumstances
the direction of the metaphor is reversed to make it work from
minor to major, from the known to the unimaginable, from the
empirical to the negative transcendent.

The assertion of a nexus between metaphor and consolation is
also an assertion of the privileged role of the poet. The word for
consolation is the root n-ḥ-m, and it is characteristic of the unrelieved dourness of Lamentations that the root occurs outside of
verse 13 only four times. All of these appear in the noun form
"comforter" (menaḥem) in chapter 1 as elements in a motif that
deepens the description of Zion's wretchedness. Her misery is redoubled because all who might comfort her, particularly her children, have been led away by the enemy. What is arresting in light
of the death and exile of Zion's comforters is the poet's evoking
of the same root in verse 13 ("that I may comfort You,"
va'anaḥamekh) to designate the potential power of his own poetic
activity. There is an implication here of a replacement of lost reality by symbol, of actual comforters by the virtual comfort of figurative language. Metaphors become the restored children of
Mother Zion. (The privileging of the poet's activity continues in
the next verse [14] in the denunciation of the false prophets who
failed to warn Zion of her iniquity. Although the reference is not
to the classical canonical prophets, who themselves decried such

delusion mongers—Ezekiel 13:10–13 is an example—there *is* a
sense here in which the moment of prophecy has passed, its powers rendered useless by the actuality of the Destruction. The kind
of discourse that is needed in the aftermath is not prophecy but
lamentation.)

What takes place in the second half of chapter 2 traces the course
of the poet's recovery. The poet turns to Zion directly and reviews
the dimensions of her humiliated and debased condition (15–17).
For the sake of her dying children the poet appeals to her to rouse
herself from her stunned prostration and cry out to God. "Pour
out your heart like water / In the presence of the Lord!" (19), he
entreats her, stressing the importance of channeling her grief into
direct appeal to God. In the remaining lines of the chapter (20–
22) Zion does indeed raise her own voice to God. In placing before God the sad results of His handiwork, Zion brings the motif
of dying children, which had been the original occasion for the
poet's breakdown, to its extreme: "Alas, women eat their own fruit,
/ Their new-born babes!" (20). Making God responsible for cannibalism as well as for priest and prophet murder and thrusting
these acts before Him—these are signs of a rhetorical ingenuity
far more effective than the mode of self-pitying complaint in which
Zion presented herself in chapter 1. Zion has ceased being merely
a trampled subject of oppression and has become truly articulate
on her own behalf. This achievement is the culmination of a process of progressive activation which has seen Zion move from being
only a mute object of description at the outset of the chapter to
becoming the living recipient of the poet's address to finally making effective use of her own voice. This is of course the poet's doing;
he has roused, involved, and instructed her. He has in a sense
transferred the burden of lamentation from himself to Zion, and
in so doing, endowed Zion with nothing less than the dignity of
self-representation through language.

Yet no matter how skillful this articulation, it can never tran-
scend the conditions imposed on it by the nature of Zion's conception as a rhetorical figure. Although Zion's voice might be pushed
to even more harrowing registers of misery, affliction, and loss,
there is at this point in the progress of Lamentations a sense in

which the function of expressivity has been carried as far as it can be taken. The text indicates that at a certain moment in the depths of catastrophe the pain that derives from the immediate experience of starvation, humiliation, and loss of life gives way to a deeper and more abiding pain: the pain that derives from the breakdown of those structures of meaning that until now have guaranteed the significance of suffering, that is, the ostensible cancellation of the covenant. To deal with this threatened loss of meaning—what amounts to a threat of caprice, gratuitousness, absurdity—Zion as a figure is simply not sufficient; a woman's voice, according to the cultural code of Lamentations, can achieve expressivity but not reflection. And now acts of reasoning and cognition are the necessary equipment for undertaking the desperate project of understanding the meaning of what has happened.

The solution is the invention of a new, male figure, the speaker of chapter 3: "I am the man who has known affliction" (3:1). This is a figure whose maleness is unambiguously declared by the use of the strong word *gever* for "man" and whose preference for theologizing rather than weeping is demonstrated throughout. A prodigious amount of critical argument has been expended in discussing the identity of this speaker, in reasoning whether the "I" who speaks does so as a personification, a collective personality that represents the people as a whole, as in the first two chapters, or as an individual, and if as an individual, whether as a historical figure such as Jeremiah, King Jehoiachin, the poet himself, or, on the other hand, as an anonymous typical sufferer, a Jewish everyman.[5] The preoccupation with this issue has not always been helpful in understanding the poem. Proposing historical identities for the speaker is the kind of speculation which is not only destined to indeterminacy but is also of doubtful relevancy to a literary analysis. To ask whether the speaker is a figure representing the people as a whole or an anonymous individual sufferer is indeed to pose a vital question, but attempts to find a single, consistent solution throughout the chapter are condemned to be defeated, not by the poem's lack of unity, but by its complexity. By a consecutive reading of the poem that attends especially to the work's rhetorical moves, I hope to be able to present a fresh perspective on these issues. The relevance to the question of catastrophe lies in the new light the poem casts on the situation of the individual and the community in their relationship to God and to the enemy in the aftermath of the Destruction.

Chapter 3 is the monumental center of the Book of Lamentations. It is three times the length of the chapters that flank it on either side; its triple alphabetical acrostic spreads over sixty-six verses. The chapter also contains the most regular use of the distinctive *kinah* meter, the limping, mourning rhythm of 3 + 2 stresses per line. The chapter is also the theological nub of Lamentations. Chapter 3 divides into three roughly equal sections, panels of a great triptych. It is in the middle panel, at the center of the center of Lamentations (3:21−39), that we witness a grappling with the preeminent questions of meaning and relationship that elsewhere in the book are avoided or preempted.

The fruits of this grappling seem, in the end, rather conventional. The speaker of the poem achieves a conviction of his sinfulness and with it a justification of God's affliction. The drama of the poem turns out, in fact, to be lodged not here, in the theological "message" at the center, but rather in the framing panels of the poem, in the ways in which are rendered the experience of alienation before the recovery of faith and the experience of reconnection after it. On the face of things, this is a good illustration of the distinction between the relative power of a stated message in relation to its dramatized meaning. Yet something more is at work in the text that alters the message itself. Rather than simply offering a heightened rendering of the theological issue, the first and third panels of the poem subtly shift the focus of meaning from the relationship between the speaker and God to the relationship between the speaker and his people. Here as elsewhere in Lamentations it is the play of rhetorical markings that signal the deeper movements of the text.

Panel one (3:1−20) records the unremitting torture of the speaker by an unnamed enemy. His flesh worn away, his bones shattered, he has been imprisoned in tomblike darkness; his very cries for help are walled up and stifled. Rendered defenseless like a stationary shooting target, he is a laughingstock to all men. The enemy, too, is pictured as an individual, a warrior in dual combat who has invidiously singled out the speaker for punishment. He appears by turns as a lurking bear or lion and as an archer who empties his quiver into the pinioned body of his victim. The ordeal has suspended the sufferer in a vacant present of exhausted despair. Stripped of a belief in any future prospect of deliverance, he has further lost the very capacity to retrieve memories of the well-being he once enjoyed, and to recall to mind the torments of the immediate past is "wormwood and poison."

Though the savage antagonist is nameless, his identity is no mystery. The name of God, the proper antecedent of the pronouns and subject of the verbs in this sequence, is finally uttered at the end of the panel when the sufferer moans, "I thought my strength and my hope / Had perished before the Lord" (18). Already in chapter 1—it should be recalled—we are prepared for making this association when God is described there directly in gladiatorial terms ("He spread out a net for my feet / He hurled me backwards" 1:13). Precisely because we are in possession of such knowlege, the conspicuous withholding of the identification, the' suppression of the antecedent, is significant. In the absence of the name, we, like the sufferer, are forced to meet God in a space in which He is reduced to existing as nothing other than a bloodthirsty soldier, a ruthless archer, even a vicious wild beast. There is no sign of metaphor to mediate the horror of the reduction, and no name, redolent of past association and privilege, to be invoked. God is unaddressable as well. "He has walled me in . . . ," cries the man, "And when I cry and plead / He shuts out my prayer" (7–8). The ordeal is an experience of being buried alive because all attempts to speak to God are repelled and stifled. The passage as a whole is an example of what we might call deflected speech. The words the sufferer utters are words that *would have been* addressed to God directly if the speaker's voice had not been shut out by a wall of "hewn stones." The deep aloneness of the speaker is rendered in the impossibility of speaking to Him. The desire that moves through the poem and produces its structure is the desire to break out of this aloneness by regaining God as a recipient of human discourse.

The turnabout begins in verse 21—this is the beginning of panel two—with the recalling to mind of a series of propositions about God's nature. The recovery is effected in two movements. The theme of the first (vss. 21–30) is the possibility of hope. If God is the source of all things, the sufferer reasons, then good as well as ill must come from Him. Since His mercies are known to be inexhaustible, a man's suffering must therefore eventually come to an end. So it is best to submit to the yoke and wait in silence for deliverance. The second movement (vss. 31–39) is concerned with the justness of God's actions. In contrast to the oriental despot who crushes and afflicts his subjects for no reason beyond his own pleasure, God never acts capriciously. God's punishments are just and meted out only to the deserving. If a man wishes to be returned to life, let him search his ways, discover the sin that has been responsible for his punishment, and return to God. "Of what shall a living man complain?" he concludes, "Only of his own sin!" (39).

There are several things that are striking about this recovery. The first is that it is seemingly unmotivated. The preceding lines describe a man for whom neither the past nor the future can be made to divulge the least sign of hope. Yet against the background of this degree-zero of despair, the sufferer recovers himself suddenly. "But this do I call to mind, / Therefore I hope," he begins and proceeds with a series of exploratory meditations that end in justifying God's ways. The suddenness of this move reveals it to be an act of will that is indeed unprepared for, in the sense that it is nourished by nothing but its own desire. In opposition to the palpable realities of his situation, the sufferer imagines a different sort of beginning. The propositions he adduces about God's nature unfold a process that is cognitive in essence; it is based not on what is experienced to be true—*that* is the persecution and alienation of the preceding lines—but on what is known to be true and can be reasoned to be true. What I wish to show is that although it is a train of reasoning that is put in motion, the momentum in the end brings the sufferer to a state of self-understanding that is deeper than mind and cognition.

This deepened understanding is the conviction of sin, and it is arrived at only at the end of eighteen verses of ratiocination. Like the withholding of God's name in the first section, the appearance of the word sin at the conclusion of panel two awakens us to its conspicuous absence until this point. The truth is that until now, and it has been a considerable time, the sufferer has failed to grasp a necessary relationship between the ordeal thrust upon him and his own actions. This is certainly the case when he meets God as a torturer poised in an act of gratuitous cruelty. It is also the case through the first half of panel two as the man counsels himself to abide patiently God's affliction though its motivation be inscrutable. The difficulty in making this linkage, which on the surface of things would seem to be the most elementary of connections—or perhaps at first the plain obliviousness to it—is one of the great problems in Lamentations. It reveals the disproportion between the overwhelming experience of the Destruction and the scant possibility of any immediate sense of deservingness. The motives for *making* the connection are clear enough. Without sin the event has no meaning, God remains gladiator and beast, His persecution an eternal rejection. Chapter 3 demonstrates that precisely because a conviction of sin is at first so unnatural, it must be won. Man stands alone bereft of God's help at the beginning of a passage back, upon whose achievement so much depends. The enabling forces released in the remainder of the chapter are an indication of the momentousness of this breakthrough.

"Let us search and examine our ways, / And return to the Lord" (40). With the extraordinary debut of the communal "we" panel three is opened. Like the other instances of withheld material in the poem, the sudden appearance of a communal voice makes us realize how gravely isolated has been the ordeal of the speaker until this point. His savage persecution at the hands of God was dramatized in the loneliness of single combat; his reasoning of God's nature was concerned only with the relationship between God and the individual sufferer, the *gever* standing alone. The constricted isolation of the "I" reminds us of another component of the experience of the Destruction. No matter how strong his previous rootedness in communal and national structures, the individual victim is stripped of these associations in the immediate aftermath of the event and left to meet the horror utterly alone. The ap-

pearance of the "we" at this point implies that the recovery of the
solidarity of community is contingent upon an awareness of sin
and a commitment to a turning back to God. In the face of catastrophe, there is no turning that is not perforce plural and collective. The discontinuity in the text at this point—the abrupt juxtaposition of the unprecedented "we" with the mention of sin in the
verse just before it (39)—stunningly enacts the very moment of
release from aloneness.

There is also no turning without someone to turn to. The fact
that God is at last addressed directly in these lines must be counted
as a breakthrough. The sufferer has spoken in his own voice until
now, but his speech has been turned back into the reflexive loneliness of soliloquy. God has been the one spoken *about* in the sufferer's discourse but never the one spoken *to*. The brutalization of
spirit had gone so far that the very possibility of turning toward
God had ceased being imaginable. The recognition of sin and the
commitment to repentance now permit the sufferer to think of
himself once again as a participant in a covenantal relationship,
and, as such, as one who possesses rights of entreaty and appeal.
The recovery of God as an addressable other is rendered in an
echoing of lines from the victimization scene of panel one and their
transposition in direct address in panel three: "And when I cry
and plead, / *He* shuts out my prayer" (8) now becomes "*You* have
screened *Yourself* off with a cloud, / That no prayer may pass
through" (44). The act of denial and repudiation is the same, but
the rhetorical direction of the two utterances is not—and that makes
all the difference. Deflected, reflexive discourse has become prayer;
complaint become supplication.

Until this point the poem has turned on the development of two
binary relations: the relationship of the voice of the individual
sufferer to the voice of the community of Israel ("I"/"we") and the
relationship of the human to the divine milieu (Israel/God). What
takes place in the concluding section of chapter 3 is the introduction into each of these structures of a third, mediating term. This
move toward rhetorical triangulation, I wish to show, is the final
and most crucial moment in the restoring of a provisional equilibrium of spirit after the Destruction.

Expecting a continued convergence of voice between the suf-

ferer and people, we meet in verse 48, characteristically without
warning, the reappearance of the "I," which speaks in its own voice
to the end of the poem. "My eyes shed streams of water / Over
the ruin of my poor people," the speaker begins (48) and goes on
to declare his intention to weep incessantly until God takes pity on
His people. In a more personal key, the speaker takes up a *De
Profundis* theme: "I have called out Your name, O Lord, / From
the depths of the Pit / . . . Do not shut Your ear to my groan, to
my cry!" (55–56). The last lines become a plea for vindication. Let
my enemies, the sufferer implores, finally get just punishment for
their endless taunts and iniquities. "Oh, pursue them in anger and
destroy them / From under the heavens of the Lord!" (66).

Who is the "I" who speaks in these lines? The overwhelming
differences between the sentiments of the speaker here and the
self-absorbed complaints of the sufferer at the outset of the poem
have led some readers to argue that these are in fact two different
figures. A specific identification of the second speaker with the
person of the poet has been prompted by the similarity between
the emotionalism over the plight of the people (48–51) and the
"breakdown" of the poet in chapter 2.[6] To split the "I," it seems
to me, is singularly to gut the force of the poem. That force is
generated by the momentum of the changing relations of the "I"
through the vicissitudes of persecution and reconciliation. The reemergence of the "I" has the effect of emphasizing the fact that
this is the same man and bidding us to attend to the transformations in his identity. This continuity of person makes a large and
significant point about the stages of the survivor's consciousness in
the aftermath of the destructive event.

Although the quantum of affliction expressed by the "I" in these
lines does not change greatly from the early lines of the poem, the
source of the affliction does change significantly. The pursuit, torture, and entombment suffered by the speaker at the beginning
of the poem are *his own*. In his isolation he imagines that he alone
has been singled out for victimization. He experiences nothing but
his own persecution. Here, in contrast, the speaker's tears are
provoked not by his own pain but by the plight of his people. This
is a great change. Not only has he achieved a capacity for empathy

but he has also assumed the role of an advocate of his people's cause before God. If the terms of this advocacy resemble those of the poet in chapter 2, it is less an indication of the identity of these two figures than a statement about the speaker's passage toward the remarkable self-transcendence represented there by the discourse of the poet.

This is not yet the end. The rhetoric of the poem has a final refinement to divulge before bringing to rest the speaker's ordeal of identity. The final stage is not the stance of advocacy (lines 48–51) with its implied distance between the articulating individual and the voiceless collective. In intoning the *De Profundis* and vindication themes from verse 52 to the end of the poem, this distance is closed. The closure comes in a curious way. The speaker once again pleads his *own* case. "Hear my plea," he shouts, "vindicate my right" (56, 59). In pleading on behalf of no one's but his own affliction, he seems to be returning to the estranged self-absorption of the poem's opening lines. It is this similarity—or rather this seeming regression—that draws us to compare the identity of the "I" at the beginning and end and to summarize those changes.

We can best get at this, I think, by recalling the two camps in the conventional debate in biblical scholarship over the identity of the *gever* in chapter 3: the argument that the figure is an actual individual, whether a historical figure or a typical Everyman, and the argument that he is a figure representing the collective, similar in conception to the personification Fair Zion. If our analysis has proved anything it is that it is less a question of affirming one or the other of these models of personhood than seeing them as constituting the poles between which the "I" of the poem makes it journey. It's precisely as an "individuated" individual that the speaker begins the poem. Isolated from the consolations of community, left to meet his fate alone, enclosed in his suffering, he is indeed the faceless man, the typical sufferer. In the stages of awareness through which the speaker moves—the resignation to suffering, the justification of God and the conviction of sin, the momentary merging with the communal voice, the breakthrough to empathy and advocacy—all these movements have chartered a trajectory of change that prepares us for the final consummation:

the sufferer becomes the people, the people becomes the sufferer. No longer does he speak on *behalf* of the people but *as* the people. He has truly become a personification, an "I" through whose singleness the pathos of the "we" becomes luminous.

The last development concerns the relationship between man and God. There is of course no question of a sign from God here or elsewhere in Lamentations; the change is located in man's view of the relationship. The change is profound. God is no longer conceived as Israel's prosecutor but—potentially—as Israel's protector against an outsider to that privileged relationship, against the enemy, who is now installed as the agent of those acts of affliction. One need only recall for a moment the opening picture of God as gladiator, poised in an act of gratuitous victimization, to appreciate the depth of this change. Already in the communal lament in verses 40–47 God had been recovered as an addressable other, but it is only here in the last lines of the poem that the bitter presence of the enemy first appears and then increasingly becomes the obsessive subject of the speaker's discourse. This is not really a change in theology—the punishment of Israel is not taken out of God's hands—but a change in the angle of perception which is dictated by the dynamics of the relationship. This relationship, with its powerfully overdetermined background in the covenant, simply cannot be reconstructed if God remains the direct source of affliction. Mediation is imperative. The burden shifts to the human other and *his* deservingness of punishment. We may be guilty, Israel cries, but so are they; let our chastisement be vindicated by their destruction.

The introduction of the enemy means also the introduction of history, and there is relief in the regrounding of the relationship between Israel and God within the terms of history. The horror of the opening lines derives in part from the sense that this is an arbitrary assault that can be perpetually repeated. Nothing ties this act to the Destruction in particular or to any historical rubric. The presence of the enemy at the end of chapter 3 does much to bring the event back into history and thereby delimit its unbounded horror.

The prayerful turning to God at the close of Lamentations represents, after all that has passed, a remarkable achievement; but it remains starkly unilateral. The clamor of Israel's release from estrangement and reentry into the rhetorical encounter of the covenant can distract but momentarily from the unmoved fact that God neither speaks nor acts. Nowhere in Lamentations is there the least trace of a divine response. Perhaps it was due to the darkening historical reality of destruction and deepening exile that divine speech could not be imagined. Yet no people can long maintain an unrequited stance of reverent appeal. In the absence of some sign from the Other, silence turns into a deafening conviction of rejection. This is the danger that the exilic and postexilic prophetic writings address. Prophecy offers consolation not just in the promise of divine deliverance but in the very fact that through the prophet again God speaks.

Such is the difference in the Hebrew Bible between lamentation and consolation. Lamentation, taken generically rather than as a particular text, can be understood as a record of man's struggle to speak in the face of God's silence. Through human discourse—be it the voice of the nation, the poet, or the individual—man seeks to express the horror and contain its effects, to understand his sin and disavow it, to turn to God for relief and redress. There is, to be sure, comfort in these measures: the mitigation of immediate pain, the working through toward recovery of the meaningfulness of experience. But this comfort remains self-fabricated and self-administered, and as such, limited in strength and duration. Consolation, on the other hand, is what is given from the outside. From across a transcendental space, God's word breaks through to man, ending the silence and confirming the persistence of the divine commitment. In the covenantal relationship, the discourse of lamentation is the discourse of Israel; consolation is God's.

There are two varieties of consolation. Classical consolation, the mode of the major prophetic traditions, promises a redemption that will unfold within the bounds of history. Apocalyptic consolation, as crystalized in the Book of Daniel and in later postbiblical literature, envisions a redemption that will take place at the end of time when history has completed its course. An example of the first—I shall return to apocalyptic presently—is the figure of Second Isaiah. Although consolation is surely a feature of the prophecies of First Isaiah, Jeremiah, and Ezekiel, it is only the text of Second Isaiah that is given over to this purpose alone. This preoccupation results in the creation of a special language whose exquisite exaltation is perhaps unique in the history of Israel.

Second Isaiah's prophecies were delivered at a crucial remove in time and place from the destruction of the Jerusalem temple, and it is this distance that determines the nature and function of his discourse. The site of Isaiah's prophecy was Babylonia; his audience was made up of the Judaean notables, priests, and officials deported by Nebuchadnezzar from Jerusalem; the time was between the years 550 and 539 B.C.E. With hindsight these years may seem to us as poised at the close of the half-century of exile which ushered in the restoration. The exiles experienced nothing of this. They saw no end to their ordeal. The passage of time could be interpreted only as deepening and consolidating the finality of their rejection by God. Their sin, they reasoned, must have been one for which no atonement is possible and therefore no hope of regaining God's supervision of their affairs. Not only had the Davidic kingship been abolished and the Temple razed, but God's special servants had been sent away into the kind of exile from which, to judge by the earlier fate of the Ten Tribes, there is no return. Their fate, it seemed to them, was also a judgment on God. Located at the imperial seat of a world power, witnesses to the splendor of the triumphal processions of the conquerors and their gods, it was natural for the exiles to believe that the Destruction was a sign of something beyond their own rejection: the eclipse of the God of Israel in the world scene.

The prophet understood the historical moment differently. It was not simply that as a man of faith Second Isaiah interpreted the exile not as a sign of abandonment but as both a punishment and an atonement for sin, and it was not just that he comprehended the successes of the Babylonian armies not as a sign of God's impotence but as an instrument of the workings of His larger purpose. But something more: the prophet discerned in the world historical events of the 540s forces that would decisively affect the fortunes of the exile community. Cyrus, king of the Persians, had begun to erode the strength of the Babylonian Empire, and his conquest in 546 of Lydia in Asia Minor, ruled by Croesus, was taken by Second Isaiah as a sign that just as God had used Nebuchadnezzar as a rod of chastisement against Israel, so would He now annoint another temporal ruler, Cyrus, king of the Persians, to be an instrument of redemption and restoration.

Isaiah saw that after the silence of half-a-century, God would resume his active role in the covenant. He would once again begin to address His people in the language of historical events and through the words of his prophets. But what of Israel? In the vacuum of divine silence, after the ordeal of destruction and exile, the prophet feared that the capacity for a believing response had so atrophied that when the moment of triumph finally arrived it would simply pass by unanswered. God would once again speak and Israel would fail to hear.

The burden of Isaiah's prophecy is to reconstruct the faculty of hearing, to recreate the conditions under which the reality of divine speech regains plausibility. The theological ideas in these prophecies are slight and frequently repeated, for theology plays a role that is secondary relative to the rhetorical means through which the prophet attempts to rehabilitate the theological imagination. These means are not what we might expect in a prophecy of consolation. Rather than soothing, reassuring, and comforting, the prophet submits his listeners to what amounts to a rhetorical shock treatment: stirring exhortations, sudden shifts of perspective, dramatic evocations, fantastic imaginings, irony, and ridicule. The rhetoric of consolation in Second Isaiah is a rhetoric of arousal.

Caught in the slough of resignation, the exiles are stunned time and again by the booming of God's voice, addressing them frontally, inescapably after all those years: "I the Lord am your God, / Who grasped your right hand, / Who say to you: Have no fear; I will be your help" (41.13).[7] The hortatory style is epitomized in the incessant barrage of imperatives: Gather together! Hark! Fear not! Awake! Arise! Cloth yourself in splendor! Shout aloud for joy!—imperatives that amass to one extraordinary command to be redeemed, a command repeated so often that the listener cannot but believe in the majesty and authority of the commanding voice. Exhortation alternates with more complex forms of manipulation. Second Isaiah continually plays with ratios of commensurability between things finite and things infinite. After evoking in chapter 40 the wonder of the creation of the natural world in which the Lord effortlessly shaped the vast reaches of heaven and earth, the prophet suddenly shifts the attention of his listeners to the subject of the nations of the world, and implicitly among them the Babylonian Empire. Suddenly what once seemed unchallengeably imposing now seems puny and impotent, mere "dust on the balance" the Masterbuilder used to construct the cosmos. In the passages on idolatry, the ratio is worked in reverse, from the finite to the infinite. Here the prophet dilates on the ingenuity and mastery of the craftsman as he creates a beautiful image, only to veer away in the direction of the divine milieu in order to expose the dependence of both image and maker upon God.

The roused audience of exiles is further won over by a strategic sensitivity to the suffering and despondency in the aftermath of the Destruction. The text of Second Isaiah displays a consciousness of its role as an antidote to the discourse of lamentation. Through echoes and quotations from the poetry of communal complaint, the prophet emphasized that it is precisely this discourse that has been superseded by the discourse of consolation. The pathos of the Zion figure, for example, reverberates in the lines

> She has none to guide her
> Of all the sons she bore;
> None takes her by the hand,
> Of all the sons she has reared.
> There two things have befallen you:
> Wrack and ruin—who can console you?
> (51:18–19)

"Who can console you?" In Lamentations there could be no possible answer to this question beyond the brave resolve of the poet to serve through his metaphors as a makeshift substitute. In Second Isaiah it is none other than God who becomes—directly and immediately—the consoler of Israel, the consoler for the suffering He Himself inflicted: "I, I am He who comforts you!" (51:12). In these lines Israel is once again pictured as a forlorn woman, and it is the resort to the Zion figure that constitutes one of the most powerful correspondences to the discourse of lamentation. The woman of sorrows—deserted by her husband, stripped of her children, violated by heathens—will have restored to her all she has lost. She will forget the "shame of widowhood" and her new children, the children of "the wife forlorn / Shall outnumber those of the espoused." Most of all, God will be not just her comforter but her husband as well.

> For He who made you will espouse you—
> His name is "Lord of Hosts."

The return of God and the reconsecration of the conjugal bond between God and Israel will signify a new covenant that will never again be broken.

The rhetoric of Second Isaiah deserves to be studied in its own right because it succeeds in building and supporting a fantastic visionary edifice which, in the end, is tethered to historical reality in only the slightest way. The exquisite trancelike exaltation of the language of Second Isaiah, together with its rhetorical tactics, conducts the listener through a new exodus and a new redemption, leading him along a miraculous highway through the desert to a rebuilt Jerusalem encrusted with precious stones, there to be reconciled with God in an unsunderable union—and all this to be accomplished imminently with the accession of Cyrus. Now, Cyrus did in fact triumph, some of the exiles did return, and in time a temple was built; however, it takes only the barest familiarity with the writings of Ezra, Nehemiah, and the latter prophets to realize that the protracted, tortuous difficulties faced by the postexilic community present the strongest possible contrast to Isaiah's visionary consummations. And it is hard to say whether this stunning gap between vision and reality served for these generations more as a ground for continuing hope or deepening embitterment. In later Jewish tradition, this discrepancy is dealt with by transposing the prophecies into an eschatological time frame, and so today when selections from Second Isaiah are read in the synagogue on the Sabbaths following the Ninth of Av, the summer day of mourning for the Temple, we read these words not as a description of what *did not* take place during the generations following the Destruction but rather, with our eyes on the horizon of time, as an exquisite statement of a millennial promise. Taken in this way, consolation, unlike lamentation, floats upward into a realm of its own, and while the later influence and interpretation of the texts of consolation determine an important line of literary history, their manifest detachment from the felt experiences of catastrophe will place them beyond the scope of the present study.

In whichever ways Second Isaiah was later interpreted, the prophet himself undoubtedly envisioned God's redemption as taking place squarely within the bounds of historical time. On this score Second Isaiah is of a piece with virtually the whole of the Hebrew Bible. Yet it would not do to conclude a survey of responses to catastrophe in ancient Israel without mentioning a point at the far end of the arc of biblical literature when the contradictions of history seemed so overwhelming that a resolution could be imagined as coming only at the end of time. This exception is the Book of Daniel.

The second half of Daniel was most likely composed within pietist circles in Palestine between 167 and 164 B.C.E., during the last years of the reign of the Seleucid ruler Antiochus IV Epiphanes and just before the rededication of the Temple after the Maccabean victories. In an effort to extirpate the Jewish religion and transform Jerusalem into a Greek polis, Antiochus abolished Jewish sacrifices and festivals, prohibited circumcision and observance of the Sabbath and dietary laws, built pagan shrines and altars, ordered swine and other unclean animals to be sacrificed, and ultimately erected a statue of the Olympian Zeus upon the central Temple altar.[8] It was not just the gentiles who stood as the enemy in the eyes of the pietists but other Jews as well: the Hellenizers, who sought to make accommodations with the new social and cultural order.

In the Book of Daniel the contemporary crisis is not represented directly. The action of the text is set four hundred years earlier during the Babylonian exile; Daniel, one of the exiles of Jerusalem, is rewarded for his loyalty to Judaism by being made the recipient of visionary prophecies that describe the events of future history. The future is presented through symbolic means as a sequence of struggles and successions among world kingdoms—Babylonian, Median, Persian, Macedonian—with the most attention given to the protracted conflicts between the Ptolemies and the Seleucids. When the End comes, these kings will perish and the turmoil of history will cease. At that time, those who in their lives had kept faith with God will be resurrected to life eternal and "shine brightly like the brilliant firmament" forever and ever, while those who had abandoned Him "will become everlasting objects of contempt and abhorrence" (12:3,2). The contemporary listener knew exactly where he stood. In the great spirals of history he recognized his time as a point poised just before the conclusion of history. In the brief interval remaining, he understood, the persecutions would increase, the last tyrant would perish in a maelstrom of strife, and the reign of eternal life would at last be ushered in. The pious had only quietly to endure the persecution, trust in their own goodness, and await the End.

Daniel and the apocalyptic mode exerted a prodigious influence on later religious writing—but not on the "normative" Hebrew traditions that are the concern of this study. The community of Qumran, the circles that produced the mass of postbiblical writing such as the Vision of Baruch and Apocalypse of Ezra, and the early Christian church were all drawn to elements of the combination in apocalyptic of quietism, judgment, and future reward. But the Rabbis, for reasons I shall soon discuss, were not so drawn. They carried over the idea of resurrection but rejected the conviction of imminent ending because it seemed to diminish the importance of moral action in the interval. Yet, if apocalyptic is not relevant to the inquiry at this stage, it will be later on. Because of its essential foreignness and antinomianism, apocalyptic was returned to by such Hebrew poets of the modern period as Uri Zvi Greenberg as a model for the transgressive historical imagination. What they took for themselves from apocalyptic was not the quietism or faith or the splendid vision of eternal life, but something else: the vision of violent, cataclysmic judgment, the vision of the Nations damned.

·2·

MIDRASH AND

THE DESTRUCTION

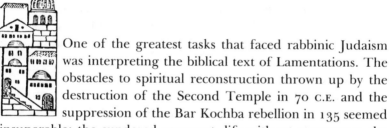 One of the greatest tasks that faced rabbinic Judaism was interpreting the biblical text of Lamentations. The obstacles to spiritual reconstruction thrown up by the destruction of the Second Temple in 70 C.E. and the suppression of the Bar Kochba rebellion in 135 seemed insuperable: the sundered covenant, life without atonement, the abandonment of future hope, the judgment of the Nations, God's silence. The Rabbis had somehow to neutralize the Destruction and defuse its subversive implications. Unless the Destruction could be absorbed into the millennial convenantal drama projected by the Deuteronomist and focused by the prophets, then the fall of Jerusalem would forever have the force of a terminal apocalypse.[1] In meeting this task the Rabbis had nothing but their own interpretive powers to rely on. God had spoken directly, and voluminously, to Second Isaiah, and the prophet had but to turn to the people and make the fact of divine speech credible. The Rabbis, in contrast, were conscious of living in an age in which the channel of prophecy had been closed and the Holy Spirit exiled from its earthly abode. Religious authorities could no longer expect to be made the direct recipients of divine revelation. Only one source

remained through which to discover God's will: sacred scripture.
The Temple was destroyed but the text remained. According to
the rabbinic theory of the text, there existed in addition to the plain
words of the scribal text a vast reservoir of latent supplemental
meanings which, in the form of an oral Torah, had also been revealed at Sinai. By using certain authorized hermeneutical procedures, it was possible for the Rabbis to release these meanings, especially those which the pressures of contemporary events made
it most necessary to release.

The text, in sum, was the ground on which the grave issues raised
by the Destruction had to be joined. Because of the closure of divine revelation, beyond possibility for the Rabbis was the direct
production of the poetic speech of lamentation or the prophetic
discourse of consolation. The only possible response to catastrophe was reading. And the text which had to be read, the text which
on no account could be avoided, was, like the Destruction itself,
the most unyielding. The Book of Lamentations, in which no word
of consolation is uttered, in which the conviction of sin and the
enumeration of sins are tenuous and elusive, in which the suffering of Israel is presented as inconsolable, in which the Gentiles re-
vile Israel without reproach, in which God Himself is pictured as
a wild animal let loose upon His people—this was the text that had
somehow to be made to yield explanation, consolation, and reconciliation. That the Rabbis succeeded in producing this reading
is a magisterial achievement.[2]

In contrast to Lamentations, which is presumed to have been
written in the immediate aftermath of the Destruction, the response of the midrash was undertaken in various stages over many
later generations. The importance of this difference is rendered
poignantly in the following passage.

Rabbi used to expound the verse "The Lord laid waste without pity" in
twenty-four ways. R. Yohanan could expound it in sixty. Could it be that
R. Yohanan was greater than Rabbi! Rather, because Rabbi was closer in
time to the Destruction of the Temple he would remember as he ex-
pounded and stop to weep and console himself; he would begin again
only to weep, console himself, and halt. R. Yohanan, because he was not
close in time to the Destruction of the Temple, was able to continue to
expound without pause. (p. 100)

The perplexity of the midrash is aroused by a seeming paradox: How is it possible that Rabbi Judah the Prince, called simply Rabbi, the compiler of the Mishnah and the preeminent sage of the period, could be bested in interpretive ingenuity by R. Yohanan, his disciple and one of the Amorites, the rabbis who succeeded the sages of the Mishnah and whose authority was considered secondary? The paradox is resolved by indicating the distance in time of each from the destruction of the Temple. Rabbi lived in the second half of the second century and the beginning of the third, and though he was not an eye witness to the horrible consequences of the Bar Kochba wars of 132–135, he was apparently close enough to hear the accounts of witnesses and to observe the effects of the disaster; R. Yohanan, living one generation later, was not burdened by the same weight of memory. To expound the verse "The Lord laid waste without pity" would have meant to give instances and applications of this scriptural image in terms of the contemporary disaster, and one would assume that proximity in time to the events would naturally make it easier to multiply the illustrations. The misrash refutes this commonsense assumption; reading and interpreting are *not* dependent upon experience and memory. In fact, rather than generating interpretations and supplying authenticity, experience and memory can act as impediments. Rabbi's weeping and self-solace represent a breakdown of his project of interpretation and its separation into the twin discourses of lamentation and consolation, as if to say that there can be no premature release from these modes, nor easy accession to interpretation. Reading and interpreting are activities that are distinct from lamentation and consolation. They depend not upon the authenticity of experience but upon will and imagination, the will to recover meaning from the text and the imagination of exegetical ingenuity, which in turn depend for their success upon time and distance.

Through these exertions the Rabbis did in fact succeed in reading Lamentations in such a way as to introduce into the text an empathetic God, extravagant sins, and self-evident bases for consolation, and these several lines of reading are the subject of what follows.

A conviction of sin in Lamentations was in no wise easy to come by. As an achievement, the *gever's* awareness of wrongdoing in chapter 3, reasoned through anguish and alienation, stands alone. What confessions are to be found there seem reflexes of piety. Though from the outside the poet can declare of Zion that "the Lord has afflicted her / For her many transgressions" (1:5), Zion herself cannot look beyond the terror of her own condition. Even in the prayerful conclusion to Lamentations, the cry of the communal chant, "Woe to us that we have sinned!" is compromised by an equivocal deferral of responsibility: "Our fathers sinned . . . / And we must bear the guilt" (5:7). If the conviction of sin in Lamentations is slight, the sense of specifically identified transgressions is slighter still. The imputation of unchastity is there, as are the allusions to the derelictions of prophets and priests, but nothing more. Although the voices of Lamentations know in vague ways that their calamity must be a punishment, they cannot name their sins; they have no precise idea what acts could have warranted such massive retribution.

For the Rabbis this vagueness became a dangerous vacancy. The steps in the retrogression they feared can be easily imagined: the elusiveness of the crimes could generate a sense of disproportion between felt culpability and the actual dimensions of the Destruction; in the space between, a feeling of gratuitousness would take root. If, in turn, the catastrophe that God had wrought was held not to be a punishment, then there could be only the explanation of divine malice, divine impotence, or divine neglect. The last was the locus of danger, for if God had truly withdrawn from Israel and retracted His providential guidance, then the Destruction must be a sign of abandonment, the terminal moment in Israel's relations with God. In order to forestall a baleful fall into despair the Rabbis found it imperative to specify, enumerate, and catalogue Israel's sins. Because the text was so unobliging in this regard, the Rabbis were compelled to dig in to the narrowest footholds and erect elaborate structures of plausibility with their powerful exegetical tools so they could establish Israel's guilt for extravagant acts of idolatry, sexual license, bloodshed, and other heinous offenses.

The rhetorical figure that governs this entire interpretive project is hyperbole. Hyperbole allows the textual trace to be magnified into an exorbitant specter and the slight gesture to be exaggerated into flagrant and obsessive performance. In Lamentations Rabbah this practice is far in excess of the normal tendency of midrash toward specification. I take as examples two midrashim about Israel's idolatry. The first is an interpretation of one of the few genuine imputations of guilt in Lamentations, the description of the wantonness of Fair Zion in chapter 1: "Her uncleanness clings to her skirts" (tum'atah beshuleha) (1:9). The Rabbis take beshuleha as a geographical designation, the Valley of Tophet, where, on the outskirts of Jerusalem, the unclean acts were practiced.

There was a great idolatrous image there placed before [the entrance to] seven chambers. Below was a copper stove and in its hand a copper basket. For the one who brought an offering of fine flour they would open the first gate; for an offering of turtle-doves the second gate; for a lamb the third gate; for a ram the fourth gate; for a calf the fifth gate; for an ox the sixth gate; for a human being the seventh gate. The priest would accept it and place it in the copper basket, light the fire underneath, and praise aloud: "May it be sweet to you! May it be pleasing to you!" Why so much [exclamation]? So that [the parents] would not hear the cries of their children and repent their deed. (pp. 71–72)

What is striking about the midrash is the way in which the gravity and the horror of the offense are systematically elaborated and deepened. As the supplicant escalates the value of his offering, he progresses deeper into the "heart of darkness" until, standing with the supreme sacrifice in hand in the innermost sanctuary, he perpetrates the supreme abomination. The parodic contrast between what transpires in this inner sanctum and the Holy of Holies of the true Temple seems clear, as does the voice of sincere prayer compared with clamorous invocations whose real purpose is to stifle the cries of innocent victims. If thus we gave over our children to foreign gods, the midrash asks, can we be surprised when later the enemy took our lives by force?

The virulent propagation of idolatry is the subject of the second example (pp. 16–17). The passage is a proem (petiḥta'), a compositional form which through interpretive ingenuity establishes a correlation between two seemingly disparate scriptural contexts. Knowing that the ultimate subject of the homily is Lamentations, the listener-reader follows with interest as the exegete takes up an obscure verse from Isaiah, first explains it as a description of idolatry, and then brings it to bear, with a wealth of support from other prophetic writings, on the subject of the Destruction. The resort to the proem form indicates how difficult it was for the Rabbis to be restricted to the Lamentations text as a resource for demonstrating Israel's wickedness. With its base in the prophets, the proem was the fit vehicle for bringing into the discussion of the Destruction the hundreds of explicit denunciatory references to idolatry that stud the text of Jeremiah, Ezekiel, and Hosea but are lacking in Lamentations.

The point of departure for the proem is the verse from Isaiah (5:8): "Woe to them who add house to house and join field to field till there is no room." After establishing that this refers to the two temples on the basis of "house to house" *(bayit levayit)*, and then to their destruction in particular on the basis of "field to field" (following Jeremiah 26:18: "Zion shall be plowed as a field"), the homilist proceeds to his main point, which is the end of the Isaiah verse, "till there is no room *(makom)*." Playing on the meanings of *makom* as both place and Temple, he poses the question, "Who caused the Place to be destroyed?" and answers, Israel, "because they left no place free from the worship of idolatry." The homilist dramatizes the infiltration and diffusion of the idolatry by showing (through texts from the Prophets) how at each stage its propagators, encountering no resistance, were emboldened to conquer new ground for their practices: they began worshipping in secret lairs and then moved to homes and then to rooftops, gardens, hilltops, and fields; a supplementary series takes the process further: from fields to crossroads, to public squares, to cities, to streets, and finally into the Holy of Holies in the Temple itself.

These two stories of idolatry move in opposed directions. The Valley of Tophet narrative moves inward from exoteric space into the heart of abomination; it describes its own world, a pocket of unspeakable worship, which is the black mirror image of the Temple and located only a stone's throw from it. In the second narrative the movement is from private spaces to public display, replicating the spread of a cancerous pollution from a hidden source to the entire body politic. In both cases the interpretive strategy is the same: stage-by-stage, systematic exaggeration and the extension of faint textual signs into an epic of infamy equal in its turpitude to the devastation it provoked.

The particular sins on which attention is lavished in the midrash are not selected at random. The Rabbis in Lamentations Rabbah evince no interest in sins against the regime of worship in the Temple, that vast cultic area to which most of the Jews' religious obligations were related, nor were they concerned with the punctilios of symbolic or ethical behavior. The focus is on three major transgressions, the "cardinal sins" of rabbinic Judaism, for which a Jew is enjoined to lay down his life rather than commit. The three are idolatry, sexual immorality, and murder. The treatment of the last two is as hyperbolic as the first. Forced once again to resort to the Prophets for evidence, the midrash draws on Isaiah 5 in order to describe the whorish ways of the daughters of Jerusalem: their alluring cosmetics, enticing adornments, and seductive manners. They were not only resistant to prophetic rebuke but they went so far as to rejoice over the fall of the city, so sure they were that their charms would purchase favorable treatment from their conquerors. And indeed, when the Destruction came these women were gathered up and installed by the officers in their chariots. But when God saw this, He caused the womb of one woman to continue to discharge blood until it filled the whole of the chariot, whereupon the soldier stabbed her with his spear and placed her in front of the carriage, which passed over her and cut her to pieces. Finally touching base in the Lamentations text, the midrash describes the clamoring of the soldiers to repel these noxious women as the moment referred to in the verse " 'Away! Unclean!,' people shouted at them, 'Away! Away! Touch not!' " (4:15).

This sanguinary exorbitance is even further magnified in a passage that comments on the preceding verse in chapter 4: "It was for the sins of her prophets, / The iniquities of her priests, / Who shed in her midst / The blood of the just" (4:13), which the Rabbis

adjust to describe the murder of prophets *by* priests. The case is
the murder of a prophet named Zechariah in the Temple courtyard—based on an incident in 2 Chronicles 24:21—whose spilt
blood remained seething above ground instead of being absorbed
into the earth. This curiosity, and the lies told to conceal the truth
about it, provoked the enemy commander to slaughter 80,000
priestly novitiates and to threaten the nation as a whole with an-
nihilation, until God took pity and caused the blood to stop seething.

It is perfectly understandable that the Rabbis should have wanted
to introduce into Lamentations the dramatic high transgressions
that figure so prominently elsewhere in the Hebrew Bible. But the
Rabbis had business of their own as well:

R. Huna and R. Jeremiah said in the name of R. Samuel b. R. Issac: We
find that the Holy One Blessed Be He may overlook idolatry, sexual immorality, and bloodshed, but He does not overlook the repudiation of
Torah, as it is said, "Why is the land in ruins?" (Jer. 9:11). [The answer
given] is not idolatry, sexual immorality, and bloodshed, but rather "Because they have foresaken my Torah." (9:12).

Now, the distinction between Torah and the three cardinal sins
seems specious, for the former is simply an inclusive term for the
latter. While this is true enough in the Bible itself, in the discourse
of the Rabbis Torah designates not just the commandments man-
dated within it but also, and principally, the *study* of those commandments, more specifically, the entire apparatus of academies
and courts and scribes and scholars of the Oral Law that in fact
constituted the regime of the Rabbis. This appropriation of the
biblical term by the Rabbis was not mere self-regard but an
expression of the conviction that the cultivation of the reading and
interpreting of the Law was central to the survival of the people,
and that failure to support this enterprise, the repudiation of Torah in its larger sense, could produce only one result. The Rabbis,
of course, scarcely devalued observance of the commandments and
faith in God, yet in laboring to expand the notion of Torah they
were capable for rhetorical purposes of giving priority to the study
component. So much so that when the Lord cries out in Jeremiah
16:11, "They have forsaken Me and not kept My Torah," the Rabbis

can gloss this as a contrastive statement. God's words become paraphrased as "Would that they had forsaken Me *but* kept my Torah, for by studying it the light which it contains would have led them back to the right path" (pp. 2–3).

In sum, whether the source of transgression was the cardinal sins, the neglect of Torah, or sundry other impieties and misdeeds, the resolve of the Rabbis in their reading was to globalize. So much so that they read into the meaningless opening word of Lamentations, *eikhah*, the numerical value of thirty-six, the very sum and signature of iniquity, holding that Israel was not exiled until they had repudiated all of the thirty-six ordinances in the Torah for which the punishment is *karet*, "premature death" (p. 41). It should be clear that the point of the Rabbis in these exaggerated indictments is hardly to heap abuse on the people or affix an indelible stigma upon its historical identity. Far from it. The purpose was to shore up the battered paradigm of the covenant, which required instances of massive wrongdoing in order to render the Destruction meaningful. The evocation of Israel's culpability was the first step in rehabilitating an apparatus which, once restored, had much more important things to say about the future than about the past.

Like sin, God's voice is the second remarkable absence in Lamentations. Yet unlike sin, the pressure to discover God's voice in the text arose less from a logical necessity than from a direct, desperate need to be assured that God's concern for Israel had not forever lapsed. The need was all the more acute because it was apparent that this time there would be no rebuilding and restoration; Israel had to live with a hope that was indefinitely deferred. This pressure, as we saw, is intrinsic to the biblical text: the speakers in Lamentations move from self-absorption in misery toward direct appeal to God, a stance won at the cost of great struggle. The failure of divine response to meet this movement is a hard truth.

Reading God's voice in the text was a far more difficult task than making explicit Israel's sins. There are no footholds in which hyperbole could plant itself and set to work. Somehow, within the crowded polyphony of voices in the text, God's voice had to be introduced. The extraordinary act of appropriation that the Rabbis undertook as a way out of this dilemma is shown clearly in a gloss on the incessant weeping expressed in the verse, "For these things do I weep, / My eyes flow with tears" (1:16).

"Oh, that my head were water, My eyes a font of tears! / Then would I weep day and night / For the slain of my poor people" (Jer. 8:23). Who speaks this verse? If it is Jeremiah, how is it possible for him to go without food, drink, or sleep? The speaker of the verse is not he but the Holy One Blessed Be He, for whom there is no sleep, as it is written, "Behold, the Keeper of Israel neither slumbers nor sleeps" (Ps. 121:4). (pp. 78–79)

Since for the Rabbis Jeremiah was the author of Lamentations as well as of his own prophetic book, once this principle has been laid down in Jeremiah—the principle that God can be made the speaker of words not plainly ascribed to Him—then it could be extended to Lamentations itself, and this with extraordinary results. For since only victims speak in the text, the appropriation of their discourse means ascribing to God the voices of the very subjects His wrath had made into victims! This is an audacious appropriation indeed, and it is made possible by the confidence the Rabbis had in the powers of their exegetical instruments. But there are limits to these powers: The only kind of speech left to appropriate after the Destruction was the discourse of lamentation. So God's voice, as it "speaks"—ventriloquizes, as it were—through the words of Fair Zion, the *gever*, and the poet of Lamentations, is perforce the voice of a sufferer as well.

The new presence in the text as read by the Rabbis is divine pathos. Transformed at the moment of the Destruction, the figure of God switches from the monitory enforcer of punishment to the dazed sufferer whose suffering derives in part from His *own* pain over the loss of His children and in part from His empathy with their affliction. The Destruction is a cosmic event that is a catastrophe for God as well as man. When in Jeremiah God utters: "Summon the dirge-singers . . . Let them quickly start a wailing for us" (9:16), the midrash emphasizes, "for *them* it is not written but for *us*" (p. 4). In the actual representation of the figure of God in the midrash there is a split along different lines, which nicely replicates a basic feature of the biblical text: the split into masculine and feminine personae. The feminine persona includes both the Shekhinah, the indwelling divine presence that reposed between the cherubim atop the Holy of Holies in the Temple, and the Holy Spirit *(ruah hakodesh)*, which seems to be the voiced, projective aspect of the Shekhinah. Unlike the holy vessels captured and paraded by the enemy, the Shekhinah is withdrawn from the Temple just before it is razed and, like the Jews, goes into exile. With great poignancy, the midrash depicts the grieving reluctance of the Shekhinah as she quits the Sanctuary precincts. At each of the ten stations in her rueful progress, she breaks down, embraces and kisses the walls and pillars, and cries, "Farewell, my Temple! Farewell, my Palace! Farewell, my beloved House! Peace to you, from now on let there be peace!" (p. 29). At the last of these stations, the Mount of Olives, according to the midrash, the Shekhinah tarried three-and-a-half years in the hope that Israel would repent, while a *bat kol,* "heavenly voice," appealed to the people: "Return, wayward children" (Jer. 3:14), "Return to me and I shall return to you" (Mal. 3:7). When no repentance ensued, the Shekhinah was enjoined finally to go into exile (pp. 29–30).

It is in the masculine aspect of God as King and Father that divine pathos is most powerfully communicated. The Master of the Universe is suddenly reduced to a disoriented, grief-stricken man of sorrows. The basic situation is usually given in parabolic terms: God is compared to a king whose sons provoked him and he in response either banished or executed them; now he sits dejected, longing for the company of his children, and regretting the need to have taken action against them. Typically, these parables supply no details as to the nature of the provocation; they concentrate on the sudden turn in inner experience from king to father and on the spirit of remorse and lost opportunity that follows. God's voice takes over the poet's voice in chapter 2 in the crucial passage that despairs of finding adequate metaphors for Zion's condition ("What can I compare to you?"—2:13); the voice exploits alternative meanings of *a'idekh* (to warn, to meet, to ornament) to bewail again and again Israel's failure to heed the various signs of

His solicitude: all the prophets, the sanctuaries, the myriads of angels He had sent to them. In another image God seems prepared
to put aside all the reproaches of the past and, were it only possible, take Israel back. God appropriates the speech of the sufferer in chapter 3 at the lowest point in his disconsolateness—this
is the concluding verse of panel one—when he recalls his recent
afflictions: "Whenever I thought of them, / I was bowed low" (3:20).
In God's mouth these unspoken bitter memories become explicit
as nostalgic remorse; "Oh, that My children were still with Me as
they were in the desert, even though they murmured against Me!
Oh, that My children were still with Me in Eretz Israel, even though
they defiled it!"

In frankly and programmatically anthropomorphic terms, God
is pictured as a man plunged into states of deep mourning and
deep isolation, from which He needs help and instruction to
emerge. God, according to one tradition, is so exhausted and en-
feebled from mourning and lamenting the loss of his first child
(the Ten Tribes), that when He must exile his youngest sons (Judah and Benjamin) the redoubled loss leaves him incapable of
mourning (p. 4). "Summon the dirge-singer . . . Send for skilled
women," He appeals for help, "Let them quickly start a wailing
for us" (Jer. 9:16). The theme of divine loneliness attaches most
boldly to the word *badad*, "solitary," in the opening of Lamentations: "Alas! Lonely sits the city" (1:1). Although this is the keynote of the description of Zion as abject widow, it is simply and
majestically transferred from the victim to the victimizer and taken
as an expression of *God's* abject condition. There is a twist. Despite
this transfer God is still dependent on man in crucial ways. God,
in this tradition, is entirely untutored in mourning and requires
instruction in its customs, as if in incurring this loss He has been
brought down to a new and human realm of experience: "Said R.
Nahman: the Holy One Blessed Be He summoned the minister-
ing angels and said to them: 'If a human king had a son who dies
and mourns for him, what is customary for him to do?' They replied, 'He hangs sackcloth and ashes over his door.' He said to them,
'I will do likewise.' That is what is written, I clothe the skies in
blackness / And make their raiment sackcloth (Is. 50:3)." And so

the Rabbis proceed to work out a virtuoso correlation between odd scriptural verses describing derangements of natural phenomena and the actual steps in the legally prescribed mourning ritual, which the Rabbis themselves had fashioned.

God's necessary resort to a human model of mourning indirectly spurs His eventual emergence from isolation. In its lengthy redacted form, proem twenty-four (pp. 23–28), though surely a collation of earlier sources, gives a distinct outline of the course of this movement. The proem begins conventionally as a dramatic realization of the verse "On that day did the Lord God of Hosts call for weeping and lamentation" (Is. 22:12). Descending from heaven to inspect the fate of His Temple, God is overwhelmed by the destruction He witnesses and cries out, "Woe to the King who succeeds in His youth and fails in His old age!" He is compared in His distress to a disconsolate father whose only son dies under the marriage canopy. To express His grief here too God summons skilled mourners, in this case the patriarchs and matriarchs and Moses himself, whom he dispatches Jeremiah to summon. The text departs at this point from the expected, conventional sequence. Abraham and Moses, for example, do appear, and discovering the Destruction, they moan and bewail the catastrophe with histrionic vehemence. But they refuse to be restricted to their role as professional mourners serving as surrogates for their Lord. Overcome by pathos for the battered children of Israel, the patriarchs intercede before God on their behalf. Abraham refutes the charges against Israel point by point and begs that his own suffering faithfulness be counted in their favor.

Moses now adduces the trials of his own life, and then utters an affecting graphic picture of the fate of Israel at the hands of their captors:

Some of them were killed; the hands of some were bound behind their backs; others were fettered with iron chains; others were stripped naked; others died by the road and their carcasses were food for the birds of heaven and the beasts of earth; and others were exposed to sun, hungry and thirsty. (p. 27)

This passage, which for midrash is unusual in its prosaic, descriptive observation, functions as a turning point in the text. The fulcrum of sympathy now shifts almost entirely away from God in the direction of the victims. This is a change that has taken place through the mediation of figures who were originally summoned to minister to the grief of God alone. Through the model and mediation of the eponymous fathers, whose only modality is the extension of sympathy to others, God is urged to emerge from His own grief and turn to the misery of His children, to pass from being a rapt object of pathos to becoming a source of pathos to His creatures.

In the end it is neither Abraham nor Moses who effects this reorientation. In a parallel to the power of child suffering to break through to the poet in chapter 2 of Lamentations, it is a female voice, the voice of Mother Rachel. With incessant tears and lamentations, she refuses to be comforted for the loss of her children, and it is to her and for her sake that God, turning fully to the misery of His people, finally promises: "Restrain your voice from weeping, / Your eyes from shedding tears, / For there is reward for your labor / . . . Your children shall return to their country" (Jer. 31:16–17).

Of Jeremiah upon his return from Egypt after the Destruction, the following is told:

> He found fingers and toes cut off and cast upon the mountains. He gathered them up, embraced, caressed, and kissed them, placed them in his cloak, and said to them, "My children, did I not warn and tell you: 'Give honor to the Lord our God / Before He brings darkness, / Before your feet stumble on the mountain in shadow'?" (Jer. 13:16)

Like God, the great prophets undergo a radical change in their attitude toward the people after the Destruction. The picture of Jeremiah repining over the scattered limbs of Israel illustrates two important features of the treatment of the victim in the midrash on Lamentations. First, the status of the Jew is transformed by the Destruction; the moment he becomes a victim, the sin and turpitude of his former state are suddenly expunged and he is now bathed in the light of pathos. Second, the moment of the Destruction signals a change in the means by which Israel as a people is given literary representation; whereas formerly the people could be spoken of as an anonymous, collective entity, with the catastrophe a process of fragmentation takes place, which makes the fate of the people renderable only in terms of discrete, individual instances.

There is a deep paradox in the fact that something as terrible as the Destruction bestows upon its victims a quality of worthiness and merit. This is not the same extravagance one finds developing later in Christianity; in the midrash there is no deliverance or transfiguration through suffering, nor any ecstatic-aesthetic aura in its description. Rather, the Destruction signals what might be called a shift in aspect, a shift in the point-of-view from which the same object is seen. The midrash explains this change through an alternative reading of a verse from Proverbs: " 'Bad, bad,' says the buyer; but once he goes on his way he boasts" (20:14). "So one finds," the midrash comments, "that before Israel were exiled, the Holy One Blessed Be He called them wicked, as it is written, 'The wicked people refuses to heed my bidding' (Jer. 13:10). Yet once Israel went into exile He began to praise them, saying, 'Now that [they] are gone, [they are] to be praised' " (p. 34). The plain meaning of the proverb concerns a buyer who disparages the merchandise while he is haggling with the seller and then boasts of the purchase when he walks away. In the rabbinic reading, the subject of the second part of the proverb is not the buyer (God) but the merchandise itself (Israel). Though Israel possesses the same sum of good and evil deeds before the Destruction as after it, this fixed measure can be viewed from either the aspect of judgment or the aspect of pathos. Like the perceptual reversals of an Escher drawing, the Destruction is a moment in which the angle of vision suddenly and decisively swings about. The midrash is capable of containing within a single imaginative discourse these two contradictory ideas of Israel damned and Israel innocent.

The aspect of pathos chiefly yields an image of Israel *after* the Destruction. But since pathos is a way of seeing rather than an absolute attribute, it can also supply an alternative past, an alternative picture of Israel before the Destruction. So in addition to the view of Israel as idolators and murderers, the mythic reach of

the midrash can also encompass a vision of the "glory that was Israel" during the high Second Commonwealth period, a vision which
stresses such qualities as populousness, urbanity, wisdom, and
cleverness. The two versions are not really in opposition; the more
generous one does not contradict the charges of social and ethical
immorality but simply does not relate to them. The focus instead
is on the social life and the institutions which, whether pure or
impure, have forever passed away. This is a variety of nostalgia,
and the literary form it assumes is the idyll, a term I use here in
the sense of a semi-idealized evocation in timeless terms of a lost
society. The function of the idyll is to make the loss more deeply
felt by an imaginative retrieval of the object. The degree of idealization is related to the attitude of the succeeding generations to
their precursors. In the case of Lamentations Rabbah that attitude
is decidedly ambivalent, though this tends not to be true in later
periods. The idyll is a literary structure that begins its substantive
career in the midrash—there are some precedents in Scripture—
and becomes a frequent component of later responses to catastrophe.

The retrospective image of Israel is in fact more remarkable for
what it ignores than for what it names. The entire world of the
Temple ritual—the priests, the Levites, the vestments, the sacrifices, the Yom Kippur service—is again conspicuously absent from
Lamentations Rabbah. This is not to say that these losses are not
lamented elsewhere in rabbinic literature, but never unambiguously. The historical question of the Rabbis' attitude to the Jerusalem cult remains a vexed one. In terms of the midrash collection
at hand, whose one subject is the Destruction, the Jerusalem that
is lost is far more worldly than cultic. A great deal of space, for
example, is given to tales of the wisdom of Jerusalemites. This
wisdom is not religious knowledge, textual erudition, or scholarly
acumen, but rather the kind of cleverness and ingenuity that one
finds commonly in the heroes of folklore, which, in the end, is exactly what these stories are. (They are implanted as a block between pages 46 and 56.) In sharp contrast to the midrash that surrounds them, these materials lack the least trace of exegetical
embeddings or relatedness to Lamentations proper. The point of

the tales is to demonstrate that the wisdom of the Jerusalemites, and even their children, excelled that of the wise men of the Nations, especially the fabled sages of Athens. In their timeless and anonymous ambience, the tales emit a naive national pride that could survive only as a memory after the great humiliation of Israel at the hands and in the eyes of the Nations.

The Holy City of the midrash is a teeming urban society peopled by citizens with exquisite manners. In light of the iconographic aura that attaches to Jerusalem in subsequent centuries, what the Rabbis chose to recall with regret might now strike us as curious. "A woman from Caesarea once took her son to a baker and said to him, 'Teach my son the trade.' He replied to her, 'Let him stay with me five years and I shall teach him five hundred dishes made with wheat' " (p. 129). Unlike the folktales, this vignette *is* exegetically anchored. When the sufferer of chapter 3 of Lamentations moans, "My life was bereft of peace, / I had forgotten what happiness *(tovah)* was" (3:17), the Rabbis take *tovah* as prosperity and, as with the baker's art, proceed to multiply the illustrations of extravagant hospitality: the eighty different courses served to R. Judah b. Batyra, the eighty kinds of birds' brains tendered to R. Abbahu by Jose Resha (p. 129). The numbers are as hyperbolic in their own right as the enumeration of Israel's sins. Recollections of the etiquette of banquets and symposia provide a further glimpse into the "happiness" that was lost. Commenting on the phrase "the precious sons of Zion" (4:2), the midrash locates their preciousness in their self-esteem and consideration for others. A Jerusalemite would not jeopardize his character by accepting an invitation to dinner without knowing who his fellow diners would be. In inviting others, he in turn would take pains to insure the congeniality of the company, and with the invitation he would specify all the courses to be served so that no one would have to eat something distasteful (pp. 141–144).

These nostalgic vignettes are like debris from a shipwreck; awash in the larger reaches of the text they recall to mind a splendor that has been forever dismantled. When the subject becomes the present—the state of the victims after the Destruction—the sense of an original whole no longer obtains. In the world of the victims, each individual or family is cut off from the institutions of national life and forced to inhabit its own grief. While the figures in the nostalgic recollections wear the aspect of typical representations of an epic past, the victims of the Destruction, often named, seem to stand by themselves. The midrash knows of two types of sufferers, common victims and noble victims, who are distinguished by their degree of idealization and by the presence or absence of their voices in the text.

The pathos of the common victim is evoked in the following passage:

> It is related of Miriam, the daughter of Nakdimon, that the Rabbis allowed her five hundred gold dinars daily to be spent on her store of perfumes and cosmetics. Still, she cursed them, saying, "Make such a [paltry] allowance to your own daughters!" (R. Aha said, "We responded with 'Amen!' ") R. Eleazer said, "May I not live to behold the consolation [of Zion] if I did not see her in Acco picking out the barley grains [from the turds] beneath horses' hoofs, and I quoted this verse in connection with her: 'If you do not know, O fairest of women, / Go follow the tracks of the sheep, / And graze your kids' (Song of Songs 1:8). Read not *gediyotay-ikh* (your kids) but *geviyotayikh* (your bodies)." (pp. 86–87)

In offering Miriam's story as an example of the type of the common victim, it should be clear that I am using commonness and nobility as qualities of character and spirit only. For elsewhere in the midrash Miriam's father Nakdimon is counted as one of the four wealthiest men in Jerusalem. This wealth is indicated in our passage by the extravagant allowance granted Miriam. If a woman was widowed or deserted, the court awarded her an allowance from her husband's estate in accordance with her station in life. Five hundred gold dinars is a fabulous sum of money, and the fact it was given daily makes the proportions so fantastic that we must read this in the hyperbolic mode as an element in the "glory that was Israel" motif. The critical attitude of the Rabbis to glory on this scale is shown in the depiction of Miriam's outrageous vanity and the comic-pathetic response of R. Aha, who would be only too happy to provide his daughters with a fraction of Miriam's allowance.

The structure of the passage operates on a simple principle of reversal: from haughtiness to degradation, from perfume to excrement. The reversal enacts the sudden shift from judgment to pathos. The effect is achieved by withholding the least moment of mediation or transition and so forcing us to experience an instantaneous swing between two extreme states. The extremes, it should be noted, are not of the same status. While one is a fabulous exaggeration from the barely imaginable past, the other presents an image of destitution and humiliation which, in the ears of the contemporary listener living in a land still under Roman domination, could have hardly seemed incredible. The passage concludes with the exegesis of the verse from the Song of Songs. Far from being an ornamental closure, the exegesis serves to cushion the shock of the reversal once it has been achieved. (It is even possible that the verse and its interpretation are what generated the story, rather than vice-versa; the classic midrashim exhibit this taut balance between narrative and exegesis.) R. Eleazer parses the verse as a conditional warning: if you fail to know the ways of Torah, most vain among women, then you will have to rummage between sheep's feet in order to feed your body. Miriam's fall is a horrible one, but it is, he points out, the fulfillment of a warning. By being tethered to the world of inscribed texts, the ordeal can be rescued from floating in a void of historical victimization.

There are many similar tales in Lamentations Rabbah, and in their power to move us relative to the economy of their means, they are some of the most sterling passages in the midrash. In most cases the figures in these tales do not bear the taint of culpability that is Miriam's burden; born to high stations in life or low, they are, simply, victims. There is the widow who before the Destruction used to donate her son's weight in gold to the Temple; in the starvation of the siege of Jerusalem she slaughtered him with her own hands and ate him (p. 121). There is another Miriam whose feet were so delicate that carpets were laid for her when she entered the Temple courtyard; the Romans bound her by her hair to the tails of Arabian horses, which dragged her from Jerusalem to Lydda (p. 86). There is the Jew in hiding, forced to subsist on the bodies of his slain brethren, who discovers that he has unknowingly devoured the flesh of his father (p. 82). In telling the stories of these sad figures, the midrash is carrying forward the burden of the Bible in a more direct and uninflected way than in any of its preoccupations. Unlike the questions of sin, divine voice, and consolation, nothing that is ostensibly absent has to be discovered and revealed; the pathos of the victims is already substantially, palpably, exorbitantly *there*. What is required by way of rhetorical treatment is only an act of translation from the circumstances of the First Destruction to the Second, a simple change of historical costume. The element that the midrash picks up and amplifies most exquisitely is the shock of Fair Zion's sudden fall from glory. The passages in which dainty, highborn ladies overnight find themselves groveling in the gutter or eating their children quite brilliantly translate and multiply the scriptural image.

Like Fair Zion, too, these figures are abject and mute. They possess no awareness of the significance of what befalls them and no resources for spiritual resistance. And just as the Lamentations text felt the need for something more and turned to the *gever* of chapter 3, so the midrash finds it necessary to produce alternative models of victimization, figures who display a more conscious and active relationship to their fate. A good picture of this class of figures, which I call the noble victims, is given as follows:

It is related that when R. Joshua went to Rome he saw a boy with beautiful eyes and a pleasing appearance who had been imprisoned to be used sexually by his captors. He stood in the doorway to examine him [to determine if he was a Jew], and he cited this verse concerning him, "Who was it that gave Jacob over to despoilment / And Israel to plunderers (Is. 42:24); to this the boy responded, "It is surely the Lord against whom they sinned / In whose ways they would not walk / And whose teaching they would not obey" *(ibid.).* When R. Joshua heard this, his eyes flowed with tears, and he declared: "I swear by heaven and earth that I shall not budge from this place until I ransom him. And at great expense he did redeem him and establish him in Eretz Israel. Some say he was a Jerusalemite, to fulfill the verse, "the precious children of Zion" (4:4). (p. 143)

Although the story is rooted in the harsh *realia* of Roman practices, it serves an exegetical purpose as well. It picks up and literalizes the sexual motif of chapter 1 of Lamentations by offering not an allegorical image of Israel's humiliation at the hands of the Nations but a concrete instance of sexual victimization. The first

section of the narrative, which extends to just before the boy's response, is really identical in structure to the stories of the common
victims discussed: a picture of a creature of privileged beauty suddenly cast into the depths of degradation, which is presented as
an example of a verse describing the people's fall.

In this case, however, the victim does not remain mute. His
completion of the verse from Isaiah makes the narrative into quite
something else. By restoring the full scriptural context, the boy
rescues the rabbi's question from its broken-hearted despondency
and perhaps even pulls it back from the verge of blasphemy. He
does so by taking the question as a real question rather than a
rhetorical one and by applying to it a real answer: let there be no
mistaking the fact that it is God who has designed our sad fate as
a just punishment for our failure to follow His ways. The irony
clearly lies in the superiority of the boy's knowledge and faith to
that of the rabbi. It is the boy, innocent in his own deeds, who is
afflicted by God in an unspeakable way; yet it is he who knows
that his suffering is not meaningless and random and who is willing to accept responsibility for the sins of his people. The boy's
steadfastness stems not from an inner grace but from a knowledge of the true compass of Scripture.

The boy's actions give him all the markings of what we call a
martyr. This is akin to several stories in Lamentations Rabbah in
which Jews kill themselves or allow themselves to be killed rather
than bow down to heathen images or be pressed into sexual immorality. They are themselves innocent, which is the crucial thing,
as is the fact that they die with words of Scripture on their tongues
that attest to their awareness of the meaning of their ordeal. Taken
together, these traditions are not numerous, neither here nor in
other midrash collections, nor in the Talmuds themselves. Yet so
accustomed are we to seeing Jewish history through the prism of
the martyrologies that flourished profusely in the Middle Ages—
and perhaps, too, through the influence of Christianity's preoccupation with the symbol and practice of human sacrifice—that we
project onto the Rabbis a concern with martyrdom and an idealization of it that are in truth not theirs. The account of the torture
and death of ten rabbis at the hands of the Romans that is read

in solemn assembly in the synagogue on Yom Kippur afternoon is a medieval poem whose embellishments and elaborations are distinctly medieval. The roots, to be sure, are in the midrash, as well as in the Book of Daniel and Second Maccabees, but there is nothing here of the details of physical agony that becomes a chief topos in later periods.

Adducing consolation from the unyielding text of Lamentations was perhaps the most difficult task for the Rabbis, and at the same time the most crucial. What is at stake is made plain in the Rabbis' reading of a verse from Ezekiel in which Jerusalem is compared to a cauldron that is to be purged of its impurities over hot coals.

"Let it stand empty upon the coals" (Ezek. 24:11). R. Eleazar said: Had the text said "broken" there would have been no hope of remedy for [Israel]; but since it says "empty" [there is hope of remedy, because] every vessel that is empty may eventually be filled. (p. 6)

The cauldron may be usefully taken as a symbol for the covenant. If after the Destruction the axis of the covenant has indeed been shattered, if the set of reciprocal obligations between God and Israel has been rescinded, then there can be no hope. But if the structure is intact though the contents be absent, then the possibility of future fullness can at least be imagined. Consolation and hope were thus predicated upon the successful rehabilitation of the covenant idea. The same task that faced the classical prophets after the First Destruction faced the Rabbis after the Second. Except, of course, that the Rabbis lacked the resource of prophecy. Their strategy in taking up this challenge was twofold. First, the Rabbis sought evidence in the text to demonstrate that, however ghastly, the Destruction was limited and therefore did not burst the provisions of the covenant. Second, the Rabbis asserted that interpretation itself, when applied with virtuosity and faith, carried the power to demonstrate through intertextual connections that the Destruction was only an episode in history and not its end.

The Rabbis move forcefully to contain the Destruction by demonstrating that in it the full decimating blast of God's anger had not in fact been unleashed. The rhetorical mode for this strategy is mediation and qualification, and this can be seen most directly in the midrash's sensitivity to the presence of metaphor and simile in the Lamentations text. Our attention is called to the word "like" in verse 2:4, "He bent His bow like an enemy"; God behaves *like* an enemy but He in His essence, argues the midrash, is not an enemy. What is true of the victimizer can also be true of the victim: "She that was great among the nations / Is become like a widow" (1:1). Like a widow, yes, but a widow in fact, no. "She is like a woman," asserts the midrash, "whose husband went to a distant country but with the intention of returning to her" (p. 45). In making these moves the Rabbis were exploiting the conspicuous workings of figurative language in Lamentations and stressing the saving difference between the figure and reality, as if to say that certain statements are *only* figures of speech and need not be taken in their plain sense. This maneuver resembles the conception of figurative language given in Lamentations 2:13 ("What can I . . . liken to you, O Fair Jerusalem?"), in which the function of metaphor is to defuse and thus mitigate the horror. This function, which is primarily directed at the victims and their consolation, coexists in both Bible and midrash, as we have seen, with another function of metaphor. That function is to amplify and sharpen, and it is directed at those to be moved rather than assuaged, usually God and the contemporary listener. Like the opposed modes of judgment and pathos, these two contrastive functions coexist in the midrash and both generate and delimit the plurality of the text.

The tendency toward qualification is part of a program to blunt the harsh extremities of the Destruction and shape it to fit the covenant paradigm. God's direct agency of some of the crueler afflictions in Lamentations is transferred in the midrash to others, to Nebuchadnezzar, Nevuzaradan, Vespasian, and Trajan (p. 124). The afflictions themselves are shown to be less nefarious than they seem, because the sins that provoked them did not exhaust the capacity for evil. "[The Israelites] did not go to the extreme of rebellion against justice, and [justice] did not go to the extreme in punishing them" (pp. 45–46). God tempered justice with mercy by exiling Israel in summer, so they would have provisions during their journey (p. 77), and He endowed the exiles with the fortitude necessary to withstand their ordeal (p. 124). Cannibalism (4:13) and rape (5:11) are, unsurprisingly, the two fates which, amplified elsewhere in the midrash, require special modulation for *this* purpose. Through a piece of ingenious interpretation the Rabbis make out that at the time of the Destruction women had ways of protecting themselves so that in the end only three women were actually ravaged by the enemy (p. 157). In the case of cannibalism, the Rabbis find ways of introducing their own metaphorical mediation; a set of circumstances is constructed whereby, Abraham-like, the women are called upon to be ready to slaughter their children but are not actually required to do so.

In the end these maneuvers are but minor adjustments that help to fit a square peg into a round hole. They may qualify the ultimacy of the catastrophe, but they do not address the central questions of what was lost in the past, what is left, and what can be regained in the future. There are, when all is said and done, points in Lamentations on which the midrash must yield to the absoluteness of the text. One of these comes in chapter 3 when God is depicted as shutting out the sufferer's supplication so fiercely that the entire possibility of prayer is negated. This is a grave matter, for if prayer itself is abrogated then what hope can be left? To handle the crux "specialists" had to be called in. "R. Hannina bar Pappa asked R. Samuel b. Nahman: 'Since I have heard that you are a master of interpretation *(ba'al aggadah)*, what of the verse, "You have screened yourself off with a cloud, / That no prayer may pass through" (3:44)?' " R. Samuel replies:

Prayer can be likened to a bath house. Just as a bath house is sometimes open and sometimes locked, so the gates of prayer are sometimes open and sometimes locked. But repentance can be likened to the sea. Just as the sea is always open, so the gates of repentance are always open. (pp. 137–138)

In taking up the challenge to recuperate this text, R. Samuel has had to stipulate that what is registered as a loss is in part true. The consolation he has to offer, which bases itself on the breakthrough to consciousness of sin and the readiness for return expressed in the verses just prior in chapter 3 (39–42), puts the emphasis on what need not be taken away by the catastrophe.

In what I regard as some of their most spectacular acts of hermeneutical recovery the Rabbis show themselves not only willing to stipulate the loss of what is truly lost but also actually to celebrate the creative durability of what remains. The occasion is a parable anchored to the verse "The Lord kindled a fire in Zion / Which consumed its foundations" (4:11). The midrash begins with the paradox presented in the opening of Psalm 79 by the juxtaposition of the superscription of the psalm, "A Psalm (mizmor) of Assaf," to the first verse, "Oh Lord! The heathen have invaded your inheritance." How, asks the midrash, can a dirge for the destruction of the Temple be labeled a psalm rather than a lamentation? The answer is given in a parable. It is like a king who built an elaborate bridal chamber for his son; but then his son angered him, and in his rage the king destroyed the bridal chamber. Afterward the king came upon his son's tutor sitting and singing and asked him how he could sing in the midst of the ruins. The tutor replies, "I sing because the king vented his anger on his son's bridal chamber and not on his son" (p. 148). The solution to the parable involves the distinction between Temple and nation: God vented his anger on "wood and stone" rather than on Israel. In light of the Rabbis' ambivalence to the Jerusalem cult, it perhaps does not seem remarkable that they could identify the people Israel as a separable entity, thus shifting attention to Israel's persistence. What is indeed remarkable is the presence in the parable of the tutor and his song. The notion of the non-ultimacy of the Destruction could have been made without this figure altogether, and certainly without the song. It is one thing to accept the destruction of the Temple; it's quite another to authorize an image of artistic gaiety among the ruins.

This apparent superfluity can be explained by taking the parable as itself a parable of the place and power of the rabbinic enterprise. The Rabbis are the tutor; their creative scriptural exegesis is the tutor's song; the necessity and propriety of their intervention in the lamentation literature corresponds to the situation of the tutor among the ruins. The Rabbis pipe a tune of reassurance because not to do so would be to concede the finality of the Destruction, and like the tutor, they can continue to play, because they alone can comprehend the full story, which the principals, the king and the son, by definition, cannot. The full story is the world of Scripture in its entirety, the vast but finite expanse of the divine word in which Lamentations is only one station; within this closed epic world, the Rabbis can potentially rescue any individual element by making it resonate with other elements. So, for example, the verse, "Your ruin is as great as the sea" (2:13), which describes the boundlessness of Zion's grief and names the very quality that makes the event intractable for the poet. For the Rabbis, the mention of the sea is enough to unlock the isolation of the verse and to connect it with a context of deliverance rather than destruction: the great miracle at the sea in Exodus 15.

Such readings, to be sure, partake in the kind of intertextuality that is the lifeblood of classical midrash everywhere and always; as a rhetorical mode applied to the juxtaposition of texts, prolepsis, the figure of anticipation and fulfillment, is a midrashic constant. But nowhere, I think, is it used with the same urgency and virtuosity as in two passages, catalogues in fact, in Lamentations Rabbah. In the first instance, it is the purpose of the Rabbis to demonstrate that "all the severe prophecies that Jeremiah prophesied against Israel were anticipated and healed by Isaiah" (p. 57). This is accomplished by taking a verse from Lamentations, such as, "How does the city sit solitary" (1:1), and coupling it with a verse from Isaiah, "A people shall dwell in Zion" (30:19), which offers reassurance and compensation for the precise loss described in the later text. With unflagging subtlety and rightness, this procedure of correlation is carried through, in order, all twenty-two verses of chapter 1 of Lamentations. In the second example the proposition to be demonstrated is that "with every thing through which Israel sinned, they were punished thereby and with that same thing they were comforted" (pp. 44–45). The Rabbis take things like the head and ears—mostly parts of the body, thirteen in all—and adduce a different verse to document each of the three moments of sin, punishment, and comfort in order to prove in outsize scale the necessarily dialectical nature of Jewish history.

Like most acts of virtuosity, these performances dazzle but do not entirely persuade. The cleverness of their means diverts but fails to supply the kind of consolation that can only derive from a sense of deep struggle with loss. These efforts at solace, in fact, stand out in Lamentations Rabbah, which, as a collection of rabbinic materials, is conspicuously deficient in statements refering to the Messiah, resurrection, and the Age-to-Come. Given the astringency of the text it is commenting upon, the most the midrash can usually allow itself, as we have seen, is the kind of mediation and qualification that, in shaping the Destruction in the mold of the covenant, prepares the groundowrk for a future eschatology.

There is, nevertheless, one passage, critically situated at the conclusion of Lamentations Rabbah, which uses the device of intertextuality in a way that leaves no doubt as to the depths of struggle from which the interpretation issues. The narrative, tied to Lamentations 5:18, is set in the years between the Destruction and the Bar Kochba Rebellion, when it was still possible for Jews to visit the Temple ruins in Jerusalem.

. . . Once Rabban Gamliel, R. Joshua, R. Elazar, R. Azariah, and R. Akiva came up to Jerusalem. When they reached Mount Scopus, they tore their clothes. When they reached the Temple Mount, they spied a jackal coming out of the Holy of Holies. They began to weep, yet R. Akiva laughed. Rabban Gamliel said to him, "Akiva, you always astonish us. Here we weep and you laugh!" He replied, "Why do you weep?" Rabban Gamliel said to the others, "Look what Akiva asks us! A jackal emerges from the place about which it is written 'Any common man who encroaches upon it shall be put to death' (Num. 1:51), and we should not weep? It is precisely through our situation that the verse is fulfilled: 'Because of this our hearts are sick, / . . . Because of Mount Zion, which lies desolate, / Jackals prowl over it' (Lam. 5:17–18)." Replied Akiva, "For the same reason I rejoice. It is written, 'I shall call reliable witnesses, Uriah and Zechariah son of Jeberechiah' (Is. 8:2). Now what connection has Uriah with Zechariah? [Uriah lived in the time of the First Temple, while Zechariah lived in the time of the Second! But note well] what Uriah said and what Zechariah said. Uriah prophesied:
Zion shall be plowed as a field,
Jerusalem shall become heaps of ruins,
And the Temple Mount a shrine in the woods. (Jer. 26:18)
Zechariah prophesied:
Thus said the Lord of Hosts: There shall yet be old men and women in the squares of Jerusalem, each with staff in hand because of their great age. And the squares of the city shall be crowded with boys and girls playing in the squares. (Zech. 8:4–5)
The Holy One Blessed Be He said, 'Behold, I have two witnesses; if the

words of Uriah are fulfilled then so will the words of Zechariah. If the words of Uriah prove vain then so will the words of Zechariah.' I have rejoiced because since the words of Uriah have come true then the words of Zechariah will also come true in the Future Time." [The rabbis] replied to him in these words: "Akiva, you have consoled us. May you be consoled by the heralds of the redemption!" (pp. 159–160)

For the reader or listener, the story of Akiva's comforting of his colleagues is charged with dramatic irony because of what we know about Akiva's life. In opposition to the majority of his contemporaries, Akiva gave legitimacy to the rebellion against Rome by proclaiming Bar Kochba the messiah. For this support he was martyred by the Romans; his flesh was torn with iron combs. History hardly fulfilled the Rabbis' wish that Akiva be consoled by the coming of the redemption. The point of the story is just that: the immediacies of history are the wrong place to look for a source of true consolation. Though history is not illusory, it still cannot be understood on its own terms. The meaning of history is guaranteed by Scripture; one observes an event in the historical world and discovers its meaning by understanding it as an actualization of a scriptural text. This is the shared ground between Akiva and the Rabbis; the difference between them lies in the degree of ingenuity and faith with which history can be "read."

The sight of jackals among the ruins of the Temple confirms for the Rabbis the bitter truth of the concluding verses of Lamentations, in which such a scene is taken as a sign of God's abandonment of Israel. As an interpreter, Akiva is more resourceful. Because of the polysemousness of Scripture Akiva knows that Lamentations need not be the necessary point of reference for the sad sight before him. Akiva takes instead a verse from Jeremiah 26 which describes the Temple Mount in a similar state of destruction. The advantage of this move is that the new verse is attributed in the text to a martyred prophet named Uriah and that this same Uriah is mentioned together with Zechariah in the second context (Isaiah 8) in which the two prophets are described as God's faithful witnesses, that is, as witnesses whose words will come true. Since history has provided a powerful and indisputable actualization of the testimony of one (Jerusalem plowed under), then the prophecies of the second (Jerusalem restored) must just as indisputably be fulfilled as well. For the Rabbis the fulfillment of Scripture in devastation engenders despair. For Akiva it brings joy, because for him any event in history, no matter how terrible, which confirms the predictive power of Scripture, is to be welcomed; in confirming a part it confirms the whole. The difference between Akiva and the Rabbis lies in the fact that they see a part and he sees the whole, and, further, that he believes in the power of his hermeneutical instruments to manipulate the elements of the whole. To see the whole is to see in Scripture the full dialectical sequence of sin, punishment, and restoration, rather than one moment in the dialectic; it is to understand that for the vision of Zechariah to come true, the dire prophecies of Uriah, *must of necessity* come true as well. To understand this is to understand a great deal. It is a wisdom that is authorized by utter faith in the truth of the divine word *and* the power of human interpretation. These conditions will not always prevail, and the Hebrew writer will not forever be able to gaze upon the ruins of his people and retrieve from the horror consolation, much less laughter.

The lesson of the Destruction taught by the Rabbis was acceptance. Yet paradoxically, acceptance did not mean that there was no place for complaint and even protest. By establishing the worthiness of Israel's punishment, the Rabbis, as we have seen, succeeded in rescuing the covenant paradigm. Achieved as a corollary was the reinstatement of Israel's rights within the historical relationship with God. After having accepted the justice of their fate, Israel could, on the strength of this set of contractual guarantees, raise serious questions concerning the Destruction.

As the record of His will, the Torah could be used against God to appeal the extremity of the punishment. For adept interpreters it was not hard to find in Scripture admonitions to humane treatment that God Himself had transgressed or allowed the enemy to do so. As a gloss on Lamentations 1:9, "for the enemy jeered *(ki higdil oyev),*" the Rabbis brought a line from Psalms: "The proud have dug pits for me, which is not according to Thy law *(asher lo ketoratkha)*" (119:85). "Which is not according to Thy law" became a refrain in a litany of testimonies to the excesses of the Destruction. For example, the common occurrence of children being murdered in the presence of their mothers is presented as an outrage against the cardinal interdiction of Leviticus 22:28: "No animal from the herd or from the flock shall be slaughtered on the same day with its young." That the Israelites were treated as less than animals is instanced by the fact that mounds of corpses from various sieges and battles received no burial. In taking the life of the beast or fowl the Torah commands that the blood be poured off and covered with earth as a sign of reverence for the life source the blood represents. Against this stood the fate of the victims who "shed their blood like water round Jerusalem, with none to bury them" (Ps. 79:3). The Egyptians at the Red Sea, "whose flesh is as the flesh of asses" (Ezek. 23:20), were granted burial, while God's people, left to putrify where they fell, suffered an ass's death (pp. 73–74).

Although this appeal is boldly rhetorical, it points to a surplus of pain that resists reassurance and consolation. What rankles is not in itself the sad disposition of the Jewish corpses but the disproportion between Israel's fate and the fate of the Egyptians. The midrash echoes the Lamentations text in placing at the emotional center of the catastrophe the experience of shame. The physical and spiritual torment could perhaps be borne if they remained the private affair of God and Israel instead of being inflicted by the uncircumcised enemy in the sight of all the nations of the earth. The loss of the Temple hurt deeply; the spectacle of heathen soldiers storming into the Holy of Holies hurt more. The exposure of Israel, the jeering of the Nations, the prospering of the enemy—these humiliations define what of the Destruction was experienced as excessive and not easily neutralized by the covenant machinery even after it was rehabilitated.

This unassimilable excess, which derives from Israel's shame before the Nations and from an abiding insecurity as to God's protectorship, is something we have not yet encountered in the vast enterprise of the rabbinic interpretation of Lamentations. While the tactical maneuvering at the level of local exegesis is complex and resourceful, the strategic goals of the project are clear throughout: to shape the Lamentations text through supplementation and subtraction to fit the classical prophetic theology concerning national sin and punishment. The covenant paradigm at the heart of this theology is exceedingly simple (whence its power) in the set of contractual responsibilities it prescribes and in its predictive vision of history; and it is in the direction of this paradigm that the interpretive lines of force in the midrash confidently lead. The shame motif is an exception, and an important one. It bespeaks a shock to the covenant paradigm that was never fully recovered from. With all their interpretive will and brilliance the Rabbis could not entirely close the gap between the classical prophetic idea that was promulgated before and after the First Destruction and the actual experience of the second great catastrophe in their own times. It is this space, a kind of margin of indeterminacy, from which issue the perplexities, questionings, and insecurities as to the ongoing relations between Israel and God.

To probe these difficult matters the midrash has need of a kind of discourse that is more resourceful than the ordinary instruments of exegesis. The same pressure was at work in Lamentations itself when the rhetorical polyphony of chapter 3 was employed to explore the traumatized dynamics of the convenantal relation. In the case of the midrash the form is the *mashal,* the rabbinic parable. Though meshalim are common in midrash as a whole, there is a particularly high incidence of them in Lamentations Rabbah. There are complex critical issues involved in the function and structure of the mashal, which are just now beginning to receive serious attention.[3] For our purposes, the importance of the mashal lies in the doubleness of its two principal features. The mashal always involves a transposing of an abstract and complex situation into one that is simple and familiar. The vicissitudes of the relations between God and the Jewish people become in the mashal the domestic politics of a royal family in which God is the king and Israel either His consort or His sons. (I take this, incidentally, as more testimony to the inevitability of a resource to models of personhood in the representation of catastrophe.) The mashal itself is divided in two: the parable (the mashal proper), which is the comparison to the royal family, and the solution (the *nimshal*), which sets out the correspondences and explains the meaning in terms of the covenant. In the transactions and gaps between the comparison and the situation being compared and between the parable and the solution, there is much room for ambiguity and implication. When it is God's justice that is being questioned the need for rhetorical indirection is paramount.

One parable, for example, holds up to God as His responsibility the indeterminateness of Israel's status after the Destruction (p. 46). Using as a point of departure the ambiguity of "*like* a widow" in the opening verse of Lamentations, the mashal compares God to a king who becomes angry with his consort, writes her a bill of divorcement, and hands it to her, only to snatch it back at the last moment. When she seeks to be married to another, he claims she is still bound to him, and when she demands her rights to be supported as his wife, he claims that he has already banished her. No motivation is given for the original anger or for the retrieval of the divorce document. These are the caprices of an oriental despot (precisely what the speaker of Lamentations 3:31–36 protests God is *not*); and they place Israel in a demoralizing double bind, neither released from the obligations of the covenant nor assured of protection by them. The role of the Nations—the other the consort seeks to marry—is more explicit in another mashal (p. 93). The exegetical anchor here is particularly important because the midrash amplifies rather than muffles the accusatory strain of the text. The verse reads: "There was none to comfort me; / All my foes heard of my plight and exulted, / For it is your doing" (1:21). In the parable Israel is a royal consort who is warned by her king neither to borrow from her neighbors nor lend to them. When the king later becomes angry with her and drives her from the palace, none of her neighbors will take her in. Returning to the palace to plead with the king, she is rebuked for insolence. In her defense she argues that her wretchedness is his doing, for had she had dealings with her neighbors in the past then she might now have found refuge among them. The point, of course, is not to suggest that Israel would have been better off had they had been permitted to intermarry with the Gentiles (the kind of dealings in question) but rather to emphasize the fact of Israel's faithfulness to the covenant in at least this matter and the role of that faithfulness in their ultimate dispossession. The last mashal of this group (p. 122) also bears on the question of the legitimacy of appeals to God after the Destruction. The situation once again concerns a consort who returns to the palace after being expelled by her husband and is rebuked by him for her effrontery. This time her defense is based on the claim that because she was the only woman who was willing to accept the king in marriage, she possesses rights that are inalienable. The king denies the fact but she stands her ground, presenting as evidence (in the nimshal) the passage found in many other sources which cites verses to show that God approached the other nations of the world with the offer of the Torah but met with rejection at each overture until He came to Israel.

In all of these meshalim there is a gap in the lack of overlap between the parable and the solution. The solution begins to explain the narrative of the parable at some point *after* its beginning; what characteristically remains untranslated and unsolved is the initial catastrophe that generated the predicament. This is always given in terms of a king who becomes angry with his wife and banishes her, and never in terms of a woman who angers her husband; the fact of the anger is given but never the cause. It may perhaps be assumed that the audience for the mashal knew perfectly well the specific culpability in Israel's history that this refers to; nevertheless, in terms of the rhetorical choices made within the text itself, leaving this unexplained has the force of promoting Israel's status as a victim of a wrath whose motivation is obscure. The worthiness of Israel is also advanced by the fact that in all the meshalim Israel has the last word. God may protest or deny but Israel's assertion stands in the end. Being right, of course, is small comfort. As in Lamentations as a whole, Israel stands ready for reconciliation, but their readiness is not met by an answering voice.

There is one parable in which a divine response is indeed sounded, and the time at which it comes and the content of what it says are both surprising. I end with what I consider one of the most poignant texts in Lamentations Rabbah. The occasion for the mashal is the crucial moment in Lamentations chapter 3 (the opening of the second panel) in which the speaker begins to move out of his despair. What exactly he recalls to mind to effect this release is elusive in the biblical text. The midrash makes the "this" very clear.

"This I recall to mind, therefore I have hope" (Lam. 3:21). R. Abba b. Kahana said: This may be likened to a king who married a lady and made a large settlement upon her (lit., wrote her a large marriage contract [ketubah], "So many state-apartments I am preparing for you, so many jewels I am preparing for you, and so much silver and gold I give you." The king left her and went to a distant land for many years. Her neighbors used to vex her saying, "Your husband has deserted you. Come and be married to another man." She wept and sighed, but whenever she went into her room and read her ketubah she would be consoled. After many years the king returned and said to her, "I am astonished that you waited for me all these years!" She replied, "My lord king, if it had not been for the generous ketubah you wrote me then surely my neighbors would have won me over."

So the nations of the world taunt Israel and say to them, "Your God has no need of you; he has deserted you and removed his Shekhinah from you. Come to us and we shall appoint commanders and leaders of every sort for you." Israel enter their synagogues and houses of study and read in the Torah, "I will look with favor upon you, and make you fertile and multiply you . . . I will establish My abode in your midst, and I will not spurn you" (Lev. 26:9–11), and they are consoled. In the future when the redemption comes the Holy One Blessed Be He will say to Israel, "I am astonished that you waited for me all these years." And they will reply before the Master of All Worlds, "If it had not been for the Torah which you gave us . . . the nations of the world would have led us astray." That is what is written, "If the Torah had not been my delight, I should have perished in my affliction" (Ps. 119:92). Therefore it is stated, "This do I recall to mind and therefore I have hope" (Lam. 3:20).

The catastrophic event in this passage is *not* the woman's banishment because of her husband's anger; it is the husband who, inexplicably and without mention of anger, absents himself indefinitely. What exactly this corresponds to in the relations between God and Israel is characteristically left unexplained in the nimshal. This indefinite absence is construed by the neighbors as permanent desertion. The woman is sorely vexed by their taunts because this interpretation cannot be refuted by the apparent facts.

In contrast to the other meshalim, here the neighbors are inviting; they wish to marry the deserted wife to one of their own. The king's astonishment at the end indicates that even with these provisions there was no natural reason to expect the consort's faithfulness.

The nimshal begins with the motif of the taunting of the Nations, whose subversive and debilitating power is based on facts about Israel's situation that are ostensibly true: the Shekhinah *has* been banished and God *has* deserted. What the Nations hold out to tempt Israel answers to this loneliness; it is not so much intermarriage that is offered but leadership and direction to fill the place of the absent Master. The synagogue corresponds to the bridal chamber and the *ketubah* to the Torah. The verse from Leviticus 26 that restores Israel's courage is remarkable in two ways. That chapter, together with Deuteronomy 25, is the *locus classicus* for the formal setting out of the covenant provisions, the whole apparatus of conditional blessings and curses. The choice of verses 9–11, which describe the reward for loyalty to the Law, implies that Israel's situation is one of blamelessness. What is promised in the biblical text, prosperity and God's dwelling among the people, is firmly rooted in historical time as the normative status of the people when they reach the Land, on the condition they prove faithful. But this is not what is meant by the midrash. With the words, "In the future when the redemption comes," the time frame of the nimshal suddenly switches from history to the eschaton, a jump that was not made in the mashal proper. The move is one of great importance. It indicates that there is no escape from Israel's bereft condition as long as history lasts. During that time, in the absence of God and his Shekhinah, Israel will subsist without direction, tormented all the while by the mockery of the Nations, who will be forever offering the protection of their leaders and gods. God the King will indeed return to His people, but not within history. In the long meantime that stretches between the present and the Redemption, Israel is not entirely alone. If they lack God, they possess His word, the document, the text which, if read with imagination and faith, can be their solace. Israel stands alone within history but at least alone with the text.

·3·

MEDIEVAL

CONSUMMATIONS

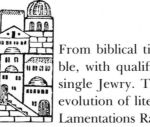 From biblical times through Late Antiquity it is possible, with qualification, to speak in cultural terms of a single Jewry. This is the case especially as regards the evolution of literary traditions. Although, for example, Lamentations Rabbah is a document of Palestinian Jewry, its outlook is carried and elaborated by the other great center of Jewish life, Babylonia. Similarly, while there exist two Talmuds, the Palestinian and the Babylonian, once the differentiae of local conditions and institutions have been taken into account, their real divergences are slight. And all rests on the common foundation of scripture and Mishnah.

In the Middle Ages this uniformity ceases to hold. Following the decline of Near Eastern Jewry toward the end of the first millennium of the Common Era, Jewish life continued to evolve within two highly differentiated spheres. The intellectual traditions of Babylonian Jewry were transferred to and cultivated in Iberia and North Africa, and after the Expulsion from Spain in 1492, throughout the entire Mediterranean basin. This culture, formed in the crucible first of Baghdad and then of Andalusia in the tenth through the twelfth centuries, is called Sepharad and the Jews in its pale Sepharadim. The traditions of Palestinian Jewry were transplanted to Italy and carried with Jewish migrations into the Rhine Valley, northern France, Germany, and later east into Poland and the Ukraine. This diaspora and its culture are called Ashkenaz and its Jews Ashkenazim. The religion of these two Jewries and their halakhic practice were by and large the same, the normative classical Judaism shaped by the Rabbis and the Geonim. The differences lay principally at the level of culture: custom, style, self-perception, and, crucially, the relationship to the non-Jewish environment and *its* culture. When the two Jewries were faced with massive collective persecution, as was sadly their lot at times, these cultural differences led to widely divergent forms of response, in deed and in text. When the Jews of the Rhineland were forced by local German bands of Crusaders to convert or die, without hesitation large numbers slaughtered their families and themselves in mass acts of ritual suicide and homicide. The texts that emerged from this period are liturgical poems that are as unflinching in their depiction of torn limbs and pools of blood as they are resolved to assimilate their subjects into the rhythms of mythic time. Faced with a similar choice, many Jews of North Africa, Spain, and Portugal temporized by making external professions of the imposed creed, Islam or Christianity. The texts that deal with their experience are neither liturgical nor poetic nor focused on concrete historical acts; these texts are rather historiosophical tracts of consolation that seek to reveal the meaning of history and often to offer reassurance that history itself will soon end.[1]

The Rhineland Jewish communities attacked by the Crusaders in 1096 had already been in existence for hundreds of years, first settled perhaps by Jews who followed the Roman legionnaires. In addition to being strong mercantile centers, such towns as Speyer, Worms, and Mainz were centers of Torah study of such importance that it may be fairly said that they were the direct successors in the early Middle Ages to the great talmudic academies of Palestine and Babylonia. Significant methodological innovations in the study of the texts of the tradition, a vast outpouring of sacred poetry, in addition to the compiling of commentaries of every sort were the spiritual and intellectual products of these scholars. In

Franco-Germany the Church despised, though tolerated, the Jews with a special theological vengeance, and the Jews in turn reviled Christianity for what in their perception were its idolatrous images, its blasphemous belief in a son of God, and what was regarded as the cannibalism of its central ritual.

Although the situation of the Jews in such an alien environment could never be secure, there was a sense before 1096 that the situation was at least susceptible of control. There operated in ducal, royal, and papal courts semi-official Jewish negotiators, lobbyists of a sort, called *shtadlanim,* who worked to mitigate anti-Jewish measures through suasion and bribery, and more often than not succeeded in averting crises by this kind of intercession from above. Frightening local incidents did occur, but inasmuch as they remained local and incidental it was possible to believe that survival among the Gentiles was negotiable. The Crusaders swept away this confidence. Legalized expropriation by a central authority could be combated; against popular riots there was little defense. The Crusaders stormed into localities as an outside force, and their fanatic-ecstatic religious hatred of the Jew stirred up and joined with the indigenous hatred of the local inhabitants. Faced with these eruptions, such local representatives of central authority as bishops backed down from protecting the Jews and left them to the mobs. Nor were these incidents isolated in time or space; within only a few months the Crusader hordes fell upon one community after another as they proceeded on their way along the Rhine: Worms, Mainz, Cologne, Trier, Metz, and farther on.

The loss of a sense of viability worked a great change in the mentality of Franco-German Jewry. Yet it was not for this that the events of 1096 etch such a sharp image in the iconography of Jewish history. Nor is it in terms of the absolute loss of life. Historians estimate that about 5,000 souls may have perished in the Crusader massacres, a gruesome fact by any standard, but still one that hardly displaces more gruesome statistics from earlier and later periods. The importance of 1096 derives in the end not from what was done to the Jews but from what some Jews themselves did, from the positive, concrete course of action undertaken in the face of the enemy. It is necessary to attend carefully to the specific nature of those acts.[2]

As the Crusader bands approached Mainz, the Jews there had full knowledge from emissaries from Speyer and Worms as to the implacable nature of the threat. Diplomacy had failed; direct bribery had no effect on men in thrall to religious fervor; for days the Jewish community had exhausted itself in desperate attempts at such means of spiritual intercession as fasting, reciting lamentations and psalms, giving charity. When the Crusaders entered the city the Jews took refuge in the episcopal palace; but the bishop's men fled and, seeing that there was no hope against the combined fury of the Crusaders and the local burghers who joined them, the Jews drew deeper into the palace. There they took counsel among themselves, and since the idea of conversion was unthinkable, exhorted each other to accept their fate as a divine decree and to die as martyrs (ʿal kiddush hashem) for the sanctification of God's name. A version of what transpired then is recorded in a contemporary Hebrew chronicle.

And in a great voice they all cried out as one: "We need tarry no longer, for the enemy is already upon us. Let us hasten to offer ourselves as sacrifices to our Father in Heaven. Anyone possessing a knife should slaughter us in sanctification of the name of the Everlasting One. Then this person should thrust his sword into either his throat or his stomach, slaughtering himself." They all arose, man and woman alike, and slew one another. . . . They lay in rows, babes and aged men together, gurgling in their throats in the manner of slaughtered sheep. . . . The saintly women threw their money outside in order to delay the enemy, until they had slaughtered their children. The hands of compassionate mothers strangled their children in order to do the will of their Master, and they turned the faces of the tender, lifeless children toward the Gentiles.[3]

When the Crusaders finally broke into the chambers in which the Jews had sealed themselves, they slew any survivors, stripped the bodies, and cast them through the windows of the palace in heaps onto the courtyard floor below. The chronicles proceed to record the martyrdoms of individual families caught outside the palace; each vignette contains a speech in which the martyr proudly bears witness to the meaning of his act and taunts his persecutors with the loathsome folly of their faith. So the words of one Master David, the Gabbai, after having lured the mob to his house with the false promise of conversion: "Alas, you are children of whoredom, believing as you do in one born of whoredom. . . . If you slay me, my soul will abide in the Garden of Eden—in the light of life. You, however, will descend to the deep pit, to eternal obloquy, condemned together with your deity—the son of promiscuity, the crucified one!"[4] Eleven hundred Jews perished in Mainz, many by their own hands or the hands of relatives. From there the Crusaders proceeded to other communities along the Rhine.

To a modern reader conversant with the rites of far-flung peoples, the spectacle of ritual suicide and homicide may not give pause. Yet within the history of Judaism before 1096 and afterwards, the self-inflicted martyrdoms of Mainz and the other communities of the Rhineland stand out boldly as unprecedented historical acts and as unsupported by—and perhaps even violating—the letter and spirit of Judaism. Now, the heroic suicides of Massada, so dramatically revealed by archeology and nowadays so widely appropriated as a political symbol, would seem to offer contrary evidence. But it should be recalled that the story of Massada is told only in the Greek writings of Josephus, which were not read by Jews until the sixteenth century. A widely read rendering of Josephus in Hebrew by a tenth-century Italian Jew called the *Yosippon* does tell the story of Massada, but with the crucial difference that in this version the Jews do not commit suicide but go off to fight to their deaths. And the suicides at Jodphata (from which Josephus the general escaped through a ruse) are presented as misguided and contrary to the precepts of Judaism.[5]

There are two issues to be disentangled here: martyrdom as the willingness to be killed and martyrdom as suicide and homicide. As we have seen in our examination of Lamentations Rabbah there was among the Rabbis a precedent for and an idealization of such figures as Daniel and Miriam and her seven sons, who in being executed by the oppressor bear eloquent and articulate witness to the meaning of their acts. Yet this attention, it was also clear, was not a preoccupation and hardly a glorying in the details and mechanics of death. The Talmud, in fact, takes up the legal question of exactly under what circumstances one is required to give up one's life or is enjoined from doing so. The issues are complex and depend in part upon the political climate, the intentions of the oppressor, and the nature of the idolatrous acts demanded of the Jew. What is significant in the case of the martyrs of Mainz is that in the face of this complexity they experienced not a whit of uncertainty as to their immediate religious duty; though accomplished dialecticians of the law, the rabbinic elite evinced no interest in exploring extenuating circumstances. If the willingness to be killed for God's name is under certain circumstances a commandment, though a heavily qualified one, the act of suicide, not to mention ritual homicide, is nowhere in rabbinic literature encouraged or required. So when the martyrs of Mainz took up ritual slaughtering knives and severed the throats of their children and their wives and then themselves, they were not actualizing some ancient ideal that had lapsed into desuetude. That these acts were in the service of an ideal goes without saying, but the means of their realization were new and unmandated, a purely voluntary and spontaneous act. It was the means themselves that became a new ideal. Here lies the importance of the events of 1096: not the fact that a new form of collective behavior entered Jewish history, but the transformation of the act, which could have remained an anomaly, into a new ideal, a norm of response to catastrophe in the imagination of Ashkenaz over the next eight hundred years, and this quite independent of the degree to which the suicides were actually imitated in deed.

It is at the level of a symbolic norm and a literary ideal that I wish to approach the Crusader martyrdoms, by first examining the documents of that generation and the one succeeding it and then by discussing their gathering iconographic force in subsequent tradition. The documents from the period are of two sorts: piyyutim, poems written for recitation in the synagogue on certain penitential or commemorative occasions, and chronicles, prose compositions that set out the events in linear sequence and were used in a similar liturgical way. Social historians have been chiefly interested in the chronicles because they constitute the first sus-

tained examples of the genre of contemporary historical writing
in Hebrew—it is no coincidence that the nature of the events warranted a new form of writing—and because as historians they are
concerned with removing the layers of literary and mythic molding to get at "historical" actuality. My concern here proceeds in
the opposite direction: from the events as they happened toward
their symbolization and stylization. The focus will therefore be on
the poems, for it is there that the processes of image-making are
most intensely at work.[6]

The great question that forces itself on the mind of any student
of the events of 1096 is, simply, why did they do it? Notions of
fanaticism and zealotry do not tell us very much and fail to explain why in earlier times Jews in similar circumstances, Jews no
less fervent in the service of their Creator, did not undertake the
same course of action. The answer lies in the special way in which
the generation that faced the First Crusade viewed itself. In the
following discussion I shall examine three thematic components
of this symbolic self-perception: themes of trial, other, and sanctuary.

It is clear from the chronicles that the martyrs consciously
understood their actions as modeled on the behavior of figures from
biblical and rabbinic lore. Of all these it was only the Akedah, the
story of Abraham's willingness to sacrifice his son told in Genesis
22, that provided a grounding in ancient texts for the idea of human sacrifice. Based on the testimonies of the chronicles, the poets
of that generation and the next developed a new genre of piyyut
called, itself, an Akedah, which retells the biblical story and draws
God's attention to the recent reenactments of that drama. For the
payyetanim what is important in the comparison between ancient
and contemporary events is the way the latter have outstripped
the former. Abraham had been called upon to perform one akedah, while the faithful of Mainz had performed eleven hundred
in one day; Isaac had to be bound upon the altar, while their sons
had willingly offered themselves unbound; though tested by God,
Abraham in the end was not required to slay his son, while their
ordeal was not just a test but also a performance, with no rams to
substitute for the human victims. Now, far from being a com-

plaint against God's justice, this comparison was urged in order to underscore the nonpareil grandeur of the generation. This was an audacious boast, and a perverse one as well. The point of the biblical story of the Akedah is, after all, to signal the supersession of human sacrifice, to assure man that animal offerings are adequate substitutes, and that what counts in God's eyes is the *readiness* to sacrifice one's firstborn, not the deed itself.[7]

This was a generation that experienced no doubt whatever as to its status. Confident in the strength and depth of its learning, in its faithfulness in the observance of the practical commandments, in the openhandedness of its charity, in the modesty of its women and the purity of its families, the generation believed itself on a par with the forefathers. God had tested their obedience as he had their ancestors', and they had not been found wanting. When we pause to compare this image of self with that of the victims and memorializers of the destructions of the First and Second Temples, what is stunningly absent is the slightest sense of sin. There are the occasional traditional pieties—*mipnei ḥata'enu harabim*, "for our many sins"—but these lack the force of anything more than stock interjections. In Lamentations the sense of sin, uncertain at first, was a crucial achievement of the text; in the midrash this consciousness was the object of an elaborate exegetical program. In the literature of 1096 sin figures not at all.

If sin is absent, then the destruction cannot be construed as a punishment. If the destruction does indeed not correlate with the behavior of the victims, the prospect of caprice and gratuitousness in the relationship between God and Israel is opened up, just that prospect that the convenantal world view of the Bible arose to contravene. Now there exists a way of maintaining a causal linkage between suffering and God's justice without involving sin. By turning things around altogether, suffering can be made consequent upon righteousness rather than turpitude: the suffering of exemplary righteous individuals as a sign of divine favor. This is an idea that goes back to Abraham's trial in the Akedah and to the doctrine among the Rabbis of *yissurin shel ahavah*, "chastisement out of love." The idea holds that, paradoxically, God tests the faith of those he knows to be already faithful. The trial is an indication of worthiness, not punishment, and its purpose is to strengthen further those who are already strong. The object of the trial is not just the individuals tested; the suffering and death of the righteous expiate vicariously for the sins of the generation as a whole.[8]

Although the idea of suffering as a trial of the righteous had a long history in Judaism, until the generation of 1096 it had never been mobilized as the dominant explanation for a historical catastrophe, nor had this idea, which seems to have been reserved for cases of individual affliction, been applied to the collective. Taken together, the various components of the idea of suffering as trial constitutes a way around the classical covenantal theology, with its unequivocal teaching that where there is destruction there must be—and it is our duty to discover—sin. The map of Jewish history, it was now being asserted, can be read otherwise. By discerning righteousness rather than sin behind suffering and self-sacrifice, one could not only save the covenant from serious threat but also further elevate and transfigure the acts of the martyrs themselves.

The trial, in the world of the piyyutim, is an opportunity given by God. The dramatic focus is not upon God but squarely upon the faithful and their success in demonstrating their worthiness. In contrast to the midrash, there is no dilation in the piyyutim upon God's experience, His loss, His mourning, His regret. This is in accordance with the conception of the opportunity for martyrdom as a kind of spiritual compliment to the generation. On Israel's part not a whisper of complaint. There is no desire that the killing go on, but as regards what has transpired thus far, we hear no word of accusation, no charge that the trial has been excessive. "There is no probing the will of God," says the chronicler, "Who gave us His Torah and commanded us to die for the unification of His blessed name."[9] God can be appealed to but not reproached.

The burden of anger, not surprisingly, is shifted from God to the enemy. This is the sort of shift we saw taking place within chapter 3 of Lamentations when, after the reestablishment of relationship, the brutal antagonism between God and man is mediated by the emergence of the enemy as a foil for Israel's pain and humiliation. The texts from the period are rife with revilement and malediction. Nowhere is there such a consummation of hatred as is the piyyut *Kelalah veshamt'a* ("Curse and Anathema"), a composition of twenty-two stanzas, a reverse alphabetic acrostic, in which God is beseeched in the following terms.

Send the sword after them so none survive. . . .
Uproot their homes, banish their shadow, raze their fortresses . . .
Make them vanish like a wisp of smoke, like molten wax. . . .
Cast them down into the nether reaches of Hell and utter oblivion. . . .
Slay them in all manner of death, vile and hideous.[10]

These are scattered lines from a composition in which the level of invective is maintained undiminished through various formal devices (the reverse acrostic, the single-ending rhyme) at an extraordinarily unrelieved pitch. The power of the poem derives additionally from the refusal of the text to grant any identity to the object of this obloquy by giving it or them the dignity of a name. The degree to which the covenant has been protected and saved from challenge is evident in the actual formulations of the curses, many of which are garnered from the language of the curses in Leviticus and Deuteronomy, in which the Israelites are told of the horrors awaiting *them* if they fail to uphold the covenant. In the piyyutim those horrors are transferred from Israel and projected outward to the persecuting other.

Although the spiritual achievement of the generation was expressed by the idea of the trial, it was hardly exhausted by it. The poets of the age did not cease to call attention to the fact that the test had not just been withstood but passed triumphantly. Yet it was precisely this measure of triumph that the figure of the Akedah and the trial could not adequately represent: the challenge and the risk—yes, but the preformance and the fulfillment—no. This surplus of meaning, this exorbitance, required taking from the lexicon of tradition a different symbolic paradigm. The paradigm could not be an individual figure such as an Abraham or a

Daniel or for that matter a group or a generation in biblical or
rabbinic annals; simply stated there was no precedent for the massive suffering of a righteous generation nor for their massive self-
sacrifice. Now, for massive sacrifice in a more ordinary and fundamental sense there certainly *was* precedent: the elaborate system of animal sacrifices in the Jerusalem temple before the Destruction. And it was to this institution that the payyetanim
appealed. I call this the *Mikdash* (sanctuary) paradigm. To explore
the significance of the Mikdash paradigm, which has not received
the same attention as the Akedah, I shall examine one of the
strongest texts from the First Crusade, the penitential poem *(seli-
ḥah)* by Rabbi David bar Meshullam of Speyer, "Elohim: al domi
ledami" (Lord: Be Not Silent to My Blood).[11] The following is a
prose translation of the central stanzas of the piyyut (the opening
section describes the massing of the Crusaders and the closing
stanza is a brief plea for divine protection).

Tender children and women gave themselves up to the binding, like
choice lambs in the Chamber of the Hearth. Oh Only One, Lofty One,
we are pierced and murdered for Your sake, for refusing to bow our heads
before the child of wantonness.

Yearling lambs without blemish were slaughtered like whole offerings,
trapped and burnt like the sacrificial portions of shared offerings. They
said to their mothers: "Do not be moved by pity. Heaven has summoned
us to be an offering by fire to the Lord."

The young struggle in agony, heaped on top of one another. [The old]
writhing in their own blood, hasten to sacrifice their fellows. Let this blood
be stirred on the terrace of Your Sanctuary. Let it boil before Your eyes
forever, [like the blood of Zechariah].

They set out before You so great a sacrificial offering that the altar was
too small to contain its measure, as babes and suckling infants were given
as whole burnt offerings. Accept Your sacrifices and remember Your offerings!

The precincts are filled to the corners with sacrificial victims: limbs and
members, heads and feet, dry matter and brains; the dear fledgling children of righteous women.

The schoolchildren are fodder for the altar, Students together with their
teachers atone for the nation. So great a sizzling sound was never heard.
Let the smell of the sacrifices of Judah please!

The priest prepare women as well as men; slaughtering, sprinkling, draining, they proceed with the rite. The souls of the holy are a pure freewill offering: the breast, the thigh, the cheeks of the head.

The tears well up and stream from every side. Those who slaughter and those who are slaughtered all groan upon one another. The blood of fathers laps against the blood of sons, as they howl their benedictions over slaughter: "Hear, O Israel!"

Let this sight come before You: young women, who put their trust in You, slaughtered naked in broad daylight; the fairest of women—their wombs slashed open and the afterbirth forced out from between their legs.

[Has the like of this] ever been seen or heard? Could anyone believe such a stupefying sight? They lead their children to the slaughter as if to a beautiful bridal canopy. After this, O Exalted and Triumphant Lord, will You hold back?

To the modern reader this delirium of slaughter, blood, and limbs must seem grotesque in the extreme. Yet to the mind of medieval Ashkenaz there was nothing hideous about it, and not because of an otherworldly derogation of human life or perverse sanguinary obsessions, but rather because of an attitude of affirmation and reverence toward the Temple service of antiquity. In contrast to their Sepharadic coreligionists, whose rationalism led to an interpretation of the sacrifices as a stage in Israel's religious development not to be reverted to in the Messianic Age, Ashkenaz experienced no embarrassment on this score. For them the sacrificial system remained always the lost quintessential emblem of the true and immediate service of God. Each morning as part of his prayers a Jew recited passages from Leviticus, Numbers, and Mishnah *Zevaḥim* enumerating the sacrifices, accompanied by the supplication: "May this verbal recitation be acceptable to You, as though we had offered the daily sacrifice in its right time and place." Thrice daily as part of the Amidah prayer the worshiper implored, "Restore the divine service to Your House and accept with favor the burnt-offerings and prayers of Israel." The scholarly elite took as an essential part of its curriculum the study of talmudic tractates concerning the Temple offerings; scholars debated the manner and method of the sacrifices—details of organs, limbs, and knives—as if the issues were absolutely alive. In short, far from there being any disjunction between spirituality and sacrifice in Ashkenazic culture, the two were the same. The Temple ritual was familiar, esteemed, and longed for.

The piyyut by Rabbi David bar Meshullam is based on a correspondence between two systems of references: the community of Israel in all its components (men and women, infants and youths, schoolchildren and teachers, brides and bridegrooms, etc.) and the order of the sacrifices in all its components (daily offerings, sin offerings, free-will offerings, etc.). Each is a kind of anatomy of the realm to which it refers. The poem proceeds by urging a correlation between an element in one system with an element in the other; the infants, for example, correspond to the yearling lambs of the burnt offering, and, dramatically, the preparation and slaughter of women and children by heads of households in anticipation of the arrival of the Crusaders corresponds to the preparation and slaughter of animals in the ancient Temple ritual. This correlation, however, is neither clear nor symmetrical. The strongest impact in the poem is undoubtedly felt in the unshrinking portrayal of the details of the slaughter and spread of blood. This is a kind of harrowing realism, the graphic representation of concrete acts. Yet on close inspection of the text, we realize that this aura of fidelity to fact derives from one side of the correspondence alone, and *not* the side we would expect, not the side that is supposed to convey the contemporary historical moment. The pious of Worms and Mainz did pronounce the sacrificial blessing and did wield ritual slaughtering knives and did slit the throats of their family member and each other. However, what they did not do from all accounts is engage in the kind of dismembering and picking apart of organs which makes up one of the dominant images of the piyyut. The depiction remains staunchly realistic, but the reality which it depicts is not the events of 1096 but the other system of reference in the poem: the cult of the Jerusalem Temple.

In the progress of the poem contemporary events are assimilated further and further into the paradigm of Mikdash. Correspondence becomes dramatic identity. The faithful of Worms and Mainz are *there* in the Sanctuary; their blood pours upon the Temple floor; their bodies pile up upon the great altar and spill over into the Temple courtyards (the *'azarot*); the priests slaughter the sacrificial victims and place them upon the woodpile, as the pleasing odor rises to God's nostrils. For the moment the millennium that separated Sanctuary from Crusade is suspended; the vast reaches of exile with their imposed alienation between God and Israel are transcended. The omnipresent "as if" could be removed, the mediating *ke'ilu* that expressed the prayerful anxiety of the worshiper as he pleaded "may my verbal prayer be acceptable *as if* I had performed the ritual offerings."

This throbbing recreation is not all. It was no ordinary day in the life of the cult that was being reenacted through simple repetition. Consistent with the proud sense of self that pervades all these texts, the generation and its exploits—as they are collapsed and concentrated into a single emblematic moment in the poem— amount to a *surpassing* of the Mikdash. Never in the history of Israel, even in the heights of its ancient glory, had the altar been piled high with so many sacrifices in one day, and, it goes without saying, never had those sacrifices not been animal proxies for the faithful but the faithful themselves. Two themes in the piyyut embody this sense of consummation. The general motion of the poem is from fragmentation to communion. At the outset the subjects of the poem exist as separate classes of individuals—women, children, fathers, schoolchildren. As the slaughter proceeds these categories are literally broken into constituent parts—"the breast, the thigh, the cheeks of the head"—resulting in the end in a massive meeting and commingling of tears and blood in which the former separateness is completely dissolved. Father and son, teacher and student deliquesce into perfect communion. The marriage imagery that appears at the end of the poem is the second theme. Mentioned briefly here as a crescendo to the entreaty for divine acknowledgment, the image of the slaughter as wedding pervades the piyyutim of the times. As an emblem of consummation, as the unification of God and the faithful in eternity, the *huppah*, "marriage canopy," draws into a rich conceptual knot the many thematic strands of the poem: the linkage between the generations, the free-will offering of love, the sacramental flow of blood, unification and sanctification.[12]

Let us stand back a moment and ask why this poem is impor-
rant. For after all our efforts to comprehend the values and consciousness of the subjects, the text remains a gruesome and fright-
ful transfiguring of self-immolation, all the more so for its
preference for symbol rather than historical fact. The significance
of the poem lies in the fact that this piyyut and others like it, more
than the chronicles, came to constitute the literary-religious norm
of response to catastrophe in Ashkenazic culture for the next eight
hundred years. This does not mean, of course, that everywhere
and always, or perhaps ever, in this vast stretch of history was this
response to catastrophe repeated. It does mean that the figure of
the martyrs of 1096 as refracted in the texts of the liturgical poets
did become the sovereign image, the norm of imitation, by which
all things were measured, adapted, or found wanting. This dominance remained unchallenged even by the historically more significant disaster of the Ukrainian pogroms of 1648.

Such a position of cultural dominance could not be achieved
without dislodging what had formerly stood in its place. This, of
course, involved no outright vitiation of the past. Daniel, Lamentations, the midrash, the payyetanic traditions of the *kinot* for the
Temple, the legends of the ten martyred sages—all remained intact, studied, and recited in the synagogue. Yet as the contemporary link that was affixed to this tradition, the piyyutim of 1096
wielded special authority because their drama unfolded under familiar conditions of European Christian persecution, and also because their radical piety achieved a new dimension in suffering
service and witness. The martyrs of 1096 had modeled themselves
on such figures from Scripture and legend as Abraham, Miriam
and her seven sons, and the Ten Sages. Because their actions, as
mythicized in the poetry, consummated and surpassed the figures
of antiquity, the martyrs of 1096 themselves became the new model
for subsequent generations.

It should be noted that 1096 does not have the same valence in
economic and social history as it has in literary history. Salo Baron
and Robert Chazan have argued that there is no substantial discontinuity in Franco-German Jewish society as a whole as a result

of the First Crusade. The towns were quickly resettled, commerce and trade were reconstructed, some of the academies went on to produce scholars of great distinction.[13] If we grant this argument—and there is no reason not to—we then find ourselves confronted by a significant and interesting divergence in Jewish history between societal arrangements and what may be called the iconographic imagination, the image-making capacity of the religious mentality. For this latter faculty, in its own terms, there is no denying that 1096 was a true turning point.

The establishment of the new norm was variously consequential in reshaping responses to catastrophe for many centuries. There occurred, to begin with, a subtle shift in the way in which texts were appropriated and interpreted. The vast energies of the midrash had been employed in the close and intensive "working over" of the scriptural text: producing etymologies for key words, correlating verses with contemporary events, reinterpreting theologically discordant statements, supplying intertextual linkages. Whatever was done was concerned with the reinterpretation and recovery of the *language* of the received tradition. In representing the events of 1096, in contrast, the payyetanim were less exercised by a close attention to the reinterpretation of language. Although they took over many of the verbal clusters and motifs from Bible and midrash, this language was used as allusion and quotation; it was left relatively untransformed through reinterpretation. This is, of course, in part a result of generic differences between midrash and piyyut and even broader changes in poetics. But it is also due to the specific nature of the events of 1096 and their representation. As depicted in the poems, the martyrs saw their actions as an emulation, a reenactment, a fulfillment of exemplary lives from Israel's antiquity (Abraham and Isaac) or exemplary institutions (the Sanctuary). The point of reference is much less the language of the past than the figures of the past. Akin to typology in the Christian tradition (with its own workings out in Scripture and midrash),[14] this consciousness understands earlier figures and institutions as types that are fulfilled in later antitypes. As the martyrs of 1096 are installed as the new types—now that they have fulfilled their precursor figures—they stimulated the growth of a new kind of hermeneutic which reads that past less through exegesis proper than through figuration.

Until 1096 the resonance of catastrophe emanated entirely from the destruction of the Temple. Mourning the Temple meant fasting at set times in the year and immersing oneself in the literature of lamentation in its various guises. This was an essentially passive process in which the Jew identified with the Sanctuary, reexperienced the pain of its loss, and consoled himself with promises of vindication and restoration. The poetic depiction of 1096 introduced a dimension that was unprecedentedly active and individual. The martyrs had not mourned the Temple; they recreated the Temple. The norm of active self-sacrifice by individuals established itself alongside the norm of passive mourning for a collective institution. It is in the Middle Ages that the martyr emerges as a literary ideal. Martyrology, writing about martyrdom, was, as we saw in the previous chapter, a modest presence in the texts of the Rabbis; it is only in medieval times that it becomes a conspicuous and capacious genre of Hebrew writing, both in the higher literary culture of the piyyutim as well as in more popular contexts, in which martyrs from antiquity and recent times were made the subject of innumerable legends and wondrous tales.

There is no exaggerating the permeation of martyrology into the fabric of Askhenazic culture. The names of the martyrs were inscribed in special books and read in the synagogue on days commemorating the disasters, and a prayer on their behalf, the *Av harahamim,* became a permanent part of the Sabbath service. But something more happened: in the generations immediately following the First Crusade the ceremony of remembering the dead began to be practiced not only in the case of renowned rabbinical martyrs of public persecution but also simply for all who died natural deaths, entirely irrespective of conditions of persecution. A bereaved son would recite the Kaddish, an Aramaic doxology, for the memory of his recently departed father or mother, in the conviction that such recitation had the power to save the deceased's soul from tortures beyond the grave. The practice gained headway in the thirteenth century and by the fifteenth a new custom emerged: the *Yorzeit*, the recitation of the Kaddish on the anniversary of the death of a relative. And soon there was further established the *Yizkor* or *Hazkarat neshamot*, the Kaddish together with various supplications for the souls of the departed, recited by all on the Day of Atonement and the last days of the Pilgrimage Festivals. Taken together, this amounts to a kind of cult of the dead that began in medieval Ashkenaz and later spread to all of world Jewry.[15] The astounding tenacity of this outlook is observable in the simple sociological fact, known to all, that in the process of secularization, and especially in the acculturation of Jewish immigrants from Eastern Europe to America, the recitation of the mourner's Kaddish with its attendant rites is the very last particle of tradition to be given up.

Anxiety was an unofficial though pervasive precipitate of the new norm. It was, simply, a norm which few could live up to. The further Crusader persecutions of 1147 and 1187 and the outbreaks surrounding the Black Death in 1348 were among many such occasions for collective and often massive witnessing of the unity of God's name through martyrdom. But nothing could match the mighty confluence of factors that had gone into the making of 1096: the purity of the religious grounding of the hatred between Christian and Jew, the frenzy of death through self-sacrifice and homicide, and most importantly, the generation's unexampled sense of its own righteousness and spiritual attainments. Once this amalgam was transfigured by the payyetanim nothing could approach it; it was a symbol pushed to its highest register. Later events had to take their place under this sign, and the gap between the two could never be unnoticed. If this was true for belated martyrs, then how much more so was it for those whom God chose not to choose, those not called to bear witness with their lives, or for those forced converts who returned to Judaism. The expiatory and eschatological components of the norm of 1096 should not be underestimated. By becoming sacrificial ash on the altar of the Lord, the martyrs believed that they not only automatically secured atonement for their sins and for those of the generation, but guaranteed direct passage of their souls to the Garden of Eden to abide there forever in God's light. For "lesser" martyrs and for those not so chosen, no ecstatic moment came when the Exile was revoked; the burden of unredemption pressed down ever more heavily. Hear these lines from a poet who wrote within the same generation as the Worms and Mainz martyrs. The lines come at the end of a poem describing the bloody self-sacrifices.

> Think not of the dead,
> For they have been set and sealed for eternal life,
> But of us, who remain accountable for our sins,
> We, who have transgressed perfect commandments.
> Eternal One! Into the protection of your wings we flee,
> For we have been left abandoned *(agunim)* and stricken.[16]

The use of a variant of the term *"agunah,"* the "chained" woman who cannot remarry because of the disappearance or unproven death of her husband, carries a strong emotional charge. The merit may devolve upon their descendants, but those left behind in this life are not relieved of dread and self-doubt. Their unease is a precursor of the survivor guilt of later ages.

The last massive disaster in Ashkenaz before the modern period was the Chmielnicki massacres of 1648–1649 in the Ukraine, and this event can serve as a final test case for our investigation of the transactions of the literary imagination with history. Before proceeding, a word about the naming and mnemonics of catastrophe in Jewish tradition. Both "1096" and "Mainz" have been used in the preceding pages as a kind of shorthand for a series of events and literary responses to events that were not limited to that year or to that location. This is a practice that is deeply ingrained in Jewish historical writing from its earliest stages: key dates and key place names have become symbols for vast and complex historical catastrophes. To a literate Jew, uttering the date 1096 (in Hebrew, vocalized as *tatnu*) or 1648 *(tah vetat)* and the town Mainz or Nemirov can evoke only one set of associations. And so a series is formed: 586, 70, 135, 1096, 1492, 1648, 1881, 1903, together with spatial coordinates: Jerusalem, Betar, Mainz, Spain, Nemirov, Kishenev. In recent times Auschwitz has recognizably come to stand for the Holocaust as a whole. Much is revealed about the nature of historical memory in this phenomenon. In Jewish history the

serial linkage of paradigmatic years and places makes a clear
statement about the way in which discrete historical catastrophes
are drained of their discreteness and absorbed into a larger tradition.

The year 1648 well deserves its paradigmatic status. It was then
that the Cossacks under Bogdan Chmielnicki joined together with
the Ukrainian peasantry to drive out the Polish landowners who
had colonized the Ukraine. The principal victims of the attacks were
the Jews, who had been brought by the Poles into the Ukraine to
administer their estates. According to Jewish sources 100,000 Jews
were killed during that year, 300 Jewish communities were obli-
terated, and many Jews were sold into slavery. In contrast to 1096,
the events of 1648 constituted a titanic dislocation of the social,
economic, and institutional contours of Jewish life. A whole segment of the Jewish world had been wiped out almost overnight.
The Jewish people as a whole felt the trauma; in Poland and the
Ukraine the reconstruction of Jewish society took generations, and
what was rebuilt never ceased to live under the spectre of Chmielnicki's memory.

The central document of the times is the chronicle *Yeven metsulah* (The Mirey Pit) by Rabbi Nathan Nata Hanover, and the
chronicle makes it clear that both in its historical actuality and its
contemporary perception 1648 was indeed different.[17] Although
in certain circumstances Jews were given the chance to escape death
through conversion, the crisis was to a much lesser degree than
1096 a naked confrontation between the truth of the Cross and
the truth of the Torah. Religious hatred was only one factor con-
tributory to the implacable ruthlessness of the Cossacks and the
Ukrainians. The chronicler's view of the situation, to put it very
simply, is that the Jews were in the wrong place at the wrong time.
The Cossacks had formed an alliance with the Tatars and coopted
the Ukrainian peasantry in order to break and expel the coloniz-
ing Polish gentry. As the visible agents of the Poles and as for-
eigners who had the most contact with the Ukrainians, the Jews
were the natural and available objects of attack, especially in the
absence of any protection from their employers. Perhaps because
of an awareness of these political factors, one finds an absence of

the kind of self-immolation that was the keynote of 1096. Although the chronicle records several dramatic vignettes in the genre of the Crusader poems, the dominant spectacle is of Jews being slaughtered by the sword of vicious gentiles, not by their own hand. Furthermore, the option of temporary conversion, when offered, seems to have been taken by not insubstantial numbers of Jews, though there is no certainty as to the figures. The fact that *Yeven metsulah* presents the speeches of rabbinical communal leaders exhorting their flocks to take the high road of martyrdom would indicate the existence of an insecure communal will in need of strengthening.

Yet, it must be said that while these discontinuities are undeniable, the dominant religious-literary response remained in the other chronicles of the times (*Tsok ha'itim* by Meir b. Samuel of Schebreshin and *Megillat 'efah* by Shabbetai b. Meir ha-Kohen) or, taken as a whole, by *Yeven metsulah* itself. In their efforts to winnow contemporary historical fact from the elaborate conventions of traditional chronicle writing, historians have left the impression that the nub of *Yeven metsulah* lies in its insight into the social-political situation of the Jews. While certainly there is useful information to be extracted from the text, the purpose of the chronicles's author, Rabbi Nathan, was to acquit himself of the responsibility to provide the relevant details of setting and background rather than to offer principles of explanation and causation. *Yeven metsulah* is written within the essential canons of the Crusade chronicles. The catastrophe is given meaning under the general rubric of *kiddush hashem,* which in the intervening time has been broadened to comprehend all who die under conditions of persecution, whether choice was present as an element or not.[18] In place of accounts of large-scale collective self-sacrifice, in *Yeven metsulah* the chronicler supplies several stories of pious virgins who go along with the approaches of their amorous captors just long enough to make dramatic and suicidal gestures of loyalty to the God of Israel. As set pieces these vignettes breathe amply of the spirit of the 1096 documents. No virulent sin, moreover, is imputed to the generation as a whole; the notion of the trial of the worthy is the pervasive tone. Nowhere is this more evident than in the concluding section of *Yeven metsulah*, which is a paean to the lost spiritual grandeur of the Polish Jewry. In the manner of a proper homiletical eulogy, Rabbi Nathan takes a set of attributes from Mishnah *Avot* (study, charity, justice, truth, and peace) and describes Polish Jewry in the excellence of its embodiment of each value. This kind of nostalgic idealization, which we called generically a historical idyll, was already in evidence in the midrash's account of the exquisiteness of Jerusalem society before the Destruction and again in the praises of the payyetanim for the peerless righteousness and learning of the Rhineland settlements.[19] The hundreds of memorial volumes, the *yizkor bikher*, of destroyed European Jewish communities in our own time are the latest sad expression of this impulse.

Once again we confront a divergence between social-economic history and the literary-religious imagination. This time the terms are reversed. In contrast to 1096, the Chmielnicki massacres constituted a real disaster, a calamity of huge proportions for Jewish society, while the iconographic spirit made do with received forms. Two facts from Hebrew literary history illustrate the persistence of this continuity and even its intensification in the centuries following 1648. Many piyyutim were composed to memorialize the massacres, but in subsequent generations these texts were eclipsed in the rites of Ashkenazic synagogues by the stronger precursor poems from the Crusader period, especially those relating to the Blois incident of 1171. There was something about the ancient authority of these poems and their expressions of radical piety that was apparently not displaceable.[20] The second fact has to do with the later reception of *Yeven metsulah*. It was extraordinarily popular; it was reprinted in every generation and the simplicity of its style gave it a wide readership. We know from allusions to *Yeven metsulah* in the contemporary literature of later periods that what was compelling to readers was not the material of historical explanation but the perennial and paradigmatic story of Jewish persecution and martyrdom. What lived on in the historical memory of Ashkenaz were the several poignant stories embedded in the larger chronicle about loyal Jewish maidens who took their lives rather than be taken by the Cossacks.

PART

·II·

THE REHEARSAL

·4·

THE RUSSIAN POGROMS AND

THE SUBVERSION OF THE

MARTYROLOGICAL IDEAL

 One of the most poignant scenes in late nineteenth-century Hebrew literature is the picture Moshe Leib Lilienblum draws of himself in the spring of 1881. By that time Lilienblum had passed through several ideological transformations: from the mitnagdic orthodoxy of his Lithuanian origins, to the religious reform of the Haskalah, and then to nihilistic positivism on the Russian model, and now at the age of thirty-eight he was, in a sense, going back to school. Lilienblum was intent on attending university and achieving a career of practical usefulness; but having never studied secular subjects, he had first to master the gymnasium curriculum. There he sat in Odessa, struggling with the rudiments of algebra, Latin, and geography, tutored by youths half his age, when the wave of pogroms that suddenly spread through southern Russia burst upon Odessa. Distracted from his studies in the months that followed and deeply shaken in his assumptions about the world, Lilienblum came to the realization that the Jews are ultimately and unchangeably alien to European society, and that rather than trying to gain

entry to that society or emigrating to other countries where the
sad tale would repeat itself, the Jews must return to their ancestral
homeland and once again make it their own. To activity as an or-
ganizer and publicist on behalf of the cause of political Zionism
Lilienblum gave the remaining thirty years of his life. His commitment to Zionism was experienced as something more than an
arrival at a final ideological resting place or the return of an alienated intellectual to his people. Lilienblum was reborn; the spirit
and will that had withered within him were recalled to new life.[1]

I have adduced the example of Lilienblum because his life is
representative of the profound duality of catastrophe and creativity that marked the pogroms of 1881 and their aftermath. The
pogroms were an eruption of antisemitic violence unprecedented
in modern times and horrible in the maiming, loss of life, and
economic disaster they left in their wake. At the same time, the
pogroms triggered the release of a great intensity of creative
energies in the Jewish society of Czarist Russia: programs, pro-
posals, ideologies, organizations, movements, migrations. Yet inasmuch as Lilienblum was a *Hebrew* writer he is *not* a representative figure because of the unrepresentativeness of Hebrew literature
itself. The masses did not read modern Hebrew; they tended to
be traditionally religious and unsympathetic to secular literature;
and the economically dispossessed among them were more inclined to emigration than to ideology. Among the intellegentsia,
Hebrew literature in association with Zionism represented only one
cultural-ideological solution to the Jewish problem; it stood alongside the Jewish socialism of the Bund, general revolutionary com-
munism, Diaspora cultural autonomism, and, later, Yiddishism as
a direct competitor in the sphere of language and literature.

I stress the minority status of Hebrew literature not to apologize
for its serving as the subject of the remainder of this study but to
remark on a significant shift in the nature of the literary object
under investigation. The literature we have dealt with until now—
scripture, midrash, piyyut, chronicle—was inscribed at the center
of a religious civilization, often serving in its liturgy. These texts
were generated by the norms of that civilization, and they in turn
became its norms. Although created in elite circles, as a canonical

literature, it was circulated among the people and accepted by them as a whole. While this traditional literature continued to be studied and produced, there arose alongside it, from the time of the Enlightenment forward, a new Hebrew literature that was conscious of serving secular ends. Philosophy and historiography had been written in Hebrew from the Middle Ages and continued to be in the modern period; added to them now were social criticism and satire and, most important, belles-lettres per se, in emulation of the autonomous status of poetry and romance in European culture.

There are two relevant facts about the new literature for our purposes. It is not, first, a sacred literature founded upon a metaphysics of inspiration and tradition. Despite the various modalities of the relationship between new and old—negation, dependence, continuity, usurpation, parody—this is an undeniable break in the history of Hebrew literature as regards the status of the documents as discourse. This holds true for the social setting of the new literature as well. Despite the significance we may give it relative to contemporary history or relative to its later successes, and despite the air of superior significance with which it regarded itself, it must be remembered that the diffusion of modern Hebrew literature remained limited to the intellegentsia and only to certain circles within it. This remained true well into the twentieth century.[2] Given these combined conditions of isolation and superiority, it is not surprising that one of the main themes of the new literature was the fate of the masses of Jews who did not read it and, as we shall see presently, the responsibility of the Hebrew writer-intellectual to them.

The differential responses of the masses and the intellectuals to the events of 1881 are crucial in assessing the significance of the pogroms as a turning point in Jewish history. In March 1881 Czar Alexander II was assassinated, and the charge of Jewish responsibility for his death was made credible by the promulgation of large-scale antisemitic propaganda by the Sviaschennaia Drushina, a secret league of reactionary nobles. It was, in fact, the other extreme of the political spectrum that supplied direct participation in the pogroms themselves. Radical revolutionary groups viewed

pogroms as progressive phenomena, expressions of popular justice that schooled the masses in revolutionary violence and helped
them to understand the nature of the system.[3] The pogroms began on April 27, 1881, in Elizavetgrad and spread to Kiev, Ber-
dichev, Odessa, and hundreds of smaller settlements in the Ukraine.
The outbreaks spread along the major railway lines. Unemployed
railroad workers and students would enter a town, mix with the
local riffraff, get drunk, and begin to destroy and loot Jewish
businesses and homes. Having got word of the violence, peasants
from the surrounding areas would come into town a day or two
later to steal property, murder, and rape. The police and local militia reacted with painful slowness, often not intervening until after
two days; sometimes some of their number participated in the
massacre. In all, several hundred souls perished in the pogroms,
several thousand were wounded, and vast economic damage was
done, amounting to tens of millions of rubles. Consequent upon
the pogroms the Imperial government promulgated a series of anti-
Jewish measures which aimed at isolating the Jews and containing
their influence, forcing them to emigrate and thus lessening the
provocation to social unrest among the general population. These
"May Laws" of 1882 strengthened the restrictions on Jewish settlement both within and without the Pale and enjoined Jews from
doing business on Sundays and gentile holidays. In 1887 the *nu-
merus clausus* was introduced, which imposed severe quotas on
Jewish attendance at secondary schools and universities. On the
first day of Passover, 1891, the Jews faced an immediate and sudden expulsion from the city of Moscow.[4]

    Yet despite the dramatic imposition of these ordeals, for the
Jewish masses 1881 was less a turning point than an event which
accelerated ongoing processes. Throughout the century the wel-
fare of the Jewish masses had been deteriorating as a result of a
geometric increase in population over a narrowing base of economic opportunity. The drift of Jews from villages and towns to
the cities, where they competed for livelihood with newly eman-
cipated Russian peasants who had made the same migration, created severe conditions of dispossession and deracination, and these
combined with other factors to lead to the beginnings of mass em-

igration. The great Russian famine of 1868–1869 was a strong motivation in its own right. In the decade *before* 1881 over 40,000 Jews emigrated to America alone. Although in the decades following the pogroms the number increased many fold, the momentum had already been set in motion.[5]

For the intellectuals 1881 was a much greater shock. In our minds the history of East European Jewry is often conceived of as an endless series of anti-Jewish pogroms. The facts are otherwise: With the exception of local disturbances in 1744 and 1768 and an isolated pogrom in Odessa in 1871, there were no large-scale outbreaks of violence against the Jews in the two hundred and thirty years since the Cossack massacres in 1648. The pogroms of 1881 were not, then, just the eruption of a perennial menace; they signaled something much more threatening. The sudden metastasis of the political situation most deeply affected those intellectuals who were committed to the hopeful prospect of the emancipation of Russian Jewry within Russian society. The proponents of Russian Haskalah, the domestication of European Enlightenment ideals in a program for the modernization of Jewish life, had been encouraged by the "whiff of liberalism" introduced by the policies of Alexander II in the 1850s and 1860s. Though a complex and varied set of programs and ideas, the Haskalah in its many streams held as a common tenet a belief in the reality and tenability of a kind of social compact: Russian society would lift the civil disabilities of the Jews in exchange for a degree of westernization ("Russification") of Jewry as regarded education, dress, occupation, and to a much lesser extent, religion. So, for example, if a Jew attended a government-sponsored school and learned languages and sciences, he would expect to be allowed to attend university, join a professional guild, and settle in a city outside the Pale like St. Petersburg. For a brief time and for a limited number of members of the middle class such opportunities were opened; but already with the Polish insurrection of 1863 and the consequent fears of a Judeo-Polish alliance, Russian policy toward the Jews came once again to be dominated by xenophobic sentiment. The late 1860s and the 1870s witnessed the renewal of reaction in government circles and virulent criticism of the Jews.

On the part of the Russian government there was, and had been, no compact. Alexander II seems to have been motivated more by conversionist hopes than by a belief in the potential integration of the Jew *qua* Jew into Russian society. Yet for Jewish intellectuals it was exceedingly difficult to admit disconfirming evidence. To relinquish the conviction that the Jews would be dealt with justly if they reformed themselves would have been to relinquish a belief in reason, and given the essential values of the Haskalah this would have been to give up a great deal. The Jewish masses, on the other hand, unfettered by ideology in this regard, sensed the shifting winds and, as we have said, bestirred themselves. With some exceptions, among them a number of proto-Zionist thinkers, the intellectuals clung to a belief in the eventual emancipation of Russian Jewry; the physical security of that Jewry, its material viability, was never put into question by them. Parallels in our century to the attitudes of American intellectuals to Russia can suggest some of the tenacity of these beliefs.

As in the case of the Crusader massacres, the significance of 1881 lay not in the absolute quantum of destruction. The waves of pogroms of 1903–1905 and 1917–1920 resulted in loss of life on a far, far greater scale. The paradigm-shattering power of 1881 lay in the reinterpretation of Russian Jewish history suddenly forced upon Jewish intellectuals. The so-called liberalization of the 1850s could no longer be regarded as a harbinger of things to come but had to be reinterpreted as a surface aberration. Instead, it was the pogroms that revealed the true conditions of Russian-Jewish relations and promised to be the dark precursor of their future as well. If the Jews improved themselves, educated themselves, made themselves productive, prettified themselves, *it would make no difference.* It could be perceived in retrospect that from the time that Russia "inherited" the Jews in the partitions of Poland in the late eighteenth century, the intention of the Imperial government had been to isolate the Jews from the rest of Russian society. This was not just a geographical and economic isolation but a juridical one as well. The Jews were forced to occupy a space outside the law. They were not protected by the same rights and privileges as indigenous Russians or even as other minorities. Being outside the law meant that the savaging of Jews was not criminal; the central government restrained this impulse for the sake of preserving internal civil order and thus central control. But once the restraint was lifted, pushed aside by the popular will or withdrawn for official motives, there could be no hope for the Jews. Belief in the very tenability of Jewish life in Russia suddenly and irreversibly had to be given up.[6]

The founding of political Zionism and the Bund, together with the plethora of other approaches to the solution of the Jewish problem, is a sign that, at the level of politics and ideology, the pogroms were responded to by the taking of vigorous and unprecedented measures. At the level of the literary imagination, however, the response was considerably more traditional. Though in poetry the confidence in reason and reform of the Haskalah was jettisoned, it was the tradition that was reverted to. Poets bypassed the modern period and reached further into the past in search of models of discourse appropriate to the new historical consciousness. The biblical traditions of lamentation and consolation unsurprisingly filled this need. As with the prophets, the attitude toward Israel reversed itself upon the destruction. From having been the object of didactic and ennobling preachments, Israel allegorized suddenly became the subject of mercy and solicitude. Take these lines written in the winter of 1882 by Judah Leib Gordon, the preeminent Hebrew poet of the Haskalah.

Why do you sob, my sister Ruhamah?
Why are you downcast, why is your spirit agitated?
Because plunderers have fallen upon your honor and profaned
   it?
If the fist has triumphed, the hand of the enemy grown mighty,
Can the blame be yours, my sister Ruhamah?[7]

The basic pattern of the literature of consolation is clear; Israel personified as a weeping, battered woman victimized by a brutal enemy. Ruhamah, an allusion to Hosea 2:3, means "the pitied one"; the consolation the poet offers is the assurance that responsibility lies not with her but with the bloodthirstiness of the enemy. Later in the poem he offers further promise of future relief, which for

Gordon, unlike more nationalist contemporaries, will come in the form of emigration to America. The same high biblical diction, the same extravagant pathos, and the same invective against the oppressor are the basic mode for such other writers of pogrom poetry as M. M. Dolitsky, and Judah Halevi Levin. An exemplary figure and the author of the most popular verses on the subject was Simon Frug, a Russified Jewish poet who began writing in Russian but after the pogroms became a Yiddish poet and Jewish nationalist.[8] In the case of the poetry on Kishinev, as we shall see later on, the response was just as traditional.

The distinctively biblical mold in which the subject of the pogroms was cast was the result of the conventions of Haskalah poetry and its linguistic ideals. In the wider literary culture of the 1880s and 1890s, it was the Middle Ages that were pushed to the center of consciousness. The ground was prepared by the rediscovery in Jewish historiography of the martyrological documents of the Middle Ages. Between 1887 and 1889 Hayyim Jonah Gurland, the government rabbi of Odessa, issued a vast compendium of annotated materials from the massacres of 1648: chronicles, piyyutim, letters, eulogies, prayers.[9] In 1892 Adolf Neubauer, the reader in Rabbinic Hebrew at Oxford, brought out an edition of Hebrew historiographical texts, among which were the powerful and affecting chronicles from the First Crusade, hitherto unpublished.[10] H. Graetz's massive *Geschichte*, which functioned in Hebrew literature like a great nineteenth-century historical novel and spoke eloquently of the epic of Jewish suffering, was translated into Hebrew by S. P. Rabbinowitz between 1890 and 1899,[11] and in 1899 Solomon Buber published his critical edition of Lamentations Rabbah.[12] The conception of Jewish history as a movement toward emancipation had now to accommodate the older notion of the recurrent, periodic victimization of the Jews at the hands of implacable enemies.

The medievalization of Jewish literary consciousness, however, was not universal. The texts of three major writers of the period—Abramowitsch, Tchernichowsky, and Bialik—constitute an investigation and a subversion of the reversion to martyrological models. It is this response to a response that forms the subject of this chapter. The counterstatement is more significant for literary history than the norm in this case because the dissenting texts are high art while the medievalizing texts are not, and because it was these writings, especially Bialik's, which constituted the norm which in turn exercised a great impact upon the response—or lack of it—to the Holocaust in contemporary Hebrew literature.

By its nature it was the prose rather than the poetry of the late Haskalah that engaged the actualities of Jewish life. The greatest prose writer of the time, Shalom Jacob Abramowitsch (known by the name of his narrative persona, Mendele Mokher Seforim) had founded his fictional enterprise upon a profound critique of the central institutions of Jewish society in the Pale: marriage as a commercial transaction, rampant overpopulation, sensualism and verbality as substitutes for power and politics, scholasticism and ignorance of the natural sciences, inhumanity in class relations— in short, his critique embraced the entire Haskalah program for reform, though with none of the Haskalah's blithe confidence in the inevitability of reform. By the time of the pogroms in 1881 the contours of Abramowitsch's fictional world were already well defined and the early versions of the major works were already written. To ask how Abramowitsch responded to the pogroms, then, is to ask how a fully formed major writer is affected by a great change in the fortunes of the reality about which he writes. This is not an easy question to answer on technical grounds because of the instability of Abramowitsch's textual production. He was hardly the kind of author who would write a book, publish it, and go on to the next; rather, he maintained throughout his career three or four major projects that he was continually expanding and revis- ing, while shifting back and forth between Hebrew and Yiddish. Fortunately, there is a datable and unilingual group of short sto- ries that Abramowitsch wrote in the 1880s and 1890s, in Hebrew, which can serve as a stable point of reference.

In the 1886–1887 story "Beseter ra'am" (Secret Thunder), set in the Mendelean town of Kabtsiel, Abramowitsch declares him- self unambiguously as to which options in the representation of the pogroms he declines to take. Like the hero of Walter Scott's *Waverly*, the Mendele figure in the story is comically unconscious for the duration of the pogrom in Kabtsiel, and since the tale is told from his point of view, the sensationalist account we most expect to be at the story's center is simply not there. The narrator justifies the omission by explaining that the events have already been well described in the " 'Book of Lamentations for Kabtsiel,' attributed to one of the troop of noisy threnodists who appeared like mushrooms after the rain in the Hebrew periodical press at the time of the outrages."[13] The reference is to nothing other than the high biblical pathos of Gordon, Frug, Dolitzky, and Levin, or at least their local imitators, the authors of innumerable chronicles and elegies for particular pogroms. Mendele treats us to a sample from the fictitious "Lament for Kabtsiel."

Woe! Ennobling houses were laid waste on the day of reproach, and tens of thousands of our brethren Israel were ruined. Those raised to the purple in palaces of delight were left naked; hungry and thirsty they wandered in the streets.[14]

Mendele proceeds to poke fun at these epic hyperboles. Kabtsiel, to begin with, is in truth a tiny place with a small population. There are no substantial structures, not to mention "palaces of delight," with the exception perhaps of the rickety one-story tax house in the marketplace. Far from being the sons and daughters of the nobility, the Kabtsielites lead a threadbare existence, and most of them have no apparent source of income; they have no property and their few valuables are pawned weekly to make Sabbath expenses. In comparing the rhetoric with the reality, Abramowitsch is not taking away from the seriousness of the pogroms and their impact; he *is* deriding the conventional literary response to them. A national literature that makes no discriminations and absorbs every negative event into the rhetoric of absolute catastrophe, that rushes to idealize and beatify what was destroyed, that takes off into the heavens of inflated ornamental language—this is not a national literature that well serves the nation.

The critical question of whether the pogroms can be or should be absorbed into the rituals of perennial catastrophe is raised by Abramowitsch in a story of ten years later, "Hanisrafim" (1897).[15] *Nisrafim* are a class of beggars, people supposedly made homeless by fire, who, on the strength of their misfortune and of letters of attestation to that effect, wander from settlement to settlement seeking alms. The premise of the tale is that Mendele, in his travels through the countryside as a bookpeddler, encounters an immense caravan of beggars, who turn out to be the entire village of Kabtsiel, Mendele's hometown, taken to the road as *nisrafim*. The theme of the story is the fundamental change Mendele undergoes in his attitude toward his townspeople in the very process of making inquiries about—and making fun of—their fate.

Before meeting up with the caravan, the narrator, Mendele, sets the mock-epic tone of the first half of the story by stating that the event he is about to recount occurred in the first year after the great fire in the community of Kabtsiel. He goes on to explain:

> The fire was inscribed in the register of the community, and by it the Kabtsielites began to measure time. They would say, for example: the birth of X, the marriage of Y, in year such-and-such to the Fire; the decree of the yarmulkes, the decree concerning the licensing of melamdim, the polluting and purifying of the putrid mikveh and river in the year such-and-such to the Fire. There are still old men and women alive from the time of the Fire, and when they used to tell of it sitting around the stove in the study house at dusk the young people would thirstily drink in their words and their eyes would glisten with tears.[16]

The epic reference that serves as the basis for the mock-epic structure in this passage is, of course, the Destruction of the Temple. Throughout the Middle Ages, Jews reckoned time both from the creation of the world and from the Destruction of the Temple. Through this linkage the pogrom in Kabtsiel is exalted to the heights of classic catastrophe and made the kind of founding, orientating event that demarcates the great epochs of history. In the catalogue of chronicled events that comes next the mock-epic space between the Destruction and the pogrom in Kabtsiel is at first not felt; it is natural, after all, for births and deaths and the like to be related to an important event in the life of a community. The gap becomes evident and then widens as the catalogue proceeds to list the anti-Jewish measures (parallel to the May Laws) that followed the pogrom. A decree concerning head coverings does not strike a note of great seriousness, and neither does a government requirement that melamdim be certified as competent to teach. The indictment of the heder system was one of the central planks in the Haskalah program, especially the profession of elementary teaching, which often served as the last refuge for the ineffectual and the ruined. The level of derision rises when the causes of an epidemic of infant death are superstitiously ascribed to sin rather than to the outrageous but tolerated sanitary conditions that prevail in the town. Instead of provoking the Kabtsielites to take stock of their situation and perhaps mobilize to alter it, the trauma of the pogrom has been domesticated, dissolved into talk, and absorbed into the comfortable glow of oral tradition. Once a terrible actuality, the pogrom has become, like the Destruction of the Temple itself, the stuff of hallowed myth.

When Mendele comes face-to-face with the Kabtsielites they are bewailing their fate with verses from Lamentations, sighing over the destruction of Kabtsiel visited upon them by God for their many sins. Confronted with the histrionics of high catastrophe and high mourning, Mendele probes a bit into the mundane specifics of the disaster. He discovers that this divinely dispatched conflagration actually began because of the negligence of one Naphtali, through whose uncleaned chimney sparks flew up and ignited a straw roof; because the houses of Kabtsiel are built one atop the other, the fire spread in a flash, and because Kabtsiel had never bothered to establish a fire brigade, nothing could be saved. The actual damage, it turns out upon further investigation, was not extensive; there were only a few real houses in Kabtsiel to be destroyed. But given the nonproductive occupational structure of the town, the ruin of these few householders spelled ruin for the many dependent upon them: the tenants who rented from them, the shopkeepers who sold to them, the melamdim who taught their children, the scribes who wrote mezuzot for their doors, and the dozen varieties of religious functionaries, the *kelei kodesh,* who eked out a living from their alms. So here they are, moaning, complaining, divided against themselves, an entire community pauperized and taken to the road.

The play on the self-deluding airs of the Kabstsielites, on their negligence, on their passivity paraded as pious trust in Providence, the satire on the flimsy vacuity at the heart of the community's economic existence, the deflationary parody of such classical Hebrew texts as Lamentations—this first half of "Hanisrafim" is topflight, classic Abramowitsch. It could have been lifted from an Abramowitsch text from thirty years earlier; its comic method remains unaffected by the dire contemporary historical matters it reflects on. This is doubly true in the case of the attitude of the Mendele figure toward his people: surely not contempt but a grinning, bantering irony that verges on derision. The second half of "Hanisrafim," however, is quite different, and the difference is entirely a matter of a shift in Mendele's stance. The situation of the Kabtsielites does not change, but *his* stance toward them changes considerably. The agent of this change is remarkable for its alluding to a key passage in the earlier literature of catastrophe. While Mendele has been conversing with Kabtsielites, a young child has curled up upon his knees and fallen asleep. The child is frail and exhausted from life on the move and the dolorous innocence of his face asleep moves Mendele to a mood of pity and generosity of spirit. The child represents Kabtsiel as a whole and by extension all Israel under the aspect of persecution. "I gazed at the child," says Mendele, "and my being melted away *(vehishtappekhah alai nafshi)*."[17] The allusion is to that point in chapter 2 of Lamentations (vss. 11,12) when the poet breaks down upon seeing children fainting from hunger in the besieged city. In both texts the child serves as that component of suffering to which no sin or guilt can be attached, pure victimhood detached from historical responsibility. In both texts as well, the spectacle of child suffering precipitates a collapse of the distance between the speaker and the subject of his discourse.

Under the aspect of pathos, which Mendele now assumes, identical structures are given new interpretations. The mutual economic dependence that he had characterized a moment ago as idle parasitism is now cast in the hues of empathy and solicitude. That an entire town should take to the road in mourning for the destruction of the houses of a few of its citizens is the height of fellow-feeling, the quintessence of gemeinschaft. Kabtsiel is one body and when a limb becomes diseased it is felt by the whole.

But what of the Jewish body politic as a whole? Kabtsielites may

take care of their own, but is not Kabtsiel but one organ in the
larger Jewish people? And if so, how can that organ be allowed to
atrophy and wither? Kabtsiel's suffering is real, its disaster docu-
mented, yet its appeals for help have fallen on deaf ears. The
community wanders through the Pale woebegone and ignored. In
the long monologue that concludes the story Mendele warns of
the dire consequences of such neglect. Pushing the body metaphor still further, he predicts that if the diseased limb of Kabtsiel
is not soon treated, the disease will infect the body as a whole. The
kind of treatment he has in mind is philanthropy. If Jews fail to
give their pennies voluntarily now, they will be forced to give vast
sums later on, and they in turn will become impoverished. The
heated apocalyptic finale of Mendele's monologue unrolls a vision
of the cancerous spread of pauperization to the whole of Israel.
For having failed to deal kindly with Kabtsiel, the rest of the Jewish world will *become* Kabtsiel.

Mendele's attitude toward the Kabtsielites reflects Abramowitsch's attitude toward his readers, and in general the attitude of
the late Haskalah writer to the Jewish masses. That attitude, like
the text of "Hanisrafim," was deeply divided between impulses of
irony and pathos, aloofness and identification, indictment and advocacy. What is striking about the two halves of "Hanisrafim" is
how entirely unintegrated they remain: The movement from one
to the other is more of a capitulation than a progression. The second half, moreover, offers no revisionary understanding of the
people's status. The suffering of the Kabtsielites becomes credible
and affecting, but no less undeserved. And like parts of Lamentations itself (the beginning of chapter 3, for example), this is an
entirely internal Jewish drama; the enemy, the non-Jew, does not
figure. This is all the more remarkable because the lesson of 1881
for many intellectuals was the frightening *unrelatedness* of antisemitism to the internal reform of Jewish life. For Abramowitsch, in
short, the effect of 1881 can be summarized as follows: The pogroms released in him an outpouring of sympathy which had the
effect of something added to his literary enterprise rather than
something absorbed. The fundamental critique of Jewish life remained unaffected. The sign of the failure of this supplement to

be absorbed is its sentimentality and didacticism, which stand in such contrast to the magisterial achievement of Abramowitsch's satire.

There is an immense distance between Abramowitsch and the young Saul Tchernichowsky: Abramowitsch, the neoclassical prose satirist, the man of the Haskalah, the scion of talmudic erudition, and Tchernichowsky, the late romantic poet, the man of modern European culture, the rebel against the classical Jewish past. Yet the compressed development of Hebrew literature at the end of the century saw their careers overlap, when one man was in his sixties and the other in his twenties. Both writers responded in their works to the pogroms of 1881 and to the climate of Jewish society in their aftermath. The joint force of their writing was to interrogate the normative response of the Jewish intelligentsia and to undermine its authority in a way that prepared the ground for Bialik's great statement after Kishinev. The specific component of the response which Tchernichowsky investigated was the phenomenon of medievalization: the tendency on the part of Jewry to read its situation as a recurrence of the persecutions of the Middle Ages. "Barukh mimagentsah" (Baruch of Mainz), a narrative poem of some 800 lines, is set in Mainz at the time of the First Crusade and is clearly based on Tchernichowsky's readings in the newly available historiographical texts.[18] The following section from the chronicle of Rabbi Solomon bar Samson is one among several passages that may have served as the point of departure for Tchernichowsky's critically divergent reworking of the materials. The passage concerns one Master Isaac the Pious bar David Haparnas, who was forcibly baptized by the enemy and afterwards sought atonement for his sin.

He came to his house and closed himself and his children within. He asked his children, "Is it your will that I sacrifice you to the Lord?" They responded, "Do with us what you wish." Isaac said, "O my children, the Lord is the true One—there is no other!" In the middle of the night Master Isaac brought his son and his daughter to the synagogue and slaughtered them before the ark for the sake of *kiddush hashem*. . . . He sprinkled their blood on the pillars of the holy ark so that their memory should come before the divine mercy seat. He proclaimed, "May this blood [also] serve as an expiation for all my sins!" He then set fire to the synagogue. He walked back and forth with his hands spread out to heaven, praying to God with a pleasing voice from within the flames. The enemies cried out to him through the windows, "Wicked man: Come out of the fire and be saved!" They extended a plank to him to grasp and be saved, but Isaac refused and was consumed, an excellent and God-fearing man whose soul reposes with the souls of the righteous in the Garden of Eden.[19]

The considerable achievement of "Baruch of Mainz" is intelligible only if we keep in mind the specific set of associations that contemporary readers brought to the poem. This literary competence depends less on familiarity with particular passages or even particular texts than on the general aura of martyrological sanctity associated with the Crusades and the Middle Ages generally as a time of Jewish courage, loyalty, and self-sacrifice. Tchernichowsky tests these associations by making us view the events entirely from within the consciousness of one man, a man whose behavior deviates from this literary norm. The formal vehicle is the dramatic monologue; Baruch stands before the fresh grave of his wife and talks to her of what has transpired in the few days since her death. Like the classic dramatic monologue on the model of Browning and Tennyson, the poem is based on a dynamic of judgment and sympathy: the judgment that the reader makes of the speaker for his violation of moral norms and the sympathy that the speaker manages to win for himself by virtue of his voice, his presence, and the disclosure of his motives. The speaker's voice, of course, controls the telling of the tale, and the reader gets the information on which to base his judgments not through a linear narrative telling but through the strategic release of information as it serves the interests of the teller. More than in other poetic forms, the reading process in the case of the dramatic monologue is a matter of sequential discovery, a piecing together of the picture as new facts are disclosed, often unintentionally.

The poem begins with Baruch's stammering, distracted account of the day of the massacre in Mainz. All is confusion in his speech; fragments of voices and faces, torches and axes mix together in a metonymical chaos that seems designed to avoid calling attention to Baruch's own actions. Baruch, as it emerges from his jumbled telling, broke down when offered the choice between slaughter and conversion; he was dragged, mortified and confused, to the church, where he repeated those formulas he now does not wish to remember but whose damning import is inescapable. This revelation comes but some fifty lines into the poem, and it has the effect of already identifying Baruch as deviant from the martyrological norm and underscoring Tchernichowsky's choice to write a poem about the kind of figure that Jewish chroniclers preferred not to chronicle. Yet by the act of conversion Baruch has not disqualified himself entirely from the prerogatives of the martyr figure. There remains the special instance of Master Isaac quoted above who, after converting, repented his deed and sacrificed his children and himself. Baruch's case, then, remains open.

Baruch's attitude toward his deed goes much deeper than regret. In one of the several units that divert the sequential narrative, Baruch's memory is suddenly jogged into a reevocation of the day of his bar mitzvah: the mingled feelings of sanctity, awe, and expectation at becoming fully part of the congregation of Israel through formal acceptance of the covenant (pp. 526–27). As the boy winds the straps of the phylacteries around his arm for the first time and recites the formula of commitment from Hosea 2, the present reality suddenly invades his reverie and is literally interspliced with the biblical verses.

> "And I will espouse you forever"—
>   And the covenant have I overthrown . . .
> "And I will espouse you with goodness and mercy"—
>   After foreign things have I wandered. . . .

Baruch views his act with none of the generosity that Maimonides sought to extend to forced converts when he forbade them to consider themselves cut off from the Jewish people and its salvation. Baruch's feelings, as becomes increasingly clear as the poem progresses, go beyond the purely religious stance of faithfulness and witness that marks even the more frenzied texts of medieval Ashkenaz. His sense of his own betrayal is absolute and unredeemable, a defilement so deep that nothing can cleanse him. A sense of sin so acute that it simply cannot be borne requires interpretive categories beyond the religious or the national; it requires, in short, a psychological explanation that invokes the concept of guilt. Far from trivializing the poem, this necessary recourse to the psychological is what the poem is most profoundly about. As more and more of Baruch's behavior is revealed, we realize that his actions are motivated not by religious zeal—though this is their sanction and camouflage—but by a racking conviction of guilt that is inalienably his own. The price of his failure to take responsibility for his actions is exacted from others; a shame too deep to be borne is made to be borne by other lives. The bloodcurdling methods he employs resemble the acts described in the medieval chronicles, but they are not the same, and in this slight yet telling dissimilarity lies the gathering subversive force of the text.

The stirrings of our suspicion concerning Baruch's motives still do not entirely prepare us for his next revelation. In his rambling indirection Baruch lets out that he has "liberated the souls of his daughters" (p. 527). This act of slaughter in itself would not disbar him from the medieval norm were it not for his daughters' reactions and the reasons he gives for his deed. In contrast to Master Isaac's children in the chronicle, with their assured faith in their father's religious aspiration, Baruch's daughters, for reasons we learn later, are not eager to be liberated. The recollection of their imploring, unrelenting eyes forces itself uninvited into Baruch's discourse and forms a second foundation of shame and guilt. When Baruch recovers himself he presents the rationale for his cruelty: He could not bear to contemplate the possibility that his surviving daughters would become married to gentiles and give birth to sons who might eventually become killers of Jews. His reasons, it is important to note, are not those of the historical fathers of the chronicles. Their concern for their children's fate was a religious concern and their hope was that the sacrificial manner of their deaths would guarantee their children's future salvation. Baruch's reasons are not only national rather than religious, but they are also self-regarding. "I could not bear the bitterness of my fate," he explains. *My* fate. The source of his motives rests closer to an anxiety for his own expiation than a concern for his daughters' spiritual, clearly not physical, salvation.

The poem now veers away from this painful subject and accommodates a substantial digression: an idyll concerning the harmony of the family's life before the massacre. The sonorous roll of rhyming couplets in the idyll contrasts sharply with the turbulence of Baruch's speech until now, with its frequent enjambment, its lines of uneven length, and frequent ellipses. The shift and its fittingness remind us of Tchernichowsky's remarkable skill with prosody and his virtuosity in manipulating prosodic forms for strategic purposes. The idyll describes life in the lap of nature: the coming of night, the performance of simple daily tasks, the delights of birds and flowers, their house, their garden.[20] The idyll is a reevocation of the past in its positive aspect, which makes the destruction more catastrophic by forcing us to experience the depth and substance of what was lost. The particular past evoked by Tchernichowsky makes an unexpected statement about Jewish history and the Exile. Where we might expect a picture of the everyday life of the medieval Jew to be painted with strokes of piety, fear of persecution, and longing for redemption, we get instead a portrait of natural man and his utter at-homeness in the bower of nature.

The idyll, in the end, is only a temporary evasion of the reality of destruction. The very momentum of Baruch's speech leads him back to the fact of loss and the terrible question of responsibility. The narrative of the idyll moves from the substantial and weighty to the frail and wispy, from the heavens at night through the house and garden to the flowers themselves. The ponderousness of natural creation comes to rest on these flowers, which, in their blameless vulnerability and attractiveness to the hand of the picker, become a transparent figure for the slaughtered daughters. "It was not my hands that spilt the blood," Baruch avers, "and plucked the tender blossom / But the hands of the enemy. . . ." (p. 535). With responsibility laid elsewhere, Baruch launches into a series of invidious and venomous curses hurled at the brutal gentiles. The language of the curses is taken from Leviticus 26 and Deuteronomy 27 as well as such medieval poems as the "Kelalah veshamta."[21] By itself this section was one of the high points of the poem for the contemporary audience, those who were able to read it in its uncensored version; its malediction of the Gentiles was daring for the literary conventions of the times, both externally and internally imposed, and it had the effect of giving vent to pent-up rage.[22] Yet read within the sequential context of the poem, this rage against the Nations—very much part of the medievalization of the response to 1881—is undercut by irony: While the Nations do indeed deserve to be damned, we know that Baruch's project of damnation has originated in his need to alleviate his own guilt.

A lush description of the depredations of vampire bats comes next, and it is here that Tchernichowsky scores his greatest success in manipulating the reader's experience of the poem. Although the description stands by itself, we assume that these noxious creatures and their foul acts must stand for something other than themselves, and in the absence of a given referent we naturally assume that the bats are a compressed and demonized symbol of the bloodthirsty Crusaders, who have just finished being anathematized. Yet we have been taken in. Renewing his address to his dead wife, Baruch begins the next section as follows:

> If only, my dove, you could become
> —And I with you
> Before my strength fails—
> That blood-sucking bat!
> Each night we would arise
> And ascend from the grave
> To drink and sate ourselves
> On blood of their cruel god.

Baruch proceeds to explain to his wife how their nightly sorties will avenge, in an entirely literal way, the blood of the raped and slaughtered innocents. It is this grotesque nightmare that finally tips the balance of our judgment of Baruch irrevocably. When he reveals his longing to become not only as evil as the enemy but even less human, Baruch forfeits the vestiges of sympathy that had at least made it possible to view his motives as mixed or ambiguous. Tchernichowsky further underscores the unbridgeability of the distance between Baruch and the figures of the tradition by making his vision a black parody of the *El malei raḥamim*, the preeminent memorial prayer of the Jewish liturgy. "O God, full of compassion, dwelling on high," the worshiper beseeches, "grant perfect rest under the wings of thy presence in the company of the holy and the pure that shines like heaven to the soul of [the departed] who has gone to his eternal home."[23] Holy and pure, the martyred soul of Baruch's wife has apparently claimed its perfect rest in its eternal home. Baruch, who can never expect to achieve so much, proposes an exact perversion of the Jewish imagining of the future reward: ceaseless activity instead of perfect rest, nightly befoulment and pollution instead of the shining of purity and holiness, self-powered flight on reptilian wings instead of enclosure under the wings of the Divine Presence.

Baruch does not wait for the afterlife to take his revenge. From his cell in the monastery he starts a fire that destroys the church and spreads to the town as well. Neither his claim to be divinely commanded in his deed, nor his delirious fascination with the progress of the fire, nor the gratuitous cruelty of his refusal to save a bird nest from the flames—none of these are necessary any longer to substantiate Baruch's madness. It is now that we learn what we have suspected but not known regarding the manner of the daughters' death. They were left to be burned to death in the general conflagration—perhaps together with the other surviving Jews of the city—instead of being ritually slaughtered in the sacrificial mode inscribed in the chronicles.

Yet Tchernichowsky's text does not end in apocalypse. Baruch is not Samson, shouting "Let me die with the Philistines!" As a monologue, the discourse of the poem can be constituted and transmitted by nothing other than Baruch's persisting speech. The fiery consummation was not all-consuming; the speaking subject survives, survives ingloriously. In that persistence, so unlike the expiatory suicide by fire of the prototype Master Isaac, Baruch emerges as new figure with its own prototypical force: the tainted survivor of modern literature.

During Passover, 1903, a pogrom in the Bessarabian city of Kishinev left 45 Jews slain, 600 wounded, and 1500 houses and shops plundered or destroyed. The occasion for a substantial international outcry, the pogrom at Kishinev gave its name to what

was actually a four-year-long series of pogroms. As a response to
the growth of radical movements in Russia, the government found
it useful to allow reactionary groups to blame the Jews for the increased revolutionary agitation. After the outbreaks at the time of
the Russo-Japanese War, by far the greatest wave of pogroms occurred after the October revolution in the fall of 1905. In one week
over 600 communities were attacked, mainly in the Ukraine and
Bessarabia; in Odessa alone 300 Jews lost their lives, thousands were
wounded, and 40,000 were ruined economically.[24]

Although the pogroms of 1903–1906 were much worse than
those of 1881, they were not entirely unanticipated. In addition to
mass emigration, the intervening years had seen the mobilization
of ideological programs whose purpose was to offer cures to ma-
ladies of which pogroms were the symptoms. It was the Zionists
and the Bundists who were the principal organizers of local self-
defense groups, which did mitigate the violence in some communities, though their effectiveness was often neutralized by the local
police and militia and by their own crude state of organization.
The twenty years since 1881 had also seen the appearance of a
growing number of Hebrew and Yiddish writers, many of whom
responded to the pogroms in the periodical press of the times.
Popular Yiddish poetry, keynoted once more by the lyrics of Simon Frug, delivered outpourings of mercy and called for chari-
table assistance. The most traditional and sentimental response came
from the branch of Hebrew literature that was by then already established in America, where publicistic denunciations of the per-
fidy of Russia and dirges styled on Lamentations were the norm.
In Russia itself David Frishman's widely read poem "David in the
Lion's Den" saw the pogroms as the dashing of the hopes for civilization at the very outset of the new century. Ya'akov Cahan
idealized the Jewish fighters of antiquity, while I. L. Baruch and
Pesah Kaplan modeled their poetic accounts of the pogroms on
the martyrologies of 1096 and 1648.[25]

Of all these writings there is only one that warrants more than
passing historical interest: Bialik's "Ba'ir haharegah" ("In the City
of Slaughter").[26] In the same measure as these poems are predictable, sentimental, and conventional, Bialik's text is astonishing,

austere, and pathbreaking. The circumstances under which "In the City of Slaughter" came to be written are worth noting. Immediately upon news of the pogrom in Kishinev, a committee of inquiry was formed in Odessa by such distinguished intellectuals as Aḥad Ha-am, Simon Dubnow, and Abramowitsch. Bialik, thirty years old at the time, was dispatched to Kishinev by the committee with the charge of investigating and recording the facts of the event and producing a detailed account to be distributed among Jews in the West. When Bialik arrived in Kishinev a few weeks after the pogrom, the rubble and debris had hardly been disturbed. Bialik assiduously investigated all the damage, took testimony from observers, interviewed Jews from leaders to workers, and ended by filling four large notebooks with transcriptions and observations. Today these folios can be viewed in manuscript at the Bialik Archive in Tel Aviv. They were never published. Instead of submitting the notebooks, Bialik published "In the City of Slaughter," a major poem of some 300 lines, which excoriates the inhabitants of Kishinev for their failure to undertake efforts at self-defense, proclaims the deaths of the victims to be gratuitous, and refuses to mourn them.

"In the City of Slaughter" is founded upon a lie. There *was* self-defense in Kishinev; it may not have been terribly great or effectual, but given the surprise of Kishinev—it was the first major outbreak of violence in twenty years—it is hardly reasonable to have expected more. The source of this contradictory evidence is nothing other than Bialik's own unpublished notebooks.[27] Diligent investigator that he was, Bialik had taken everything down, including descriptions of the attempts to fend off the attacks. Yet the claims of historicity were apparently secondary to the higher imaginative prerogatives Bialik wished to take. In the hyperbolic mode of the Rabbis and the payyetanim, Bialik sought to make iconographic use of Kishinev by draining the event of its particularity and by informing it with symbolic power. Bialik wished to make Kishinev stand for something massive and millennial, and the "higher truth" superseded the contingent truth of the note books.

The following English version by the Canadian Jewish poet

A. M. Klein can stand on its own as a poetic composition. Klein has happily succeeded in conveying Bialik's juxtaposition of a high biblical diction with restraint and austerity in description.[28]

IN THE CITY OF SLAUGHTER
(from *Songs of Wrath*)

Arise and go now to the city of slaughter;
Into its courtyard wind thy way.
There with thine own hand touch, and with the eyes of thine
    head
Behold on tree, on stone, on fence, on mural clay,
The splattered blood and dried brains of the dead.
Proceed then to the ruins, the split walls reach,
Where wider grows the hollow and greater grows the breach;
Pass over the shattered hearth, attain the broken wall
Whose burnt and barren brick, whose charred stones reveal
10 The open mouths of such wounds, that no mending
Shall ever mend, nor healing ever heal.
There will thy feet in feathers sink, and stumble
On wreckage doubly wrecked, scroll heaped on manuscript,
Fragments again fragmented—
Pause not upon this havoc; go thy way.
The perfumes will be wafted from the acacia bud
And half its blossoms will be feathers,
Whose smell is the smell of blood!
And, spiting thee, strange incense they will bring—
20 Banish thy loathing—all the beauty of the spring,
The thousand golden arrows of the sun,
Will flash upon thy malison;
The sevenfold rays of broken glass
Over thy sorrow joyously will pass,
For God called up the slaughter and the spring together:
The slayer slew, the blossom burst, and it was sunny weather!
Then wilt thou flee to a yard, observe its mound.
Upon the mound lie two, and both are headless—
A Jew and his hound.
30 The self-same axe struck both, and both were flung
Unto the self-same heap where swine seek dung;
Tomorrow the rain will wash their mingled blood

Into the runnels, and it will be lost
In rubbish heap, in stagnant pool, in mud.
Its cry will not be heard.
It will descend into the deep, or water the cockle-burr,
And all things will be as they ever were.

Unto the attic mount, upon thy feet and hands;
Behold the shadow of death among the shadows stands.
40 There in the dismal corner, there in the shadowy nook,
Multitudinous eyes will look.
Upon thee from the sombre silence—
The spirits of the martyrs are these souls,
Gathered together, at long last,
Beneath these rafters and in these ignoble holes.
The hatchet found them here, and hither do they come
To seal with a last look, as with their final breath,
The agony of their lives, the terror of their death.
Tumbling and stumbling wraiths, they come, and cower there.
50 Their silence whimpers, and it is their eyes which cry
Wherefore, O Lord, and why?
It is a silence only God can bear.
Lift then thine eyes to the roof; there's nothing there
Save silences that hang from rafters
And brood upon the air:
Question the spider in his lair!
His eyes behold these things; and with his web he can
A tale unfold, horrific to the ear of man:
A tale of cloven belly, feather-filled;
60 Of nostrils nailed, of skull-bones bashed and spilled;
Of murdered men who from the beams were hung,
And of a babe beside its mother flung,
His mother speared, the poor chick finding rest
Upon its mother's cold and milkless breast;
Of how a dagger halved an infant's word,
Its 'ma' was heard, its 'mama' never heard.
O, even now its eyes from me demand accounting,
For these the tales the spider is recounting,
Tales that do puncture the brain, such tales that sever
70 Thy body, spirit, soul from life, forever!
Then wilt thou bid thy spirit:—*Hold, enough!*

Stifle the wrath that mounts within thy throat,
Bury these things accursed,
Within the depth of thy heart, before thy heart will burst!
Then wilt thou leave that place, and go thy way—
And lo!—the earth is as it was, the sun still shines;
It is a day like any other day.

Descend then to the cellars of the town,
There where the virgin daughters of thy folk were fouled,
80 Where seven heathen flung a woman down,
The daughter in the presence of her mother,
The mother in the presence of her daughter,
Before slaughter, during slaughter and after slaughter!
Touch with thy hand the cushion stained; touch
The pillow incarnadined:
This is the place the wild ones of the wood, the beasts of the
_field
With bloody axes in their paws compelled thy daughters to
yield:
Beasted and swined!
Note also, do not fail to note,
90 In that dark corner and behind that cask
Crouched husbands, bridegrooms, brothers, peering from the
cracks,
Watching the martyred bodies struggling underneath
The bestial breath,
Stifled in filth, and swallowing their blood.
Watching from the darkness and its mesh
The lecherous rabble portioning for booty
Their kindred and their flesh.
Crushed in their shame, they saw it all;
They did not stir or move:
100 They did not pluck their eyes out, they
Beat not their brains against the wall,
Perhaps, perhaps, each watcher had it in his heart to pray,
A miracle, O Lord, and spare my skin this day!
Those who survived this foulness, who from their blood awoke,
Beheld their life polluted, the light of their world gone out—
How did their menfolk bear it, how did they bear this yoke?
They crawled forth from their holes and fled to the house of
the Lord,

They offered thanks to Him, the sweet benedictory word.
The *Cohanim* sallied forth, to the Rabbi's house they flitted:
110 *Tell me, O Rabbi, tell, is my own wife permitted?*
And thus the matter ends, and nothing more;
And all is as it was before.

Come, now, and I will bring thee to their lairs
The privies, jakes and pigpens where the heirs
Of Hasmoneans lay, with trembling knees,
Concealed and cowering—the sons of the Maccabees!
The seed of saints, the scions of the lions . . .
Who, crammed by scores in all the sanctuaries of their shame,
So sanctified My name!
120 It was the flight of mice they fled
The scurrying of roaches was their flight;
They died like dogs, and they were dead!
And on the next morn, after the terrible night
The son who was not murdered found
The spurned cadaver of his father on the ground.
Now wherefore dost thou weep, O son of man?

Descend into the valley; verdant, there
A garden flourishes, and in the garden
A barn, a shed,—it was their abattoir;
130 There, like a host of vampires, puffed and bloated,
Besotted with blood, swilled from the scattered dead,
The tumbril wheels lie spread—
Their open spokes, like fingers stretched for murder,
Like vampire-mouths their hubs still clotted red.
Enter not now, but when the sun descends
Wrapt in bleeding clouds and girt with flame,
Then open the gate and stealthily do set
Thy foot within the ambient of horror:
Terror floating near the rafters, terror
140 Against the walls in darkness hiding,
Terror through the silence sliding.
Didst thou not hear beneath the heap of wheels
A stirring of crushed limbs? Broken and racked
Their bodies move a hub, a spoke
Of the circular yoke;
In death-throes they contort,
In blood disport;

And their last groaning, inarticulate
Rises above thy head,
150 And it would seem some speechless sorrow,
Sorrow infinite,
Is prisoned in this shed.
It is, it is the Spirit of Anguish!
Much-suffering and tribulation-tried
Which in this house of bondage binds itself.
It will not ever from its pain be pried.
Grief-weary and forespent, a dark Shekhinah
Runs to each nook and cannot find its rest;
Wishes to weep, but weeping does not come;
160 Would roar, is dumb.
Its head beneath its wing, its wing outspread
Over the shadows of the martyred dead,
Its tears in dimness and in silence shed.
And thou, too, son of man, close now the gate behind thee;
Be closed in darkness now; now thine that charnel space;
So tarrying there thou wilt be one with pain and anguish
And wilt fill up with sorrow thine heart for all its days.
Then on the day of thine own desolation
A refuge will it seem,—
170 Lying in thee like a curse, a demon's ambush,
The haunting of an evil dream,
O, carrying it in thy heart, across the world's expanse
Thou wouldst proclaim it, speak it out,—
But thy lips shall not find its utterance.

Beyond the suburbs go, and reach the burial ground.
Let no man see thy going; attain that place alone,
A place of sainted graves and martyr-stone.
Stand on the fresh-turned soil.
Such silence will take hold of thee, thy heart will fail
180 With pain and shame, yet I
Will let no tear fall from thine eye.
Though thou wilt long to bellow like the driven ox
That bellows, and before the altar balks,
I will make hard thy heart, yea, I
Will not permit a sigh.
See, see, the slaughtered calves, so smitten and so laid;

Is there a price for their death? How shall that price be paid?
Forgive, ye shamed of the earth, yours is a pauper-Lord—
Poor was He during your life, and poorer still of late.
190 When to my door you come to ask for your reward,
I'll open wide: see, I am fallen from my high estate.
I grieve for you, my children, my heart is sad for you.
Your dead were vainly dead; and neither I nor you
Know why you died or wherefore, for whom, nor by what
  laws;
Your deaths are without reason; your lives are without cause.
What says the Shekhinah? In the clouds it hides
In shame, in agony abides;
I, too, at night, will venture on the tombs,
Regard the dead and weigh their secret shame,
200 But never shed a tear, I swear it in My name.
For great is the anguish, great the shame on the brow;
But which is greater, son of man, say thou—
Or liefer keep thy silence, bear witness in My name
To the hour of My sorrow, the moment of My shame.
And when thou dost return
Bring thou the blot of My disgrace upon thy people's head,
And from My suffering do not part,
But set it like a stone within their heart.

Turn, then, to leave the cemetery ground,
210 And for a moment thy swift eye will pass
Upon the verdant carpet of the grass—
A lovely thing! Fragrant and moist, as it is always at the com-
  ing of the Spring.
The stubble of death, the growth of tombstones!
Take thou a fistful, fling it on the plain
Saying, *"the people is plucked grass; can plucked grass grow again?"*
Turn then thy gaze from the dead, and I will lead
Thee from the graveyard to thy living brothers,
And thou wilt come, with those of thine own breed,
Into the synagogue, and on a day of fasting,
220 To hear the cry of their agony, their weeping everlasting.
Thy skin will grow cold, the hair on thy skin stand up,
And thou wilt be by fear and trembling tossed;
Thus groans a people which is lost.

Look in their hearts, behold a dreary waste,
Where even vengeance can revive no growth,
And yet upon their lips no mighty malediction
Rises, no blasphemous oath.
Are they not real, their bruises?
Why is their prayer false?
230 Why, in the day of their trials
Approach me with pious ruses,
Afflict me with denials?
Regard them now, in these their woes:
Ululating, lachrymose,
Crying from their throes,
We have sinned! and *Sinned have we!*—
Self-flagellative with confession's whips.
Their hearts, however, do not believe their lips.
Is it, then, possible for shattered limbs to sin?
240 Wherefore their cries imploring, their supplicating din?
Speak to them, bid them rage!
Let them against me raise the outraged hand,—
Let them demand!
Demand the retribution for the shamed
Of all the centuries and every age!
Let fists be flung like stone
Against the heavens and the heavenly Throne!

And thou too, son of man, be part of these:
Believe the pangs of their heart, believe not their litanies.
250 And when the cantor lifts his voice to cry:
Remember the martyrs, Lord,
Remember the cloven infants, Lord,
Consider the sucklings, Lord,
And when the pillars of the synagogue shall crack at this piteous word
And terror shall take thee, fling thee in its deep,
Then I will harden My heart; I will not let thee weep.
Should then a cry escape from thee,
I'll stifle it within thy throat.
Let them assoil their tragedy,
260 Not thou—let it remain unmourned
For distant ages, times remote,

But thy tear, son of man, remain unshed!
Build thou about it, with thy deadly hate
Thy fury and thy rage, unuttered,
A wall of copper, the bronze triple plate!
So in thy heart it shall remain confined
A serpent in its nest—O terrible tear!—
Until by thirst and hunger it shall find
A breaking of its bond. Then shall it rear
270 Its venomous head, its poisoned fangs, and wait
To strike the people of thy love and hate!

Leave now this place at twilight to return
And to behold these creatures who arose
In terror at dawn, at dusk now, drowsing, worn
With weeping, broken in spirit, in darkness shut.
Their lips still move with words unspoken.
Their hearts are broken.
No lustre in the eye, no hoping in the mind,
They grope to seek support they shall not find:
280 Thus when the oil is gone the wick still sends its smoke;
Thus does an old beast of burden still bear its yoke.
Would that misfortune had left them some small solace
Sustaining the soul, consoling their gray hairs!
Behold, the fast is ended; the final prayers are said.
But why do they tarry now, these mournful congregations?
Shall it be also read,
The Book of Lamentations?
It is a preacher mounts the pulpit now.
He opens his mouth, he stutters, stammers. Hark
290 The empty verses from his speaking flow.
And not a single mighty word is heard
To kindle in the hearts a single spark.
The old attend his doctrine, and they nod.
The young ones hearken to his speech; they yawn.
The mark of death is on their brows; their God
Has utterly forsaken every one.

And thou, too, pity them not, nor touch their wound;
Within their cup no further measure pour.
Wherever thou wilt touch, a bruise is found.
300 Their flesh is wholly sore.

For since they have met pain with resignation
And have made peace with shame,
What shall avail thy consolation?
They are too wretched to evoke thy scorn.
They are too lost thy pity to evoke.
So let them go, then, men to sorrow born,
Mournful and slinking, crushed beneath their yoke.
Go to their homes, and to their hearth depart—
Rot in the bones, corruption in the heart.
310 And when thou shalt rise upon the morrow
And go upon the highway.
Thou shalt then meet these men destroyed by sorrow,
Sighing and groaning, at the doors of the wealthy,
Proclaiming their sores like so much peddler's wares,
The one his battered head, the other his limbs unhealthy,
One shows a wounded arm, and one a fracture bares.
And all have eyes that are the eyes of slaves,
Slaves flogged before their masters;
And each one begs, and each one craves:
320 *Reward me, Master, for that my skull is broken,*
Reward me, for my father who was martyred!
The rich ones, all compassion, for the pleas so bartered
Extend them staff and bandage, say 'good riddance' and
The tale is told:
The paupers are consoled.

Away, you beggars, to the charnel-house!
The bones of your fathers disinter!
Cram them into your knapsacks, bear
Them on your shoulders, go forth
330 To do your business with these precious wares
At all the country fairs!
Stop on the highway, near some populous city,
And spread on your filthy rags
Those martyred bones that issue from your bags,
And sing, with raucous voice, your pauper's ditty.
So will you conjure up the pity of the nations,
And so *their* sympathy implore.
For you are now as you have been of yore
And as you stretched your hand so you will stretch it,
340 And as you have been wretched so are you wretched.

What is thy business here, O son of man?
Rise, to the desert flee!
The cup of affliction thither bear with thee!
Take thou thy soul, rend it in many a shred,
With impotent rage, thy heart deform,
Thy tear upon the barren boulders shed,
And send thy bitter cry into the storm!

In its own time "In the City of Slaughter" was read as a violent rebuke hurled by the poet Bialik at the people Israel. Although this may indeed be the deep message of the poem, it is so completely at odds with the surface structure of the text, especially as regards who is speaking and who is being spoken to, that the issue of what the poem is fundamentally about has to be opened up and questioned. The proper point of departure for such an inquiry is the rhetorical arrangements of the poem, the arrangements that are brought into being by the text's first line: "Arise and go now to the city of slaughter." The imperative mood of the verbs, and the existence they require of a speaker who commands and a listener who is commanded, constitute a rhetorical structure that remains unchanged throughout the poem. The imperative mood means that the discourse of the poem is not lyric expression or narrative description but dramatic speech, utterances made before a listener whose presence is dramatized within the text. The unchangingness of the imperative mood further means that the listener is never allowed to respond by bringing his own speech into the text, a fact which makes "In the City of Slaughter" properly classifiable as a monologue in the imperative mood. This exclusion implies the existence, also, of a will constantly being curbed, a task constantly being imposed, a response constantly being stifled.

Who is this imperatorial speaker who monopolizes the discourse of the poem? His identity can be inferred from the more obvious identity of the addressee. The high biblical idiom of the poem and the formulas of address ("son of man," "Arise and go") and many other cues make it clear that it is a prophet who is being spoken to and, therefore, that it is God who is speaking. The poem, then, is a monologue in which God issues a series of mandates to a prophet. The status of the poem as God's monologue means that even though the poem ridicules traditional religious hopes and travesties the image of God as the dispenser of future rewards, God remains the speaker of the poem. God's voice constitutes an unironized—or perhaps, transironic in the sense of *beyond* irony— framework of value *within which* the poem's famous and flagrant impieties, derisions, and sacrileges are enacted. It is against the people's self-regarding and self-enfeebling conception of God that the mockery is directed rather than against the referent of that conception, Who in fact issues calls for accusation and rebellion against Himself. Yet in the ontology of the text this sovereignty is, of course, qualified by the existence of a prior source of authority. This derives from the distinction between a dramatized figure within the text, God, and the producer of the text itself, namely, the poet. It is a matter of no small presumption on Bialik's part to write God's words and to write a poem that presents itself in the guise of divine revelation. It is a measure both of the persistent power of the idea of God and of its usurpation by the romantic artist who moves to appropriate it for symbolic use.[29]

There is a greater presumption. God is God, but is Bialik His prophet? There is an unmistakable identity set up between the prophet-addressee and the poet Bialik. The poem is about the poet's responsibilities in responding to catastrophe, and more specifically, about Bialik's mission to Kishinev. By casting this theme in terms of biblical prophecy and by himself assuming the persona of prophet, Bialik set up a series of expectations, some of which he fulfills in earnest and others of which he tampers with. Like prophecy, it is implied that the poetic mission is imposed upon the poet from without rather than projected by his own will, and further, that the mission is invested with the kind of sacred authority that cannot be supplied by the poet's own subjectivity. The price for this high sanction is the vitiation of the poet's will. He is moved from space to space in the poem like a counter on a board, while being systematically enjoined from following the promptings of his own heart.

At the center of the prophetic vocation is the preaching of the word of God. The prophet is not called simply to enjoy a special private relationship to God; he is a vessel through which God's will is communicated to Israel so that Israel may be chastised or consoled. The prophet exists for Israel's sake, not for God's. He is chosen for his faculty of pathos; the people's whoring after other gods fires him with the fury of denunciation because of his profound concern for the dire consequences of such actions; and when the people reel from the tortures of their enemies, the prophet feels their pain and is moved to comfort them.

In the poem it is just this most central function of prophecy that God countermands. To address the people, to rebuke them or reassure them, to vent his rage or impart his empathy—at every turn this is what the prophet is ordered *not* to do. The interdiction concerns expression, not feeling. He must witness the horror of the slaughter and the greater horror of the behavior of the bystanders and survivors and feel his prophetic rage mount with every sight, yet he is forbidden, for reasons we shall learn, to do what a prophet does, to communicate that rage to his people. The act of communication never takes place; though there is an explosive release in the last lines of the poem, it is solitary and onanistic.

Yet what of the people? Is not "In the City of Slaughter" a poem essentially about the Jews of Eastern Europe, their bankrupt traditions of quietism, their political ignorance, their venality in the face of persecution, their exploitation of religion? And though they may neither speak nor be spoken to, are they not the very subject of God's discourse and the stimulus of the poet's feelings? Yes, certainly. But the conspicuous exclusion of the people from the communicative act must alert us to the fact that the obvious and commonsensical subject of the poem is not its only subject. "In the City of Slaughter" is a poem with two themes. Beneath the manifest question of the condition of the people lies the question of the romantic poet, the sources of his authority, the nature of his responsibility to the nation, the fate of his burden of feeling in the face of the unspeakable. In the course of the poem the manifest is displaced by the latent. This displacement grows as the poem progresses. The poem is organized into units according to the cycle of one day (from morning to evening) and according to a series of physical sites through which the poet is moved—the attics, the cellars, the stables, the cemetery, the synagogues, and so on.

In each unit the poet is instructed to inspect the traces of the pogrom and imagine its reality; he is encouraged to allow this imagining to fill him with wrath and fury, but he is enjoined from giving vent to these feelings and is instead moved to the next site. However, although in the first sections of the work what the poet sees, the people and the pogrom, is the focus, it is the deepening crisis of the seer that comes increasingly to occupy the dramatic center. Let us therefore examine first Bialik's presentation of the theme of the people and the pogrom and then the gathering drama of the poet.

Bialik makes us see the pogrom with the same effectual restraint that marks all his operations in the poem. Raised on the pogrom literature burlesqued by Abramowitsch, the contemporary reader comes to the poem with an appetite for high pathos and figurative exorbitance. He finds instead a text that systematically declines to feed this hunger. "In the City of Slaughter" contains almost no explicit metaphors. The poem is written in the metonymical mode. When we do come across one of the poem's half-dozen similes (in 348 lines), we savor some release from the unremitting focus on stones and feathers and broken glass, on *things*, a release into some realm of reality outside the world of the pogrom. Instead, the experience of reading the similes is like stepping on a land mine. Take the figure at the opening of the poem:

. . . attain the broken wall
Whose burnt and barren brick, whose charred stones reveal [resemble]
The open mouths of such wounds, that no mending
Shall ever mend, nor healing ever heal.

(ll. 8–11)

The unsettling effect of Bialik's metaphors derives from the realms of objects they conspire to confuse. The pattern often involves a comparison of inanimate objects to ones that are animate but hardly human. Here the holes in walls that have been burnt through to the bare brick are likened to festering, incurable wounds. Material damage is bad enough but at least it is final; comparing it to an animal or human wound introduces a quality of infectious persistence, which is made all the more ghoulish by giving the wounds disembodied, humanoid mouths. (There is a play here on *'anush* "incurable" and *'enosh* "human.") In a figure in ll. 130–34 that recalls Tchernichowsky, the crisscrossing of boundaries between the human and the inanimate and the noxiously humanoid is still more complexly grotesque. In the stables where much of the slaughter took place, the scattered piles of carriage wheels, which are established as a metonymic stand-in for the enemy, are compared to an encampment of sated vampire bats, "Their open spokes, like fingers stretched for murder,/Like vampire-mouths their hubs still clotted red."

These strong effects, these little gruesome explosions of meaning, are effective in their rarity, and they suggest the kind of poem, perhaps a Tchernichowskian text, that Bialik chose not to write. The ruling passion of "In the City of Slaughter" is metonymic. Whereas metaphor establishes similarity between things otherwise different, metonymy makes equivalences according to contiguity or association, that is, between part and whole, cause and effect, thing and attribute. In the figure above, the comparison of the open-spoke wheels to vampire bats is a type of metaphor; the wheels as a substitute for the murderers are an example of metonymy in which the instrument stands for its agents. Metonymy is Bialik's major strategy for presenting the pogrom because of the possibilities it affords for indirection. Walking through the city of slaughter the poet is forced to observe the detritus of the massacre: the blood-splattered and brain-splattered walls, the burnt-out houses, the mounds of broken glass, the omnipresent feathers from slit bedding. He is forced to observe, in short, the traces and effects of the event but not the event itself. Even when the poet imagines the scenes of carnage in retrospect, it is in terms of axes and eyes alone (ll.46–51). The spatial organization of the poem is part of this strategy. Each of the sites through which the poet is moved has its own floating ambience of horror that suggests the events but does not dramatize them. A text that is alluded to but not introduced is part of a metonymic procedure as well. Literary allusion, to be sure, is the very stuff of Bialik's poetic language, the essential technique used with virtuosity for all purposes. What is especially relevant is Bialik's ability to suggest the resonances of the entire Jewish literature of atrocity without himself having to cover the same ground:

> A tale of cloven belly, feather-filled,
> A tale of nostrils and nails, skull and mallet;
> A tale of murdered men who from the rafters were hung;
> A tale of a babe beside his mother flung . . .
> A tale of an infant halved . . .

I have made the translation on lines 59–65 more literal here to stress the sense of catalogued repetition that comes from the anaphoric "A tale of . . . (ma'aseh be-. . .)" that begins each line in the Hebrew. The catalogue as a whole evokes—in the most parsimonious way—an entire body of literature: Lamentations, the midrash, the piyyutim and chronicles, as well as the contemporary journalistic accounts of the pogroms, and it indicates the degree to which in this elaborate literary tradition each instance of atrocity has itself become a conventional set piece, a topos. To recall it to mind, the reader need only be supplied a few charged words.

Metonymy is a technique of annoyance. Metaphor purveys the aesthetic pleasure of suddenly seeing a similarity between unlikely objects. Metonymy frustrates by deflecting us from the thing itself and allowing us access only to its residuum, its atmosphere, its paraphernalia. Bialik's motives for so rigidly enforcing the metonymic mode are several. It is an attempt to find a way out of the dilemma first faced by the poets of Lamentations: how to thwart the dulling effects of convention and convey the true horror of horror. True horror resides not in language but in the mind; supplying a few metonymic details invites the reader to complete the picture with materials from his own inchoate reservoir of fear. To say "tale of nostrils and nails" is to say quite enough to imagine the worst—much worse than could have been explicitly rendered. Yet for Bialik the summoning of terror and atrocity remains a subsidiary objective in "In the City of Slaughter"; he is concerned less with the slaughter than with the response to the slaughter, how the purgative rituals of weeping and mourning can neutralize the sense of outrage and draw the horror into the quiescent folds of the tradition. So, while Bialik does not minimize the slaughter, he does not seek to feed this Jewish appetite for breast-beating and a good cry. And as readers *we* are as suspect in this regard as Abramowitsch's Kabtsielites and the survivors satirized later in the poem. By failing to provide a direct description of the pogrom Bialik declines to supply the gratifications of representation and forces us to make do with the understatement of metonymic fragments.

This fragmentariness of description is one of the factors that makes for the poem's inner generic tension. "In the City of Slaughter" plays on the idea of epic. The high seriousness of its subject plus the unironized rhetorical framework involving God and prophet endow the poem with an epic tenor and an epic ambitiousness, as does the high biblical diction and rigorous spatial and temporal organization of the composition. Indeed the term *poema,* which implies epic intention, was used by Bialik to describe his work. Yet his harshest contemporary critic was quick to point out how many of the essential properties of epic are wanting in "In the City of Slaughter."[30] There is no completely realized picture of external events, and few epic similes, while there is much travesty and low comedy. Most problematic is the absence of epic action; there is no hero who does anything. And because there is no project undertaken, there can be no sense of tragedy consequent upon his failure, perhaps in the sense that the Crusader chronicles are tragic, and thus transcendent, because of the active nobility of their suffering. Now, whatever Bialik meant by calling the work a *poema,* it is evident that the point of the poem is the absence of just that sort of transcendent action or transcendent suffering promised by epic. "In the City of Slaughter" is not about tragic defeat but failure to initiate. It is neither an epic nor a mock-epic. It is rather an antiepic, which proposes its own, negative, principles of meaning.

The indirection of metonymy performs the additional function of keeping the perpetrators of the pogrom out of the poem. We see only the instruments, the sites, and the effects of the destruction, not the destroyers themselves. Disembodied, they exist only through the ax, the wagon wheel, the hammer. This enables Bialik to eliminate the enemy as a touchstone of antipathy and abomination and to force the reader to transfer those emotions to the interior drama of Jew and Jew, God and His people, the poet-prophet, his sender and audience. The refusal to allow the reader egress from this impacted family scene is one of the great autocratic coercions of the poem. It is an exclusion, it should be recalled, that is well precedented in the classical literature, where, except for cries for vindication, the interpretation of catastrophe was largely kept within the internal dynamics of the covenant and its partners. Bialik's motives may not be the same as the tradition's, but his move is one of almost liturgical familiarity.

The use Bialik makes of the texts of the tradition, especially the martyrological traditions, is perhaps the most celebrated aspect of the poem. "In the City of Slaughter" is a perverse summa of motifs and allusion put to parody. Nearly every line blushes to disclose a mangled quotation or a discordant textual resonance: *menusat herev* ("flight from the sword," Lev. 26:36) becomes *menusat 'akhbarim* ("flight of/from mice," l.121); the martyred Rabbi Akiva's dying witness "[God is] One!" *(yats'ah nishmato be'ehad)* becomes the stabbed infant's appeal "Mama!" *(yats'ah nishmato be-'immi,* l.66). There are hundreds of such small effects, and proper study of the ways in which they inflect their sources would yield an entire taxonomy of deformations, stunning in its virtuosity. How variously and to what effect Bialik works within the space between the original and his invention is indeed a subject unto itself, and a vast one. Common to all these maneuvers is the manipulation of the reader's familiarities and expectations and the manipulation of levels of tone and diction. An example of this in a more extended passage is the cellar rape sequence in ll. 78–112. The first third of the passage (ll. 78–89) is entirely in earnest. The traditional and contemporary literature that describes such scenes is evoked not to be undercut but to be done one better. Bialik is showing that when it comes to terror and pathos he can push the register of affect very high when it suits him; and even this through metonymic references to soiled cushions and bloodied pillows and by the understated bestiality of such a line as "Before slaughter, during slaughter, after slaughter!" This is the one place where the enemy is imagined and vilified; there is even in ll. 81–82 a noni-ronic reference to a set of well-known midrashim on Hosea 10:14, "When mothers and babes were dashed to death together." Now, as the momentum of outrage is in full force Bialik suddenly shifts the subject to the cowardly menfolk in the cellar hiding places. Our repulsion, once aroused, is not stayed but transferred onto the Jewish males, whose criminal inaction is now made to seem more ghastly than the loathesome deeds of the goy. The description of the abominations of the goy is continued but we now see them as relayed through the eyes of the bystanders. Forced into this van-tage point, our perception as readers becomes soiled and compro-mised. The tone of the passage, which began earnestly in pathos and turned to contempt, crosses over with the "Perhaps, perhaps" of l.102 into ridicule and sarcasm. The seriousness of even the contempt is undercut in the end; the passage concludes (ll. 111–12) with the sense of the absurd futility of a world unchanged by atrocity, the final note of most of the early sections of the poem. In short, by treating us to the earnest rape scene in the beginning with its traditionally identified victims and perpetrators, Bialik has drawn us in to a very different distribution of blame and feeling than we were originally prepared to make. The cemetery scene (ll. 175–208) uses a similar lure—the ritual of visiting the graves of the righteous—to set up the reader for what is perhaps Bialik's most sardonic burlesque, the parody of the expectation of after-life and future reward, the conviction so fundamental to the mo-tives and experience of medieval martyrs.

With so much parody and travesty, what is left in the poem that is serious? "In the City of Slaughter" has often been taken as an indictment of the Jewish past and a repudiation of the habit of passivity as reflected in the martyrological traditions. There is a need to make discriminations in this matter. The poem's dazzling rhetorical effects should not lead to a confusing of passivity with the tradition, of the conduct of the moment with the precedents of the past. The Jews who cower in the outhouses and pigpens are called "the sons of the Maccabees!/The seed of saints, the scions of the lions (ninei ha'arayot sheba-"av harahamim" vezeraᶜ ha-"ked-oshim")," (the reference is to 1096 especially). But the sobriquets are used in the ironic sense that these Jews are the betrayers of this inheritance. The spiritual courage and defiance involved in the ideal and practice of *kiddush hashem* is not impugned as much as the self-serving arrogation of that sanction and its application to a shameful want of courage and defiance. Martyrdom as a response to catastrophe was appropriate in its time; its persistent idealization in the modern age is a cover for a failure of nerve and a blaspheming of the memory of the truly great. What was once classical is now degenerate, the vital now effete. The same applies to more theological concepts. Immortality per se is not travestied as much as the readiness of the survivors to accept the assurance of a future reward as an easy consolation. Bialik, in brief, negates not the texts and ideas of the tradition but the liturgical use to which they have been put. To be sure, this is not a small negation. To interpret new disasters liturgically, to absorb them into a millennial drama, to draw off their destabilizing force, to be quieted by promises of redemption and to persevere in faith—what was appropriate and even creative in its own time has become pretext and evasion.

To put one's finger on the poem's center of gravity requires looking to the theme of God and prophet. God, as we have said, may parody Himself as a bankrupt householder with bare cupboards but He remains the speaker of the poem and we believe at least in the poem. The instructions God gives to the poet-prophet concerning his task form the "transironic" theme of "In the City of Slaughter." The poet's crisis is real and engaged, while the people's crisis, despite all the weeping and howling, is dodged. Like the people's, the poet's ordeal demands the discarding of a no-longer appropriate set of practices for a new role, a new definition of the poetic vocation. The lineaments of that role are adumbrated in the early sections of the poem. The poet is instructed—as Bialik in his researches did indeed do—to expose himself to and inspect every detail of the massacre; to wade through the bloodied feathers, to see the brain-splattered walls, to take in his hands the befouled cushions, to hear the tales of atrocity, "Tales that do puncture the brain, such tales that sever/Thy body, spirit, soul from life, forever!" (ll. 69–70). Yet when the cry of pain and outrage uncontrollably rises to his lips he is commanded to stifle it and keep silent, and he is transferred elsewhere to inspect yet another site of slaughter.

These forced confrontations climax in the stables among the carriage wheels where the poet is faced with "Terror floating near the rafters, terror/Against the wall in darkness hiding" (ll. 139–40). It is explained to him that this speechless, infinite sorrow is the Spirit of Anguish *(ruah dakka)*. (In a similar way the poet's sympathetic soul is briefly externalized and personified as a dark Shekhinah, grief-stricken yet unable to weep; this is an internal allusion to such earlier works of Bialik as *Levaddi*.) The poet is instructed to closet himself in the dark barn with the sorrow, to commune with it *(vehityahadeta)*, to incorporate the sorrow into himself and fill himself with it (ll. 165–67). When the day of his desolation comes, when his own resources of wrath have been exhausted, he will be able to rely upon the sorrow he had earlier taken on and be revived in his rage, as if drawing from a poisonous well *(ma'yan tar'elah,* this phrase is missing in the translation). In the meantime, the sorrow will remain within him, pressing and gnawing like a nightmare. Though he would "proclaim it, speak it out," his "lips shall not find its utterance" (l.174).

Two moments of release are finally granted in the concluding sections of the poem; one is potent but imaginary, the other real but futile. The poem is preoccupied in all its parts with the suppression and release of feeling. What is the meaning of this preoccupation? Bialik, it might be argued, is carrying forward the great Abramowitsch theme of the sublimation of feeling into speech rather than action. The satiric scenes of the poem concern the popular clamor for channeling the anguish of persecution into outpourings of lamentation and consolation rather than enduring the anguish and translating it into the realities of political organization. Less evident is the complicity of the poet-prophet. His ringing denunciations and soothing assurances had been absorbed into the dynamics of breast-beating and catharsis, and had been used more to oil the machinery of delusion than play havoc with it. The fulminations of a national poet like Judah Loeb Gordon had in time come to be ignored or taken for granted, and so Bialik, the inheritor of that mantle, had been obliged to perform the standard prophetic service in an hour of crisis by excoriating the enemy, beatifying the victims, and comforting the survivors, or even for that matter by reproaching the people for their passivity. The interdiction of expression touches the most fundamental conception of what it means to be a romantic poet. Not unlike the prophet, the poet is endowed with an exquisite sensitivity to the stimuli of the world, which in turn moves him to express the feelings called forth from his soul; this is the sympathetic rapport between the poetic soul and the *anima mundi*. What is more, it is the world that needs and benefits from the outpourings of the poet's soul and from the great truths they contain. To permit feeling but forbid expression is a move of great consequence. This wedge has been driven into the poet's being because expression itself has become suspect. Giving constant release to his feelings is doing what comes *too* naturally. The venting and dispersion of his discourse serves, as in the case of the people, as too comfortable a purgation; it is a discharge, moreover, that comes to no account, so easily is it neutralized and absorbed into the self-serving expectations of its listeners.

National crisis requires a rude reshaping of the poetic vocation. The commanding voice of the poem calls upon the poet to work against the grain of his nature: He must forswear release and allow the sorrow and the wrath to collect within him. As the pressure builds, his anguished feelings will undergo a process of acidification, by which they are reduced to a bitter essence of rancor and bile. This now becomes the wellspring of the poet's imagination; this is the *ma'yan tar'elah*, the poisonous fountain, the black muse. Ll. 264–71 present an alternative image of this dark essence as a weapon rather than a source. The stifled fury, the unshed tears, the repressed cry are pictured as a venomous serpent coiled within the bronze vault of the poet's heart, which God will harden like the heart of Pharoah. When the serpent has been driven mad by thirst and hunger, it will be sent forth to "strike the people of thy love and hate!"

As baleful as they are, the fountain and the serpent are images of potency and replenishment. Something grows in the breast of the poet, even if it is the malignancy of malediction. In contrast to this negative transcendence stands the sterility of the survivors of the catastrophe. Their hearts are "a dreary waste,/where even vengeance can revive no growth" (ll. 224–25). God has left off hoping that suffering will engender embitterment and embitterment curse and vengeance against the enemy—and against God Himself. The people are disconsolate, mumbling the formulas of consolation. They are moved from this inertia, however, in the apocalyptic vision of beggary with which the theme of the people is brought to a close. When they get up from their mourning on the next day, they finally bestir themselves; but they move not in order to take stock, to rethink, to organize, but in order to make themselves into *nisrafim*, professional traveling beggars who make a living by exploiting their misfortune. Domesticating catastrophe by mercantilizing it is a prospect that is pure Abramowitsch, but Abramowitsch without the humor and pathos. Bialik pushes further into the absurd grotesque: As if their own wounds and stumps are not enough to arouse profitable sympathy, the survivors flock to the cemetery to dig up the bodies of the slain and fill their knapsacks with the bones of their brethren to be hawked as relics at country fairs.

"In the City of Slaughter" ends finally in release but no connection. As the poet-prophet was enjoined to journey to the city at the opening of the poem, so at its conclusion is he ordered to abandon the city for the wilderness. Throughout the poem the wilderness had been the symbol of both the consummate indifference of nature to the outrage of the pogrom (ll. 36–37) and the arid void of the survivors' souls. The wilderness takes on the final association of the place prophets go when their missions have been thwarted. Yet for Bialik's poet-prophets there is no renewal of the calling, no revelation, no still small voice. He is given only to rend his soul into shreds like the metonymical debris of the pogrom and let all the carefully starved wrath finally explode. But the explosion is drowned out by the storm, which obliterates all meaning and message. The word never connects with the people; the viper, once released, is borne off by the wind.

The image of onanism has a special resonance in Bialik's career.

The futility of poetry as communication anticipates Bialik's growing difficulty in writing poetry and the silence that overtakes his
poetic production altogether by 1911, while the poet is still fully
in midcareer. "In the City of Slaughter" records the cancellation
of one rhetorical option along the way to silence. Since the 1890s,
Bialik had used the persona of the biblical prophet as a way of
addressing national concerns. In the Kishinev poem, Bialik takes
this strategy farther than he ever had, and in the end exhausts it.
Not the horror of the events as much as the insensibility of the
listeners discredits the model of prophet and people. The silence
is complete. It is with God alone that the prophet is left at the
conclusion of the poem, and from this God, who is essentially a
rhetorical principle of high seriousness and truth, no living speech
can be expected.

Yet for the poem, as distinct from its creator, its words were not
carried off by the storm. Published after the first round of a protracted series of pogroms between 1903 and 1906, "In the City of
Slaughter" did actually foster the organization of Jewish self-defense in the outbreaks that followed. The poem did much, in addition, to further the cause of Zionism among the young men and
women of the Pale. In the later imagination of the Yishuv the poem
became a proof-text for the degeneracy of the diaspora mentality.
In our own day, "In the City of Slaughter" has found perhaps its
most ironic employment as a contemporary addition to the martyrology of the Yom Kippur liturgy.[31]

The indictment of the martyrological response to catastrophe in
the works of Abramowitsch, Tchernichowsky, and Bialik, in conclusion, founded a powerful new literary norm which exerted its
greatest impact after the Holocaust. Although the Holocaust was
an incalculably greater historical tragedy for the Jews than the pogroms, the image of Jewish cowardice had already been fixed and
the recourse to classical consolation literature discredited. Together with other factors, the new norm helps to explain the complexity of the response in the culture of the Yishuv and the State
to the Holocaust and the great silence, with the exception of
Greenberg and Appelfeld, in Hebrew literature.

SURVIVORS AND BYSTANDERS

INTRODUCTION

It is astonishing to note how persistently Hebrew literature has avoided the subject of the Holocaust, particularly during the decade after the war. . . . Only Uri Zvi Greenberg confronts it head on and deals with the experience of Israel and his conflicting feelings about it in his wonderful collection of poems *Streets of the River.* The literature of the War of Independence generation approached the subject of the Holocaust with all the wariness of one scrutinizing an unfamiliar reptile. This caution was prompted by an overwhelming lack of comprehension, a sense of shame and guilt. Nothing could have been further from the experience of the War of Independence than that of the Holocaust. The writings of the Holocaust survivors themselves, such as Katzetnik, were isolated and enclosed in their own ghetto.

Only with the appearance of Aharon Appelfeld at the end of the fifties did Holocaust literature begin to acquire depth and direction. He brought it out of the ghetto where Hebrew literature had placed it. I remember Appelfeld reading us his first stories in his little room in Jerusalem. Instantly we all felt that here is a new artistic code that lets us grasp this experience through its own creative merit. We need not make allowances for it; it stands up to artistic criteria like any other true work of creation.

A. B. Yehoshua
Yedi ʿot aḥaronot
November 2, 1979

 With the necessary qualifications, Yehoshua's appraisal is accurate: between World War II and the Eichmann trial in the early sixties there are no significant works of Hebrew literature which directly engage the Holocaust, with the major exception of Uri Zvi Greenberg. Now, prolonged silence after a major trauma would not be startling if it was a case of any literature but Hewbrew (Yiddish, too, of course) and if the silence could be construed as the shock of loss rather than the avoidance of confrontation. From its rebirth as modern literature, Hebrew had regarded itself as *the* national literary language, with a responsibility to monitor the fortunes of the Jewish people as a whole. Even when the institutions of Hebrew literature relocated in Palestine between the wars and the life of the Yishuv emerged as an important theme, the condition of European Jewry remained a major preoccupation. Yet in the works of the young writers who came to dominate the literary scene in the fifties, this concern dramatically ceases to hold. Take the thousands of pages of fiction of the era's premier writer S. Yizhar, and of the Holocaust you will find nothing.

Before examining the reasons for this silence, several qualifications are in place. The period under discussion did witness the publication of information about the destruction of European Jewry in journalistic, documentary, and memoiristic accounts, sometimes in fictionalized form; but this was not, as Yehoshua says, high imaginative literature which could claim importance by virtue of its achievements as art rather than the special pathos of its subject.[1] What serious works of literary art were available to the Hebrew-reading public at the time were Hebrew versions or translations of literature written in other languages, principally Yiddish. Examples are the poetry of Yitshak Katznelson and Abraham Sutzkever. Poetry in general was a more hospitable medium than prose fiction for discrete and fragmentary responses to the Holocaust. Many Hebrew poets—among them Fichman, Shimoni, Shteinberg, Shlonski—whose careers began before the war, wrote some poems about the catastrophe, usually in a traditional vein of lamentation. But, again, among these works there are few examples of sustained poetic attention and few texts which could be considered strong poems in relation to a poet's earlier, major work.[2] In fiction, finally, Agnon stands as a complex partial exception. After the war, he wrote two stories which function as alternative and opposing "sequels" to the image of Buczaz presented in the pre-Holocaust *A Guest for the Night;* he also has several symbolic tales whose themes are guilt and the repurification of the soul after catastrophe. Although interesting and impressive, these short texts figure most importantly within the integral study of the corpus of Agnon's work, in which the Holocaust is not a central preoccupation.[3]

Self-evident but in need of repeating is the sad fact that the Holocaust is in part itself responsible for the silence on the fate of European Jewry in the Hebrew literature of this period. If the destruction had not been so nearly total, then numbers of writers like Kovner, Pagis, and Appelfeld would have come to Israel. They would have formed a stream of European-born Hebrew writers who would have shared Israeli literary culture with the new generation of Sabra writers. This did not happen; and Hebrew literature in the fifties became largely the story of the younger native writers, usually called the Palmah generation writers, after the name of the elite fighting units in the War of Independence. The central figures include S. Yizhar, Moshe Shamir, Aharon Meged, Haim Gouri, Natan Shaham. A conjunction of ideology and historical circumstance moved this group of writers to the center of Hebrew literary culture, pushing to the sidelines the generation of Agnon and Hazaz.

In the collective portrait of the Palmah generation the fact of nativeness is central. Born in the late twenties, most of these writers were the children of the pioneers of the Third Aliyah. They were either born in Palestine or brought as small children, or, in a few cases, educated in Zionist youth movements abroad. Of Europe they had no personal experience, nor memories of its Jewish life; most had little contact with grandparents, who had stayed behind. Raised in Hebrew (pronounced in the Sephardic accent of the Yishuv), their speech registered the developments of a living community. This was reflected in the range of cultural allusion in their written style. Their secular gymnasium-style of education, though it included Bible and Jewish history, left them alien to the world of Talmudic erudition, which had been a principle frame of reference in previous generations of Hebrew writers. The Socialist-Zionist ideology at the core of their broader education called for a substantial transvaluation of Jewish life. Friendship, solidarity, moral conscience, romantic love, democracy, social justice, this-worldly productive labor—these are the values that supplanted a Scripture-centered universe in which worship and study were sufficient pursuits and in which Zion was a religious ideal rather than a political goal. The society being created in the Yishuv was conceived of as a new departure. The new kind of Jew, who was a citizen of this new reality, consciously defined his stance toward the world of power and the question of self-defense as the antithesis of the passive creatures stigmatized in Bialik's "In the City of Slaughter."

The War of Independence in 1948 overtook these young people when many of them were barely twenty years old; it was the sudden ending of youth. The war forced them to undergo in a condensed moment early in their lives the kinds of experiences that most men do not encounter in a lifetime: the fear of death, the limits of courage, the loss of comrades, the moral dilemmas of war, and love in the shadow of mortality. This, the central traumatic and orientating event of the Yishuv as a whole, coincided with the initiation into adulthood of a generation, and this concurrence had important consequences for Hebrew literature. When these young soldiers began to write on the themes of the war, their work had a special poignancy and power because of the authority of their experiences. The generation moved to the center of literary culture in Israel at a very young age; and their concerns displaced the broader range of Jewish themes of such writers as Agnon and Hazaz. Because the War of Independence had intervened in their lives before university studies, travel, and family, the issues raised by the war remained ever central to their literary outlook. In the fifties their themes were the dilemmas of the young state: the integration of immigrants, the institutionalization of the pioneering ideal, the problems of charismatic leadership, the fulfillment of the individual on kibbutz. As public tasks continued to make substantial demands on the members of this generation, the question of the existential needs of the individual also emerged as an exigent motif.

Where was the Holocaust in all of this? The truth is the Holocaust figured very little in the literary production of the generation. By their own account, their response was in deeds and not in words. By organizing the *Briḥah*, the illegal immigration to Palestine of refugees and survivors, they were doing, they felt, whatever could be positively done in the aftermath of the destruction. The creation of a Jewish state and the defence of its independence, moreover, were the great tasks facing the Jewish people after the Second World War and the most eloquent "answer" to the Holocaust. Without denying these arguments, it is necessary to point to ideological and psychological factors which acted to affect and complicate attitudes toward the Jews who died in Europe. Essential to secular political Zionism was a deep rejection of the political structure, economic relations, and religious culture of East European Jewry. For the younger generation this principled negation of the Diaspora *(shelilat hagolah)* became, in the absence of first-hand contact and family memories, a strong hatred of the Diaspora *(sin'at hagolah)*. The very image of the "ghetto Jew" represented the essence of what was corrupt and soiling in Jewish life, nor was this even a viable community, according to the Zionist analysis. Eroded by assimilation on one flank and exposed to the ravages of antisemitism on the other, European Jewry was thought to be destined sooner or later either to wither or be swept away.

However, no one guessed when and how it would happen. The dominant emotion elicited by the Holocaust among the Palmah writers was shame: shame over the impotence of the Yishuv to affect the lot of their murdered brethren, and shame over what they perceived to be the submissiveness of European Jews in their extermination. *Katso'n latevaḥ*, "like sheep to the slaughter," was the condemnatory tag which, for many, extracted and summarized the meaning of the event. For fighters who had risked their lives for the creation of a proud new reality, this spectacle of what they believed to be millennial Jewish passivity on a massive scale was a shame too deep to be borne, much less articulated. It was shame, and not the shock of loss and the grieving over the destruction, that caused the conspicuous avoidance of the Holocaust in the literature of the period. Allowed to speak in this silence were the powerful stereotypes and rhetorical norms of Bialik's text, as the classic statement on the Jews and their suffering in Zionist literature. The error, of course, was in permitting an analogy to be inferred between what had recently happened in Europe and the historical circumstances behind "In the City of Slaughter." When Bialik wrote, the political ledger was still open, and it was reasonable to think that self-defense could be a significant factor in future responses; the severity of the poet's condemnation had a monitory function. The fact that the Holocaust was different, and the ways in which it was different, would have been discovered if the literary imagination had been employed in these years in the intimate investigation of the awesome and immense world of the Holocaust. Sadly, this was a project broken off at its roots.

For the young writers an inhibiting factor was the absence of a personal knowledge of and connection with the destroyed world of European Jewry. Older writers, in contrast, though less central to the literary norms of the times, were in a position to differentiate between the culture of European Jewry, which they rejected with unstinting ideological zeal, and the Jews themselves, whose loss they could mourn passionately, though not always effectively. A good example is the dedication, written in the style of Hebrew tombstone epitaphs, to a poem of lamentation by Shimshon Meltzer (born 1909, emigrated to Palestine, 1934):

To the memory of the righteous and innocent of my town, at one with God and with themselves, who in my childhood loved me, spoiled me, and sought to guide me in the right path. But I turned away from them to the path of the free-thinkers, together with all the youth, and so caused them much pain. The Lord Who knows men's hearts knows how much I have grieved over this. *For it was not from them that I sought to separate myself, but from their lives, the life of the Exile.* Let their souls be bound up in the bond of life. (My italics.)

In the literature of the Palmah writers, the few European Jews who are depicted are the survivors featured in such plays as Natan Shaham's *Hesbon hadash* (A New Reckoning) (1954), and Aharon Meged's *Hana Senesh* (1958). The plays turn on the contrast between the values represented by the survivor (expedience, self-interest, fearfulness) and those represented by the native Israeli (health, hard work, comradeship).[4]

It is only fair to point out that literary values on this score mirrored the larger political culture. In the fifties the Holocaust was at most a shadowy presence in the institutions of the state. Although the Chief Rabbinate fixed an official date (the tenth of Tevet) to commemorate Holocaust victims, the government itself temporized. During these years there was virtually no attention paid to the Holocaust in the curricula of the state-run schools. A national day of commemoration was established in 1952, yet it was not until 1959 that the form of the observance was fixed. As evinced in Kenesset debates, there was considerable ambivalence about establishing a national shrine and memorial; when the government finally set up the Yad Vashem institution in 1953, it acted in part out of fear that its leadership in world Jewish affairs would be usurped by efforts to create memorials outside of Israel. Even once these institutions were established, the emphasis was clearly placed on marking the instances of uprising and resistance during the Holocaust period, rather than remembering the millions who died in mechanized forms of slaughter.[5]

Ironically, it was such a display of power that brought an end to the nearly exclusive focus on resistance. The Ben Gurion government's capture and trial of Adolf Eichmann was intended to show to the world the power of the state of Israel to deal with the enemies of the Jewish people as a whole. Internally, however, the effects of the protracted trial in 1961 on Israeli society were quite otherwise. The testimony of the witnesses for the prosecution constituted the first time that survivors were given a public forum in which to tell their stories. For the first time also a comprehensive public picture was pieced together of the full dimensions of the Nazi murder apparatus. The trial was an event of great significance: It was a catharsis for the survivors and a confrontation for Israeli society as a whole. And for the Palmah writers, no less than others. From the early sixties onwards, Israeli literature has witnessed a number of attempts to come to terms with the Holocaust on the part of writers who had hitherto avoided engagement, as well as writings on the Holocaust on the part of survivors who had hitherto not let memory speak. These attempts at engagement and recollection, mixed in their character and achievement, form the subject for the concluding chapter of this study.

The two intervening chapters belong to Greenberg and Appelfeld. These writers constitute the two great exceptions—to return to the remarks of Yehoshua—to the silence of Israeli literature on the Holocaust. The case for their exceptionality rests not only on the superior achievement of their work as art, but also on its scope. In contrast to the isolated Holocaust novel or poem cycle of others, Greenberg and Appelfeld have each created a large, sustained, and coherent body of work, and through it a lost world.

·5·

URI ZVI GREENBERG IN

STREETS OF THE RIVER

 Uri Zvi Greenberg's *Streets of the River* is the single most important work on the Holocaust in Hebrew literature. Yet in no sense is it a poetry freshly invented as a response to the Holocaust. By the time of the war Greenberg (1894–1980) was already a middle-aged poet with many books of poetry behind him and a highly evolved, idiosyncratic style, and it is this mode of writing that Greenberg endeavored to apply to the challenge of addressing the Holocaust. The attempt, however, runs into trouble, and the continuity is only imperfectly made. What is most significant in *Streets of the River* is just this: Greenberg's faltering hold on the adequacy of his poetry and the measures he takes to recover his vocation.

The crucible of Greenberg's work was the Great War. The measure of death and destruction suffered by Jews during the First World War, the Russian Revolution, and the Russian Civil War was far greater than any previous calamity in modern Jewish memory. Between 1881 and 1882 several hundreds perished; between 1903 and 1905 several thousands; between 1917 and 1920, 60,000 Jews died, and died as Jews in antisemitic pogroms, not as soldiers in the uniforms of one or another of the sides. The massacres were accompanied by the uprooting of communities and the forced relocation of populations; the revolutionary regime destroyed and restructured the fundamental institutions of Jewish life. Although the earlier two waves of pogroms had produced shock and outrage, the fabric of Jewish society held. The later events ripped it apart.

For Hebrew writers these convulsions meant that Eastern Europe could no longer be a setting for the revival of a national literature in Hebrew. After sojourns in Berlin, Warsaw, and Paris, Hebrew writers who had fled Russia after the Revolution established themselves in Palestine. By the late 1920s, the major organs and apparatus of Hebrew literature—the publishing houses, the journals, the writers themselves—had been transplanted to Tel Aviv and Jerusalem. Much Hebrew literature written between the wars— Lamdan's *Massada*, Hazaz's sketches from the Revolution and his play *In the End of Days*, Agnon's *A Guest for the Night*—describes an apocalyptic moment caught between the certain disintegration of European Jewish life and an unproved hope for redemption in Palestine.

No one seized the apocalyptic moment with the same force as the young Uri Zvi Greenberg. His poetry and manifestoes record the electrifying horror of his experience as a young conscript in the Austrian army on the Serbian front and later with his family as near-fatal victims of Ukrainian massacres in Lewów.[1] It was the revolutionary aesthetics of German literature of this period, Expressionism, that definitively stamped Greenberg's verse. Although he had published poetry in both languages from 1912 onward, it was with the appearance of the Yiddish volume *Mefisto* in 1921 and his first Hebrew volume, *Emah gedolah veyare'ah*, in 1925 that the dissonances and hyperboles of the new idiom were announced. The explosive original energies of Greenberg's poetry of the twenties were released by a fusion reaction between a new poetics and an old vision, between the violent stylistic antinomianism of Expressionism and the equally violent vision of destruction and deliverance in Jewish apocalyptic.

To see this fusion close up I bring two stanzas from the opening poem of the sequence "Mas'a el eropah" (Oracle on Europe), published in book form in 1926.

From our ancient rage we are nourished, lads! From the overflow
    of our messianism the world is nourished
And from Jewish love with its fundamental rancor, when God spills
    our blood among the Seventy Kingdoms:
For only the knife-wielding Nations can smell the warm sheep's
    bodies behind the Jews' clothing.
They know that the time for slaughter has come when they see
    the new moon rising like a reddish apple
Over our houses in the land—

From the hidden past of the nation, from the depths of the
    slaughterhouse of the generations, the prophet is ordered to go
    out to the public gate.
He is commanded: Arise and immerse yourself in freshly spilt
    blood, for you have been baptized!
Your cloak too shall be made of blood as if it had never been white
    from your mother's wash
And the howl of your red conscience, pierced like a sieve,
Howl it out!! As if it were a mouth in the body of a man cut open.[2]

The feel of this poetry is in its intensely rhetorical outcry. It is utterance that is flung out as an assault, an aggressive communication, chanted in the communal we, or, as in the second stanza, addressed frontally to the poet-prophet himself. Graphically it is a poetry of exclamation marks and italicized stresses. The aggression is effected by the use of hectic hyperboles, the ceaseless piling up of unabashed exaggerations, extreme statements, overgeneralizations about *all* gentiles and *all* Jews. Accuracy of description is not an aim of this discourse; it is responsible not to the representation of the external world but to the projecting outward of the deeper truth of the poet's subjectivity. The landscape of this inner world, especially its colors, is not the landscape of nature; here conscience is red, the rising moon a reddish apple. (The sonal similarities in Hebrew between red, *adom, adamdam,* and blood, *dam,* reverberate.) The content of this subjectivity is anxiety, turbulence, and violence. The stance of rancor and vengefulness re-

flects the affliction and damnation that have been the poet's fate
and the experience of those he speaks for at the hands of the world.
The lexical fields from which the metaphors are drawn, together
with their unnatural, oxymoronic yokings, reflect the violence both
of the past suffering and the future vengeance: anger as nourishment, history as a slaughterhouse, a cloak of blood, conscience
riddled with holes, a scream like the mouth of a wracked body.
There is a calculated transgression of the separation of levels of
diction: archaisms (*makulin* for slaughterhouse) mixed with neo-
logisms (*matspun* for conscience), high classical allusions (Joseph's
cloak dipped in animal blood) with homely references (mother's
wash), and the use of words certain to shock the sensibilities of the
reader (the reference to baptism in a Hebrew poem). And, of
course, the great lengths of the lines of the poem (up to thirty syl-
lables in the Hebrew), their irregularity, and the new rhythm in
which they demand to be read.[3]

Now, though there are elements here that are idiosyncratic to
Uri Zvi Greenberg, the predominant texture of the poetry is woven
out of the techniques and obsessions of Expressionism, much the
same way the unique speech-act of an individual draws upon the
ideal lexicon of his language. Once supplied with the Jewish re-
ferents it might be possible to synthesize Greenberg's poetry from
a gleaning of Benn, Kaiser, Heym, Trakl, and other German poets.
It is just this connection that is the point; it is a transformative
connection that enabled Greenberg to seize an aesthetic correla-
tive to his vision of Jewish experience. In this vision, according to
the lines above, the essence of Jewish being, its very nourishment,
consists in two feelings: rage (here rage against victimization by
the gentiles and the humiliations of history, elsewhere against God
and existence) and longing for redemption. In his thrist for Jewish blood the Gentile is hyperbolically defined; for him Jews are
nothing other than sheep to be slaughtered when the moment
permits. That moment is the central event in the apocalyptic conception of time, the "time of slaughter" (*mo'ed lishḥot*) with which
the present is fatefully pregnant. Jewish history is the history of
slaughter, a martyrdom of blood rather than tears, a past more
sanguinary than lachrymose. As in the piyyutim of 1096, blood is

the great connective image and red the color to which all things are reduced and compared.

The fit between this vision of history and self and the transgressive poetics of Expressionism need not be elaborated. Looking back at Bialik's Kishinev poem of some twenty years earlier, also a poem of wrath and slaughter, destiny personal and collective, one is struck by how much has changed in the very conception of what poetry is and how it means. But more: In vision and idea there is a break from Bialik on several scores. Bialik continued the great insistence of the classical traditions on keeping the interpretation of catastrophe internal to the drama of the Jewish people and its God and of the Jewish people and itself. The authors of Lamentations and midrash labored to make the role of the enemy secondary, and his devastations instruments of divine supervision rather than signs of divine abandonment—though, despite their labors, the pain of deep humiliation before the Nations could never be entirely expunged. For the heroes of the martyrological literature of the Crusades, in the heat of their divine service, the other existed only behind a veil of contempt and malediction. After 1881 and 1903, for all the popular change of heart, Abramowitsch and Bialik essentially carried forward the internal Haskalah critique of Jewish society on the counts of worldly innocence and political passivity. One of the great suppressions of "In the City of Slaughter" was the forcible exclusion from the text of the presence and agency of the enemy, with the concomitant placement of the full weight of catastrophe upon the response of the victims. Greenberg's poetry constitutes a reversal of this exclusion. It is as if the countertheme of shame and accusation had resurfaced and ballooned into an epic obsession in its own right. Again and again, in hundreds of poems, the vision is repeated: the besotted gentile, his murderous nature, the history of blood, once the Romans, now the Slavs, later the Arabs. Although such an outlook hardly needed fresh confirmation, the immense scale of the pogroms of 1917–1920 made it hard to believe in the adequacy of the measures of self-defense urged by Bialik and less difficult to give credence to a specter of eternal enmity—slaughter repressed, slaughter unleashed—between Gentile and Jew.

For Greenberg there is a way out. Beyond the cycle of victimization there burns a vision of deliverance, and it is this eschatology that constitutes his second departure from Bialik. This vision—elaborated elsewhere in the poetry and present here only in the reference to messianism—is not the divine deliverance of classical Jewish thought but a self-willed and self-achieved national greatness. Allied to Zionist notions of national revival but magnified sevenfold, Greenberg's future leaps toward a restoration and triumph of biblical glory and potency. The howl of terror is matched in the Greenberg corpus by its obverse: the constant longing for redemption, the omnipresent *kosef*, the soil in which the roots of the eschaton take hold.

For all the differences from Bialik, there remains the great continuity embodied in the figure that emerges boldly in the second stanza: the poet-prophet and the drama of his calling. Like redemption, he is not divinely sent as in the fiction of the Bialik poem; history itself, the blood of the centuries, imposes the vocation. But the knowledge to which the poet is condemned is the same. He alone among the people grasps the meaning of the suffering he beholds, and this understanding bars him from a preoccupation with his private miseries. Of private afflictions, Greenberg asks earlier in the same poem, "What can an individual say that Job has not said already?" Like the speaker at the end of chapter 3 of Lamentations, the poet has *become* the people in such a way that collective suffering is experienced as personal pain. The coming into this task is marked in both poets by a consecration of blood, exposure to the catastrophe and contamination by its real effects, though Greenberg's evocation of Christ in his allusion to baptism *(nitbalta)* and to Joseph's coat, if only for its shock value, insists on his difference. If in Bialik's poem the exposure to these horrors pierces the brain *(maʿasim nokvim et hamo'ah)*, here too the knowledge riddles the poet's head like a sieve. Here the howl of the red conscience and the great dread; in Bialik the spirit of anguish and the venomous rage with which the poet-prophet is bidden to commune. Wrath and embitterment for both become the new muse, the permanent wellspring of poetic energy.

But here the convergence comes to an end. Greenberg *believes* in his role as prophet; he inhabits it. For Bialik the prophet is a rhetorical pose, a persona assumed for the purposes of a particular poetic situation. Moreover, for the Bialik figure there is no release of expression. The coil of wrath is wound tighter and tighter until all life is strangled; it explodes in the end only in private onanistic rage, in the wilderness away from the city whose inhabitants have forfeited their worthiness to be recipients even of the prophet's rebuke. In Greenberg there is no danger that the rage will be spent through expression; it is a natural endowment that no prodigality can exhaust. Expression is the essence of Greenberg's poetry, the very substance of its calling. Whereas the poetry of "In the City of Slaughter" is a private communication between God and the prophet which we as readers only overhear, every line of Greenberg is directed outward, flung at the listener. His words aspire to be nothing less than "dumdum bullets fired at the Nations of the World."

Uri Zvi Greenberg escaped Poland for Palestine two weeks after the Nazis marched into Warsaw in 1939. Greenberg had emigrated to Palestine in 1923 and then in the thirties returned to Poland as an editor and writer for Revisionist Zionist newspapers; by the end of the decade writing poetry had given way almost entirely to Yiddish articles documenting the coming crisis and pleading with Polish Jewry to flee Europe. His family—father, mother, sisters and their families—stayed behind and perished. In Palestine during the years of the war, Greenberg, extremely prolific until then, published nothing at all. By the late forties a steady stream of poems on the destruction of European Jewry began appearing in newspapers and journals, and it was clear that many of them had been written during the years of ostensible silence. In September 1951 Schocken issued a volume which included revised versions of these poems with the additon of many others; it was called *Reḥovot hanahar: Sefer ha'iliyot vehakoaḥ* (Streets of the River: The Book of Dirges and Power).[4]

Streets of the River is a remarkable book. It aspires to comprehend both the themes of the self and the themes of the collective in the face of catastrophe: the ordeal of personal loss and the cri-

sis of poetic calling on the one hand and the destruction of an entire nation and the visionary prospect of its renewal on the other.
It contains an extraordinary range of verse—narrative, dramatic,
lyric, balladic, ecstatic, hortatory—and sustains their orchestration
in a composition of some four hundred pages. Most remarkable
about *Streets of the River* is that it records what Hebrew literature,
in the main, does not: an attempt to face the Holocaust and to
grapple with the enormity of the loss through stages of denial,
nostalgia, and resignation; a taking up of the burden of the prophetic word of malediction and apocalypse; and finally, an acceptance of the changed conditions of existence and creation. The results of Greenberg's struggle, his political vision, will attract some
and repel others. What remains true is the origin of the journey:
its starting point in an absolute exposure to the fact of loss. This
is an encounter that was declined by the major figures of Hebrew
literature. There might have been as many outcomes to this encounter as there were ideologies, temperaments, and poetics at play
in Hebrew literature of the time. As it turned out, there is only
Greenberg's path in *Streets of the River.*

Central to Greenberg's encounter is time. *Streets of the River* records the movements of an imagination as it meets and struggles
with a terrible knowledge. The book is a representation of how
that process takes place over time; therefore an awareness of just
where one stands in successive stages of response is always essential to the reader's experience of the poetry. There is an explicit
chronological armature that fixes the poetic action at various points
between 1939 and 1945, but the real sense of sequence comes from
connections that are internal to the texts. Not only do many of the
major poems begin with the last line of the preceding poem, but
many become intelligible only when understood as the realization
of possibilities that have been opened by what has gone before, or
as evasions and displacements that swerve from what can be evoked
but not abided.[5] *Streets of the River* is a book, not a collection, and
it demands to be read with attention to its whole composition. This
is not the kind of modernist text that encourages synchronic readings, nor does the selecting of individual poems for close reading
enhance appreciation. Many of the poems do not stand up on their

own, and their separate scrutiny makes it possible to mistake one moment in a dialectic for the process as a whole.

Whole readings, however, have not been the book's general fate. *Streets of the River* is a large work and a difficult one, and its dismemberment was encouraged by the critical idealization of the "poem itself" and by the essentially periodical and nonsystematic way in which literary criticism is sometimes written in Israel. By far the most important fact about the work's reception is that *Streets of the River* was the only one among all of Greenberg's many books allowed by the poet to become the possession of a wide audience.[6] The works of the twenties and the thirties were suppressed after their small initial press runs and available thereafter only on library shelves or passed from hand to hand in photocopy. And so with the poetry of the fifties, sixties, and seventies, which appeared in newspapers but which Greenberg never permited to be collected. He did release his book of Holocaust poetry in a large edition reprinted several times, and, unsurprisingly, *Streets of the River* became the best known of Greenberg's works. This accessibility, together with the thunderous rhetorical quality of the public poems, made them open to anthologizing. In view of the general dearth of literature on the Holocaust in Hebrew, the poems filled a need for declamatory materials in the secular liturgies of commemoration that were developed for Yom Hashoah and other occasions. Transmuted into liturgy, Greenberg's Holocaust poems shared the paradoxical fate of much of the literature of destruction of other times and other places: their status as literary texts was undermined as they were appropriated into an awesome sacred discourse.

Such conferring of sacredness is a defense as well as a compliment. It absorbs the work of art into the existing orders of meaning rather than allowing the work to create its own. To listen to the inner voice of *Streets of the River* means to be exposed to a series of troubling questions about the responsibility and experience of the bystander to catastrophe, the bystander who is kinsman and brother to the victims (both the individual and the collective, the poet and the Yishuv); about the possibilities and means of purification from the ordeal of loss and guilt; about the function of myths of apocalyptic damnation and deliverance in the response to catastrophe and about the problems of their authentic realization; and about the pressures of the catastrophic event upon the boundaries of the identity of the individual ego. To allow these questions to speak through the text one must attempt to take *Streets of the River* as Greenberg constructed it; one must read it, or at least begin to read it, as a whole from beginning to end.

Although I attempt to present a schema for a reading of the whole, in the compass of this essay it is of course possible to follow Greenberg's path only in selected places. I have chosen the two lyrical cycles in *Streets of the River* in which the personal voice is favored over the public voice. The subject of the first cycle (pp. 47–158) is the breakdown of Greenberg's prophetic persona under the stress of loss and his faultering attempts to recover his powers. The analogue in the classical literature is the Book of Lamentations and the ordeals of the poet and the *gever* in the immediate aftermath of catastrophe. The second cycle (pp. 203–236) deals less with the poet than with the image of the slaughtered, especially the poet's family, and with his attempt to purge their image of shame and defilement. Although neither exegetical nor liturgical, the analogue is to the midrash's strivings to recover from the Destruction a basis for hope and survival.

The first major poem in *Streets of the River* is an invocation, the proper beginning to an epic composition. "Le'eli ba'Arnon" (To My God by the Arnon) (pp. 15–18) announces the poet–prophet's reconsecration to his mission, appeals to God, declares the sources of his poetic authority, and meditates on his spiritual biography. The poet's self-conception, according to the poem, is entirely at odds with biology and nature. He comes into the world in a miraculous incendiary birth, Moses-like, tending God's herds along the banks of the Arnon River. (The Arnon is a river in Transjordan that forms an outer boundary of the biblical Land of Israel; in addition to being a Revisionist political symbol, the Arnon represents in Greenberg's verse a pure and indigenous Hebrew poetics as opposed to the literary fashions of Gentile Europe. Greenberg had sojourned among the Nations and drunk from alien springs; but now he returns to the source of his inspiration and his powers.) Also like Moses he is called to God through a burning bush, ablaze forever with a rage that lashes out and burns within. This is God's fire, and he alone is equal to its intensity: "Who else will sing the song of fire in this generation?" (p. 18). His is a lonely distinction. Denied the comforts of sonship and society, he stands poised— "In the Snows of Poland, 1939" is the poem's subtitle— before the terrible task imposed by the coming catastrophe.

Still, for all its charged sense of present crisis, Greenberg's ordeal has little about it that is new. The *poète maudit,* pledged by God in blood and fire, sworn to the Hebrew muse—all this is a restatement of Greenberg's myth of his poetic persona which has been carried over from the poet's work of the twenties. "To My God by the Arnon," moreover, is Expressionist in spirit and technique. It is no more or less pure Hebrew utterance than was the rest of Greenberg's Expressionist verse from that decade. Accepting this poem as an invocation, it is not difficult to imagine the epic on the theme of the Holocaust that such an invocation might introduce: a fiery jeremiad against the gentiles, a majestic lamentation for the victims combined with reproaches for ignoring the poet's warnings, exclamations of torment arising from the poet's accursed calling, together with an undaunted conviction of the truth of that calling and the undiminished potency of his poetic word.

Fortunately this is not the book Greenberg finally wrote, or at least not the best parts of it. If Greenberg had gone on according to such a caricature—and Greenberg at his most rhetorical so easily lends himself to caricature—then *Streets of the River* would have been only predictable and unaffecting; even more, it would have been a statement that the Holocaust could be fitted in to the established world of Greenberg's poetry and assimilated into his self-dramatizing grandiloquence, that the Holocaust would be made to stand as a confirmation of the poet's prescience in predicting catastrophe and as a proof of the unassailability of his prophetic calling. Greenberg attempted this. In the several poems that follow "To My God by the Arnon" the poet proceeds to operate in his Jeremiah persona. In the manner of the prophetic oracle, he coins dual symbolic epithets for Israel (*ʿami-yaʿar, ʿami-yam,* pp. 38–

39), to indicate the people's forest-like vulnerability to the ravages of the enemy and sea-like deafness to warning and reproach. The term *heseḥ daʿat,* "distraction and insensibility," is introduced to epitomize the perilous and culpable innocence of Jewish life in the Diaspora (pp. 42–43). In contrast, Greenberg evokes the spirit of the Jewish rebels against Rome; from their ground bones he proposes the baking of *matsot* of rebellion to feed those who hunger for Jewish sovereignty (pp. 44–46).

Although the next major poem continues in this vein for much of its fifteen pages, there occurs a shift in subject and tone midway through "Keter kinah lekhol bet yisraʾel" (A Crown of Lament for All Israel) (pp. 47–62). At first this seems like a bemused wandering from the main argument, but soon it becomes a major derailment of Greenberg's hurtling rhetoric. He never quite resumes this rhetoric in the same way, and this juncture becomes the real beginning of what is new in *Streets of the River.* "A Crown of Lament for All Israel" opens with a panorama of East European Jewry, barefoot and defenseless, marching en masse to its death. After sustaining this image for a considerable time (pp. 47–53), the poet pauses to wonder if perhaps among this throng are his father, mother, and sisters. Unbidden, several real and recognizable faces suddenly detach themselves from the imaginary and anonymous crowd and step forward. The effect is twofold: to modulate—though not yet collapse—the ambivalent and sardonic distance from which the poet speaks of these victims, and to begin to shift from the air of outraged amazement at their behavior to the response of the involved witnesses: God and the Jews of the Yishuv. There follows a paroxysm of self-disgust, in which the material prosperity of the Yishuv during the war years is reviled with the same sarcasm applied just before to the credulous innocence of European Jewry (pp. 55–56).

The tone then moves from outrage to despondence. The faces of father and mother and sister cannot be suppressed; consciousness of their fates insinuates itself into every present moment. The poet cannot see the rain of the Palestinian winter without thinking of the Polish snows that blanket the open-trench graves. Life becomes haunted. In words that recall Alterman in *The Joy of the Poor,* Greenberg avers that the dead are not dead; they come back to us

When we walk in the street, sit in the garden,
In the theater hall and at café table,
When we turn to each other in laughter,
When a man goes to bed at night . . .

(p. 57)

A new figure from among the dead now comes forward not only
to haunt but to accuse. Shmuel, Greenberg's sister's only son, asks
how the poet could have abandoned them and gone off to Jerusalem without arousing King David and pleading with the Patriarchs, and how, without his family, he can go on with the daily
round of living. The poet is shattered and confesses his guilt and
his impotence; he knows not how he will continue to live. This is
the moment of breakdown, the failure to proceed with the bardic
task, and it recalls the crisis of the poet in chapter 2 of Lamentations; in this moment Greenberg's imagination, like the marching
victims at the poem's outset, is utterly defenseless. Far from being
capable of grand rhetorical gestures, his mind is laid open to horror.

At the center of the horror rises an image of his mother and his
sisters stripped naked by the Germans and then left unburied in
open pits (p. 58). Upon this scene, the poet, son and brother, gazes
daily from the defilement of his own survival. The shame and impotence released by this image, which recurs obsessively throughout *Streets of the River,* are feelings so deeply charged that the poet
can remain with them for but a moment. To escape, he embarks
on two different routes of evasion, strategies which seem to move
Greenberg's imagination beyond its debilitation. The first is a reverie of burial. The poet imagines his sister escaping from the
transports into the forests where, though finally worn out by the
lust of the peasants, she is at last put to rest in a proper grave; or,
of her own accord, she drowns in the Jordan-like waters of a river
(pp. 58–59). Awakening from this fantasy, Greenberg is confronted even more pitilessly with the shame of the unburied dead.
The crisis widens, as the poet experiences all aspects of his life as
compromised. How can he pray when God turned away from *their*
prayer? How can he eat and love and laugh when below him lays
the trench of their bones? Worst of all, how can he persevere in

his poetic calling? How can he continue to be (for the Jewish people) the poet of rage, force, and majesty?

It is, however, Greenberg's own earlier oracles of grandeur that become the basis for Greenberg's recovery at the conclusion of the poem (pp. 61–62). Like the sufferer of chapter 3 of Lamentations ("But this do I recall to mind / Therefore do I hope"), Greenberg lifts himself from despondence by a willed negation of the present reality. In its place he asserts a vision which, on the basis of the past, must ineluctably become the future. That past is not only the ancient biblical glory of Israel but also the poet's own past, the force and power of the prewar Greenberg texts. Both together empower the poet to regain the messianic heights and to speak in incantatory tones of the kingship that is Israel's manifest destiny. This is the crown that culminates the lament for all Israel and transforms the dirge into a final moment of consolation.

"A Crown of Lament for All Israel" presents a microcosm of the imaginative dynamics of the whole of *Streets of the River*. The poem discloses three essential movements. In the first, which describes the great procession of Jewish victims, the poet performs a bardic function, where bardic suggests a poetic discourse that is public, declamatory, and expansive. Further, it imitates the oral in its repetitions of epithets and formulaic descriptions; it is rhetorical in its use of hyperbole and exclamation, and balladistic in its documentary and narrative ambitions. In bardic discourse the poet speaks from the assurance of a certain calling, and that certainty creates a distance between the poet's voice and the subjects of his discourse, whether they be the victims, the enemy, or the bystanders. This is not a distance of objectivity—with Greenberg that is never the case—but of power. The poet's subjects are under the sway of the controlling energies of his poetic self and are not allowed to challenge that control.

The second movement is initiated with the vision of the faces of the family members. This is an involuntary memory erupting from less-conscious levels of the imagination. The distance collapses. The poet's experience of himself shifts from bard to son-brother; the controlling powers of the self falter. Having hitherto been the master of horror for suasive ends, the poet becomes engulfed by the horror and by the primitive emotions of shame, impotence, and guilt produced by it. There emerges a metaphoric correspondence between the victims' nakedness at the moment of death and the nakedness of the poet's imagination, now stripped of its defenses. The discourse in this movement is essentially lyrical, in that it becomes speech about the self. The poem's subject returns to the speaker himself and to his struggle to regain control of his imagination. That struggle centers on the question of vocation and on the crisis in the poet's capacity to discharge his (self-assigned) bardic function. Reveries of exorcism and purification, such as the vision of the sister's burial, are efforts to deny actual reality. To the degree that they focus on the family members and occur as events within the poet's reflective consciousness, they can be said to belong to the lyric movement; then such evasions turn back to face the world outside once more, initiating the poem's final movement.

The third movement is a return to bardic discourse, but with a difference. The subject is the future destiny of Israel, and, as these are public and national concerns of expansive, epic dimensions, the poet is cast into a mode resembling the opening descriptions of Israel's present fortunes. In both cases there is a distance that separates the poet from what he is describing. But while the opening of the poem addresses what is real, the close is concerned with the not-yet-existent: the one is grievous and defiling, the other, longed-for and inspiriting. In the depiction of the Jews marching to their deaths is a self-imposed distance of judgment and shame, a buffer against what is *too* real; and the rhetorical effects thus permitted involve exaggeration, ridicule, mock disbelief, irony, inversions of biblical sources. In contrast, the concluding quasi-eschatalogical picture of Israel triumphant implies a distance not only between the real and the not-yet-existent but also between the real and what, in the immediate shadow of the Holocaust, was entirely unthinkable—to anyone but Greenberg. The precursor for this discourse is Second Isaiah and his luminous prophecies at the bleakest moment of the Babylonian exile. Like Second Isaiah, Greenberg strives to project the virtual existence of the future reality and, like the prophet, relies on the dramatic and figurative powers of language to create a poetic rhetoric that is rousing, incandescent, exorbitant, incantatory.

The success of the poet's visionary campaign is a critical question throughout *Streets of the River*. The authority for Second Isaiah's vision was revelation and faith; for Greenberg it is history and politics. Success rests on the nature of the balance between the second and third movements of the poem. Does the shift from the lyric-private to the oracular-national signal an achieved hope that results from the integration and acceptance of personal emotions? Or does this shift represent a sudden withdrawal from these painful feelings and an escape into evasive fantasies of vindication and restoration? Is there an imaginative transcendence of catastrophe or a premature ideological closure? A summary determination cannot be made; indeed, just this kind of question can be answered only through a continuous reading of the book as a whole. For while the shift to the apocalyptic-eschatological in such an early poem as "A Crown of Lament for All Israel" may indeed be an evasion, the outcome may be different in poems coming after a more sustained grappling with private pain.

What emerges from "A Crown of Lament for All Israel" is a thematic and formal opposition between two orders of discourse: bardic and lyric. Rather than conceiving these two terms as a static binary opposition, it will be most useful to focus on the temporal rhythm created by their repetition, with a difference. This constitutes a three-part pattern:

bardic (history) → lyric → bardic (future)

The meaning of *Streets of the River* as a whole, it is my contention, is produced, at various levels, by the alternation of the bardic and lyric modes. That alternation creates a patterned series of public assertions, undercut by involuntary withdrawals into private concerns, followed by recoveries of public discourse in a new mode. This sequence is repeated both at the level of the microstructure and at the level of the macrostructure of the work. Thus, a single or multiple repetition of the bardic → lyric → bardic pattern may structure an individual poem. Or one individual poem, or many poems together, may belong entirely to one of these movements—

a structure that accounts for the shape of *Streets of the River* as a whole. The following outline suggests the proportions and distributions of these materials, and will serve as a useful reference for placing particular poems to be discussed. ("Bardic" here is used in both its historical and future modalities.)

THE STREETS OF THE RIVER

PAGES	BARDIC	LYRIC
1–62	The Catastrophe and the Autobiographical Myth	
63–158		Family, Loss, and Testing and Transfiguration of Vocation
159–202	The Reckoning: Israel and the Nations	
203–236		The Return of Pathos: Purification ("The Eyes of the Spirit in the Eyes of the Flesh")
	The Reckoning Resumed:	
237–275	A. God	
276–297	B. Israel, the Martyrs, and the World	
298–341	C. The Poet and his Audience.	
342–388	The Aftermath: Redemption and Silence	

Two facts become evident here. The lyric-personal mode accounts for just a third of the poetry of *Streets of the River* and is to be found in the earlier rather than the later sections of the work. Such a distribution prompts a general statement about the theme and structure of the work: *Streets of the River* is about a threat posed to the poet's bardic self-possession, derived from an engulfment in personal loss; this breakdown comes soon after the prophet-poet undertakes the project of discoursing on the catastrophe; the threat is then sufficiently neutralized or exorcised to permit a prophetic reckoning with God and the world, which is sustained for most of the second half of the work.

However, like paradise, vocation regained may be more important than vocation lost—but in the end less interesting. Judged internally, Greenberg's recovery of his prophetic posture is the work's achievement and consummation. Yet it is the breakdown, though secondary in bulk and position, that draws our attention. It should not be surprising that the lyric discourse of *Streets of the River* produces stronger poems than does the epic national impulse. Especially in terms of a study of literary responses to catastrophe, concentrating on the lyric poems has special justification. The selection of what to study and what to put aside from among the many and elaborate traditions of destruction in Hebrew literature has been governed by a principle of discontinuity. We have focused on those moments alone when the existing paradigm of meaning has been shaken by destruction and on the means by which the literary imagination works to redraw the paradigm, either in the received form or in a new configuration. So with Greenberg. Although we shall follow the shape of *Streets of the River* as a whole and suggest the basic features of its preponderant bardic rhetoric, the emphasis instead will be upon the poems in which Greenberg's received self-conception is destabilized and in which the struggle is undertaken to regain the public prophetic voice—however altered by experience.

The first of the two major lyric sections in *Streets of the River* (pp. 63–158) describes an ordeal of the imagination that passes through the following moments: the disintegration of the poet's confidence in his autobiographic myth; the flooding of his mind by nostalgia, abandonment to guilt and the anguish of separation; the seduction of death and its rejection; and an attempt at a willed recovery of poetic identity. This movement, like most of Greenberg's poetry, is hardly a linear progression. Interspersed with the lyric moments are assertive, balladistic, and choral poems each of which

represents a retreat from unbearable knowledge, and which together form the pervasive systolic-diastolic rhythm of *Streets of the
River.* Moreover, when Greenberg returns each time to the encounter with pain and doubt, he does not resume where he left
off but, as it were, falls back several rungs, and he must again experience his ordeal before proceeding onward.

Greenberg's is a poetry of megalomania. It is a poetry consumed by the task of producing an autobiographical myth. That
myth, founded in the twenties and reinforced in the thirties, is about
a young poet who foresaw the doom of diaspora Jewry and made
a redemptive ascent to Eretz Yisrael, where, because of his vision,
he alone wrote a poetry expressing and mastering the truth of
Jewish destiny. Yet now, just as history is extravagantly confirming his prophetic prescience, Greenberg's confidence in his poetic
project founders. And it is the specter of the dead parents that
precipitates the breakdown.

> Yes, I saved this body of mine when I fled the house of
>   father and mother . . .
> But I did not save my soul . . .
> A soul faint and rank and embittered by tears,
> Plucked of its feathered glory, its wings cropped.
>
> (p. 63)

His escape from Europe, the poet knows, was necessary and justified, as was his abandonment of his parents and their way of life
and his establishment in Palestine. But now there is no sense of
triumph in it, and no vindication. The price of physical survival
has been a degrading and disfiguring of his spirit. Greenberg pic-
tures himself as a once magnificent and gorgeous bird which, now
mangy and bald, is capable of neither display nor flight.

Greenberg's prewar self-myth was also predicated upon the existence of an antagonistic audience for his poetry. "I howled out
my verse," the poet recalls, "and rolled through your streets / Like
a wheel of fire [igniting] your complacent days" (p. 74). And the
audience, in its turn, reviled and maligned the poet in its midst.
"They" are the Jews of the Yishuv, and their sin was indifference
to the crisis of European Jewry and a refusal fully to pursue their

sovereign destiny in Palestine. Now, when Greenberg is in the position of self-righteousness with regard to his readers, he is struck by the purposelessness of such a stance. The Jews with whom he presently longs to communicate are not the members of the Yishuv, but his bretheren perishing in Europe. And the kind of poetry he wishes to address to them is not reproach but lamentation. Yet, alas, there is no possibility for such communication. He is here and they are there. He is like a "man standing by the shore / And raising a cry for drowning figures / Far out in the middle of the reddening ocean" (p. 75). Rather than the salvation he once thought it to be, Palestine now constitutes a separation. Those at hand no longer concern him and those he would address are beyond reach.

Stripped of an audience, Greenberg's words are forced back upon themselves. He thus stumbles unwillingly into a lyric discourse; losing his prophetic posture also means losing his autocratic control over language. Off balance and undefended, the poet is prey to forces from levels of the imagination that are less susceptible of control: memory, dream, terror, and guilt. His first encounter is with nostalgia. "Ki zeh kevar bekhi" (For This Is Already Weeping) (pp. 80–82) invokes reverie to revisit the world of his childhood at its height. In the absolute presentness of dream-time the eye of the poem passes through the yard and the garden and enters the house to find the mother and father happily waiting to greet their children who have just returned from playing in the woods. It is Friday afternoon; the family sits down to the Sabbath meal and intones table hymns. All is radiant. The mother carries the children in her arms to bed and tucks them in. "It is the holy Sabbath in our home" (p. 81). But having reached this consummation, the reverie collapses in the fullness of its own realization, and the poet returns abruptly to the actual present with its inescapable recognition—echoed in the poem's title—that all this has already become weeping. His family's house is now inhabited by a gentile family, which cooks pork and drinks wine from *his* family's pots and Sabbath goblets, and there is nothing that he, in his shame, can do.[7]

Greenberg's nostalgic fantasy recalls a genre we have met before: the idyll. The exquisiteness of Jerusalem society before the

Destruction, the ideal piety of Polish Jewry in the 1648 chronicle *Yeven Metsulah,* the coming of night to Baruch's house in Tchernichowsky—these idylls function like Greenberg's reveries of childhood, not just to esteem what is destroyed, but to stage that moment of horrible awakening from reverie to reality and then to enforce the irreversibility of the loss. But before that boundary is encountered, the idyll embodies the longing to return to the past and merge with it. In Greenberg this is the desire to be once again the son of his father and his mother. For the reader of Greenberg's prewar poetry, who recalls how central was self-declared orphanhood to the poet's rebellious expressionist posture, this sudden longing for refiliation is startling.

Reverie is not dream and nostalgia is not nightmare. After a sequence of choral hymns—the by-now familiar systolic retreat from lyric—the stratum of imagination that next emerges is deeper and less wish-fulfilling than the waking fantasy of repatriation. A grotesque image becomes the kernel for a dream narrative: the laughing face of an animal in a snowy woods (pp. 95–97). Naked, wizened, dirty, and wildly hirsute, the creature is nonetheless recognizable as Greenberg's nephew, his sister's son, who, though supposedly killed by the Nazis, is alive in the dream-altered state. The poet addresses the boy-creature, reassuring him that now all will be well and offering him pieces of challah. Although he takes the food, the creature not only fails to recognize the poet, but cowers before him as before a man who can harm him. At first dressed in his Sabbath best, the poet now strips off his clothes and covers both himself and his cousin. The poet becomes one "who happened into the woods and remained there forever" (p. 97).

Although this "forever" is qualified in the poem's postscript, the effect is to enhance the credibility and the persistence of the poet's transformation. "There are times when I turn around at a party and suddenly wonder: / Who brought me in here from the snowy woods?" (p. 97). The transformation is presented as a kind of introjection. The poet has so intensely identified with the pathos and the horror of the laughing creature in the forest that he has taken it into himself and made it part of his being. He, at times, is *it,* is *there.* Yet, however strongly Greenberg identifies, he manages only to incorporate the horror into his being but not to communicate with the victims of the horror. The locus of his pain is in the nephew's failure to recognize or acknowledge the poet and to readmit him into the family circle. Greenberg stands hale and well-fed in his best suit before the naked cowering animal who is his nephew; in the truth of the dream there is an otherness that cannot be bridged, a shame admitting no mitigation, and it is this distance that most wounds. Although the poet may give away his food and his clothes, the reversal he seeks to effect, that transforming incorporation, is possible only unilaterally and only outside the dream, as a conscious act of will.

The poet's separation now becomes a major theme of *Streets of the River*. A masterful poem, "My Sister Dukhifaz" *(Aḥoti dukhifaz,* pp. 104–108), brings the reality of separation out of the dream world and places it within the context of the poet's life in Palestine. *Dukhifaz* is a coinage of Greenberg's meaning golden bird. It is the name he gives to a bird scampering on his windowsill, which he imagines to be endowed with the soul of his dead sister; and this identification in turn evokes, in miniature, the whole sequence of loss, nostalgia, and shame that is by now so familiar. The visitation of the bird is a parodic device that inverts the famous poem of the young Bialik, "El hatsipor" (To the Bird) (1891). In Bialik's text, the bird is a visitor from the Holy Land to a pogrom-torn Diaspora and, as a messenger from Zion, is a harbinger of deliverance. In Greenberg the bird is the opposite of hope, and the distance traveled is reversed. Where Bialik longed to be translated from Russia to the bird's home, Greenberg's achieved home in Zion is no solace. Rather than redemption, Eretz Yisrael represents an abyss of separation.

Greenberg's aloneness in Zion is both ironic and pathetic. The Yishuv in the forties is laboring, building, and prospering. Far from condemning this activity, the poet views it as at least a partial fulfillment of his own will, of the program of manifest destiny laid down in his prophetic preachments. Yet amidst this teeming activity, Greenberg alone is riven with pain (p. 105). They are briskly self-preoccupied and he is possessed by a vision of destruction; they go about their daily rounds and half his soul stands naked in a

Ukrainian forest. So he turns to the bird, his sister, as his sole possible confessor, and pours out his heart. But it soon flies off, just a bird after all. The solitude of the poet in the wake of the bird's departure is deeper than before but more self-possessed; the conscious reflection that concludes the poem is characteristic of most of the poems in this sequence: an imaginary event—a reverie, a dream, a supernatural visitation—in which the mind is possessed, then followed by a drawing of lessons and a reassertion of conscious will.

Greenberg's sober reflections at the end of this poem are especially significant: "I could not raise them from the abyss on wings of poesie, / One as poor and bereft as I, rich in song!" (p. 107). The awkwardness of these verses is deliberate; Greenberg is mocking the megalomania of his own poetic persona. While Greenberg's poetry has hardly pretended to powers of resurrection, he has hoped for a poetry of necromancy, a summoning of spirits that would populate the abyss between the poet and the object of his love and mitigate the anguish of separation. But the dead are dead. "Rich of song" (*ʿashir hashirim*) is a play on "Song of Songs" (*shir hashirim*); it makes the sardonic point that if Greenberg's extravagant poetic endowment is to be of use, the poem goes on, his poetry must cease striving to communicate *with* the dead—a function that assuages the poet's desolation—and must begin exerting its energies *on behalf of* the dead.

Greenberg is now on the border between lyric and lamentation. This is the second great shift in the discourse of *Streets of the River*. The first was the poet's dislodgement from his swaggering bardic-prophetic stance and his fall into the undefended space of lyric. As harrowing as were the experiences of shame, abandonment, and separation, the concomitant loss of Greenberg's identity as a poet was, in another sense, just as serious. Now he seeks to regain his vocation and to accede to a poetic discourse which, though chastened by the destruction and in its service, entails a return to the public-bardic posture. Yet, while the first shift was an abrupt fall, the way from lyric back to vocation is tortuous. It is a journey made in painful fits and starts, which in its own right makes up part of the assertion/regression pattern of the book as a whole.

In the poem of consecration that inaugurates this movement, Greenberg states that the new prophetic task is nothing less than

To weep, to hurt, to measure and compute the horror
For which there is no measure, gauge or calipers: The force of
the sea at full current.

(p. 109)

The impossibility yet necessity of using language to describe and lament a catastrophe that is boundless—this cry of the poetic witness is familiar to us in each age, beginning with the poet's exclamation in Lamentations: "What can I compare or liken to you, O Fair Jerusalem? . . . For your ruin is as vast as the sea: who can heal you?" (2:13). As in Lamentations, the sea is the figure of incommensurability. Like the biblical prophets, Greenberg professes his unworthiness and seeks to evade the call to prophetic office; and like them too, he finally accepts the burden of the word. But if this affirmation is stirring, it is not entirely convincing to the poet himself; the consecration must be repeated many times. Meanwhile, Greenberg searches for sources of strength to bolster his commitment. Historical-ideological support is the easiest to find. Greenberg has but to recall the revelation at Sinai and the warring tribes of Israel in order to feel reconnected to a tradition of chosenness and of bravery (p. 109). (A full-scale enterprise of constructing a counter-tradition of power and resistance is deferred until after the great lyric cycle is completed, beginning on p. 159).

Finding a source of emotional strength is much more difficult. The issue again is the parents. The poet realizes that the self-confident fury of his prewar poetry was not autonomous; his prophetic word, preached from Jerusalem, depended for its vehemence upon the existence of his father *there*, in the Exile, and upon the father's traditional faith as he turned daily in prayer toward his son in Jerusalem. It is clear that now the requisite for regaining his public, prophetic vocation must be releasing himself from the toils of personal grief. This involves a final and profound acceptance of the separation from his parents: not only their death but also the impossibility of communication with them through the alchemy of the imagination. Acceptance means that the sustaining axis between there and here, father and son, is broken. "When my mother and father's house still stood under God's heavens / I was not alone in the world, I was not cut off" (p. 111). How can Greenberg resume the burden of the prophetic word in this state of redoubled solitude?

To resolve this dilemma, the poet searches for something of the father's that can be incorporated by the son: an elected patrimony that offers both compensation and connection. This is the same task of recovery the Rabbis of the midrash set for themselves when they attempted to salvage some positive message from the Destruction after stipulating what had been truly lost. For Greenberg, this is no minor task. Despite his veneration of his father, he does not venerate the principal values of his father's life: patient perseverance in the Exile and unquestioning adherence to traditional practice. In the poem "Lekol kinorotenu" (To the Sound of Our Violins) (pp. 119–125), an essence which can be recovered is finally discovered. The poem, ballad-like in form, is presented as the transcription of an experience that took place at sunset on the 5th of Nisan 1945, as Greenberg sat in an open-air café by the sea in Tel Aviv and allowed the memories of his lost family to wash over him. Amidst these reflections the poet comes to connect the sound of the violins being played in the café with the voice of his father, a cantor by profession, who used to accompany fiddlers at weddings. What then follows is an episodic chain of associations which evokes the special role of music in Jewish life. From the twin moments of triumph and destruction, from the trumpets of the tribal conquest of the Land and the hung harps of the Babylonian exiles, a paradoxical Jewish music was distilled, which is epitomized by the Jewish wedding. The fiddle music at weddings at once celebrates new unions and new futures and weeps for the destruction of the Temple and for the Exile. For this music of simultaneous affirmation and lamentation Greenberg invokes the Hassidic term for wordless melody: *niggun*. Niggun has great utility for Greenberg, not only because of its contradictory properties but because it bridges the father's world of tradition and the son's icon-breaking modernist verse. Liturgy is not poetry, to be sure, but as niggun they both share a similar function in the flux of Jewish destiny.

It is the poet's brokenness of spirit which is chiefly assuaged by the construction of a renewed poetic vocation, in which the recovery of niggun is a first step. But what of the victims? Acceptance of their deaths may be the requisite for renewal, but does acceptance mean leaving them to decompose in the open graves of Eastern Europe? Those graves never stop haunting Greenberg, and as he consolidates his own reemergence into public poetry, he turns his mind increasingly to what is a poetic equivalent of *tohorat hamet*, the purification of the corpse in preparation for burial. Purification is the theme of the second great lyric cycle in *Streets of the River*, "The Eyes of the Spirit in the Eyes of the Flesh" (pp. 203–236). The beginnings of that undertaking are already present at the end of the first cycle, in the poem "Beshmei shamayim" (In the Uppermost Heaven) (pp. 128–141). Through a kind of conjured transformation, Greenberg translates the dead from their graves to the heavens and imagines the millions of murdered Jews marching in a great procession in the skies over a *Judenrein* Europe. Naked and barefoot, they march silently, unaccompanied by the *kleyzmorim* who once brightened their processions; the silence continues until the poet begins a melody, a niggun, which is taken up by the vast heavenly chorus. Among the throng are the poet's mother and father, and they are imagined performing the Sabbath ritual in their heavenly sphere. Greenberg's image of the dead is still mixed here with elements of nostalgia, and, as such, is exposed to incursions of reality (p. 141); nevertheless, this sequence suggests that the work of purification will move towards a beatifying of the dead, a raising of them aloft, a making of them into holy icons.

As for the poet's final arrival at prophecy, the last distance cannot be crossed alone. For all his own efforts—the acceptances, the renunciation, the sublimations—Greenberg presents the final step as being effected by higher means. Revelation is at the center of the major poem that closes the lyric cycle; "Ḥazon leil geshem" (A Rainy Night's Vision) (pp. 143–150) is an apocalypse, not in the

simple sense of a vision of future times, but in the classical generic
sense of the Book of Daniel: the temporary death of the body and
the soul's guidance and instruction through the agency of an
enunciatory angel. Like apocalyptic literature, too, the contents of
the vision, the ciphers of the revelation, are not easy to read, and
perhaps deliberately so.

What remains clear, at least, is the necessity of revelation. This
need issues from an acknowledged failure of the poet's all-too-hu-
man visionary capability. Like "My Sister Dukhifaz," the poem
commences with a meditation on an everyday occurence. The winter
rain on a dreary night in Tel Aviv begins a chain of associations
concerning the solvent action of water, a meditation that ends—
this seems the final destination of all meditations in *Streets of the
River*—in the crushing thought of the unburied souls in the forest.
In defense against this, the poet produces a grotesque fantasy: The
torrents of rain become torrents of tears, and, instead of dissolving, they swell all that come into contact with them. The tears permeate the collective graves, swelling the corpses until the graves
break open from the bloating skeletons. These assume a fantastic
mass and, dirigible-like, float upward. Together they crowd the skies
of Europe and wreak a smothering vengeance upon the gentiles.
The motives of shame and impotency are so transparent that the
fantasy soon collapses. What the poet would put forth as a visionary vengeance is revealed as the paltry wish-fulfilling fantasy it is.
"Our weeping has no force," he admits; his vision, by itself, possesses expressive but not effectual power.

This complaint has been sounded before, but this time there is
a difference. Suddenly, the poet's material body, like his futile vision, collapses, while his spirit escapes and sails free, navigating its
way across the sea in the direction of the *over there* which has so
painfully lain beyond his reach. In its flight the spirit meets the
angel Zaamiel, "the muse of great and true Hebrew poetry" and,
when asked about its journey, the spirit replies that it goes to weep
at the graves of the fathers. What follows is a lament of some fifty
lines (pp. 145–147), which is a tired, dispirited repetition of all
the complaints of *Streets of the River;* without conclusion, it fades
away. Attention now passes to the angel, who has stood by silently

and allowed the poet's lament to exhaust itself. Zaamiel, an invention of Greenberg's, bears a name that associates God *(El)* with a combination of "my rage" *(za'am)* and "my people" *('am)*. This is the angel's first apparition to the poet; he is revealed in a radiant heroic aspect and addresses the poet by name.

Zaamiel's revelation is a turning point in *Streets of the River.* The angel promises to transport the poet that very night to the land of the gentiles—yet not for the consummation so deeply desired: the death-communion with the parents. The poet will be translated there in order to be shown the full essence and dimensions of the horror, which exceed the categories Greenberg has hitherto been able to project from his limited imagination; with this comes the assurance that his eyes of spirit will be reinforced in such a way that they can withstand the vision they will be vouchsafed. The force of the horror derives from the fact of its being anterior to language. "It is the silence before there were words in the world / Analogies fail before the power of what they analogize" *(meshalim hadelim kovol 'otsmat penei nimshalim,* p. 148). The sights he will be shown are located at the very "genesis of terror and anguish; a vision of things still in their raw primordiality *(behiyuliutam)."*

It is the nature of this dreadful gnosis to remain secret; the fulfillment of the promised revelation is beyond the poem. What remains exoteric in Zaamiel's disclosures concerns, therefore, not the terrain that lies prior to language, but models of discourse for speaking of the horrors once they have been bodied forth from their infernal primordial origins. After invoking the illustrious figures of Jeremiah and Ezekiel, Zaamiel wraps the poet in his cloak and transports him to the land of the Destruction. There the poet hears in succession three invisible speakers. The first is the voice of a classical biblical prophet, launched into a fiery diatribe against the leaders of the people who had betrayed their responsibility in paying no heed to the coming destruction. The second is the voice of a mocker of the people *(lets'am,* Greenberg's coinage), who jocularly praises God for bestowing death upon His people, as a sweet cessation from the tyrannies of the Nations. The last voice belongs to a prosecuting angel *(mal'akh mekatreg),* whose obscure speech seems to be a call for apocalyptic justice.

Who are the three speakers? Their words represent nothing other than the principal components of bardic-prophetic discourse: malediction/reproach, rhetorical irony/wit, and vindicatory apocalyptic. This is the discourse that was lost, eclipsed by the actualization of predicted events and displaced by lyric self-involvement. And this is the discourse—directed outward, rhetorically resourceful, and powerfully combusted—to which Greenberg, after much anguish and self-exploration, has returned. Yet, most important, this final poem in the lyric cycle demonstrates that for all the poet's exertions, the final accession to prophecy is achieved by the bestowal of a transcendental supplement, Zaamiel's revelation. That supplement, to be sure, is not given entirely from the beyond. The recipient is the persona Greenberg the poet, while the grantor is a mythic creation of Greenberg's as well, the historical author of the poem. Nonetheless, this fictive revelation makes a statement about the special resources that must be granted to language if there is to be any possibility of effective response to catastrophe.

Between the two lyric cycles in *Streets of the River*, Greenberg sustains his prophetic voice for a dozen canny and aggressive poems. These poems call for Israel's vindication and return to power; their techniques include both monumental catalogues and ironic wit. But Greenberg cannot long maintain the strong effects of the public theme before plunging back into lyric self-involvement. The poems that follow constitute a distinct unit entitled "'Enei hanefesh be'enei habasar" (The Eyes of the Spirit in the Eyes of the Flesh) (pp. 203–236). This is the last sustained lyric sequence in *Streets of the River*, in whose final one hundred-and-fifty pages the high bardic mode predominates. Although brief, this section contains some of Greenberg's most beautiful poems. The themes differ from the earlier lyrical cycle. There the emphasis was on the ordeal of the bystander-poet: impotence and shame, the denial of loss, the pain of separation, the breakdown of vocation. Here the emphasis is on the victims and the ways in which their image can be cleansed and restored through the powers of the poet's imagination.

But the practice of poetic vocation breaks down once more. The

nature of that role, as it was achieved and consolidated in the poetry thus far is rendered in an elaborate image:

> I am the architect of this sorrow, weighing bricks
> For the awesome temple from which emissaries will depart
> To light torches in the time when memories grow dim,
> Like the pits our dead lie in, shroudless . . .

(p. 205)

The poet sees himself as a master craftsman governing his materials and their deployment. Each gesture contributes to the construction of a poetic edifice which is both sacred and imposing and
which stands free of the poet, enduring beyond him. In the future, when recollection of the present destruction fades, this monumental structure will possess the power to rekindle memory. The
simile of the last line remains slightly askew. It is not clear how
the pits resemble the dimming memories, or even if the latter are
the proper referent of the analogy; and although one could trouble to offer plausible interpretations, there is a larger point made
by this faltering of signification. The theme of the stanza as a whole
is the calculated force of Greenberg's poetic production as it moves
from the poet to his media, to the accomplished work, and, in the
future, into the world. The pits of the naked dead flout this
movement and drag these efficacious energies back into the abyss.
The abyss had been the original motive for the poet's exertions,
and now it again threatens to repossess his achievement.

The poet is unmanned and exposed to the same onslaught of
pain and desire that undid him before. "The rod of my wrath was
broken when my people were broken," he complains; since the
subject and stuff of his song have perished, how can he sing (p.
203)? He has been left by their loss like a tree whose branches have
been cut off (p. 207). Nostalgia reasserts itself in the form of an
idyll on the sweetness of adolescent love in the shtetl—with the
inevitable incursion of reality at the poem's end (pp. 210–211). Next
comes a ghostly reverie of communion in which the poet imagines
himself a grown son returning after his travels in the world to the
embrace of his father and mother (pp. 212–213).

Yet for all this, there is a critical difference between this expe-

rience and the one that occurred before, and not just in the proportions:

> Spring poured through me as if I was transparent
>   from all sides and open from all sides;
> And transparent and open, too, was the ambient reality.
>
> (p. 206)

This is an image of exposure in which the self is stripped of its
integuments and exposed to the elements, but here the connota-
tion of the exposure is positive. The membranes of the self are
permeable: unguarded rather than defenseless. Instead of a raw
vulnerability there is a susceptibility which suggests that what now
lies beyond will impress itself without the crushing actuality of the
wintry recent past.

The calmness with which Greenberg stands within the flow of
memory and desire contrasts sharply with the agitated desperation with which he first met the experience of loss. The transpar-
ency of his stance makes the imagination receptive to epiphanies
of restorative images rather than grotesque visions. This influx
comes in a series of poems called "Songs from the Rim of the
Heaven" (pp. 214–218). In the delicate plasticity of their language
and in their mythic fabrication, these songs are the consummation
of the lyric moment in *Streets of the River*. This is the first:

AT THE RIM OF THE HEAVENS

> Like Abraham and Sarah by the terebinths of
> Mamre before the precious tidings, and like
> David and Bathsheba, in the king's palace,
> in the tenderness of their first night—
> my martyred father and mother rise in the
> West over the sea with all the aureoles
> of God upon them. Weighed down by their
> beauty they sink, slowly. Above their heads
> flows the mighty ocean, beneath it is their
> deep home.
>
> This home has no walls on any side, it
> is built of water within water. The
> drowned of Israel come swimming from all

the corners of the sea, each with a star
in his mouth. And what they speak of there,
the poem does not know; only they know who
are in the sea.

And I, their good son, am like a lyre whose
radiant melody has been stopped, as I stand,
towering with Time, on the seashore.
And at times the evening and the sea run
into my heart, and I run to the sea. I am
summoned, as if to the rim of the heavens,
to behold: on either side of the sinking globe
of the sun, he is seen, she is seen: my father to
the right and my mother to the left; and beneath
their bare feet flows the burning sea.[8]

"At the Rim of the Heavens" is unusual among Greenberg's visionary poems. The figure of the poet and his emotional state are secondary to the revealed image. In the first stanza the water-born image of the parents is the content of a sudden, unique epiphany. Linked to the setting sun in the last stanza, the image then becomes a regular, recurrent event. If the first part is concerned with the healing and purifying of the martyred by water, the second is concerned with fixing this purified image into a source of solace and an object of veneration.

The aspect of the parents, suddenly revealed, is dazzling. Rather than being presented as aging, abject, and parental, they shine forth wholly eroticized. They are poised at a moment which looks forward to the production of holy offspring (Isaac, Solomon, the poet). Yet it is a moment arrested here and now, in an eternal present of nuptial ardor. To view the parents under the aspect of innocent domestic sexuality, moreover, implies that their physical bodies are unmaimed and undefiled by atrocity—or returned to this state by the thaumaturgic ministrations of the imagination. The vision takes place on the shore of the Mediterranean. The martyred couple are sighted on the horizon over the water. Their gradual rising and falling is linked to a flux in them of divine luminosity and beauty, as if these qualities acted as forces of gravity. What at first seemed like a movement between the sea and the sky is now blurred as the couple is located within or between the waters, recalling the upper waters and lower waters of Genesis 1.

Their sea-house in the deep resembles the diaphanous partitions of the poet's experience of the spring described just above. Here the permeability of boundaries has become complete fluidity. To this demesne without walls, of which the martyred parents seem the proprietors, come the slaughtered of Israel from all corners of the world. The star in their mouths can be taken as a sign of divine approval or as a trace of the earlier trajectory of their journey (the heavenly processions of pp. 128–142, for example). That they converse *(saḥim)* once they arrive suggests the restoration of a social order; and this, together with the mouth-held star, gives the parental sea-house the sense of a final destination and assembly point for souls which have undergone a long cleansing and curative process. Here poetry cannot eavesdrop, and the poet's serene acknowledgment that this is a realm beyond his reach contrasts sharply with the anxious emprise of his imagination in earlier poems. The poet's imagination, in fact, has been entirely eclipsed by what he has seen. The simile for his response in the third stanza is flagrantly synesthetic. It mixes light and sound in a way that recalls the sensory confusion of the Revelation (Exodus 19) and suggests the absorption of the poet's art into a higher order of experience. Rather than describing an action, these lines register the sufficiency and rightness of the poet's presence, his readiness and his kinship.

Until this point the poem has described a visionary event of extraordinary singularity. Yet the consolation offered by the poem resides not in this unique occurrence but in the prospect of the event's becoming a process. What is described in the last stanza is neither a simple sunset nor a miraculous visitation but a fusion of the two, which has the force of a naturalization of the supernatural. From this moment onward, as evening falls, the luminous figures of the father and mother will be there flanking the sun as it sinks over the sea: their apparition and the sunset are one event and the event will recur. This is a great moment in the poet's recovery. Until now every event in the external world stirred painful associations that eventually led back to the decaying corpses.

Now it seems possible to be comforted by the stability and recurrence of the world.[9]

The nexus between water and regeneration is made explicit in the series of lyrics that follow about the Sea of Galilee (pp. 122–126). The movement from the Mediterranean to the Galilee is a further step in the process of domestication. The Galilee is Israel's own, an inland sea; unlike the ocean, it can be fathomed and encompassed, and it is sweet. The regeneration it effects applies to the poet as well as the martyred. A day's hike around the lake brings Greenberg under the spell of divine gaiety cast by the place and grants him a kind of holiday from grief. The influx of sensory beauty creates a stirring of pleasure in his body, which had remained insensate and disassociated since its collapse in "A Rainy Night's Vision." The feminine attraction exerted by the Galilee introduces for the first time a note of sexual desire, as if the existence of a lost sense is suddenly being discovered. The holiness and antiquity of this desire is conveyed by the playful conjecture that, although God did not make the Galilee the site of His Revelation, He must surely have immersed Himself in it before proceeding to Sinai.

The move from the poet to the martyred is made through the legend of Miriam's well, the miraculous spring which provided Israel with water throughout the sojourn in the desert and which, after the Conquest, came to rest in an unknown location within the Sea of Galilee. Greenberg fabricates his own continuation of the legned: On the night of the New Moon there gather at the well the crushed and mangled dead, especially the subjects of Nazi medical experiments, those bearers of unspeakable atrocity. They immerse themselves in the curative waters of the spring and are restored. Joining legend to legend, Greenberg further imagines Jacob's ladder with its base in the Galilee and its top inclined against the Golan. On the rungs of the ladder, the healed and purified souls rest after their immersion, glowing with the spectral light of moon and stars, overlooking the sleeping Yishuv (p. 225).

Like the first lyric cycle, "The Eyes of the Spirit in the Eyes of the Flesh" concludes with the reaccession to poetic production through music; earlier, the symbol was the fiddle and niggun of Jewish weddings; here it is the strains of the great organ of the destroyed Temple (p. 226).[10] Yet with the consummation of the lyric moment, there remain one hundred and fifty pages of poetry in *Streets of the River*. This is the expansive domain of Greenberg's prophetic voice. It is comprised of accusations against God's justice, vilifications of the gentiles, reckonings with the poet's detractors in the Yishuv, reveries of vindication and scenarios for retribution. Some poems, such as "Le 'eli be'eropah" (To My God in Europe) (pp. 237–252), are masterpieces of satire; others devolve into harangues whose effects are washed away by an unstinting torrent of overworked words and images. Even this public rhetoric is not uninflected; as in the whole of *Streets of the River* there pulses the systolic/diastolic movement between aggression and musing, between public reckonings and private dramas. One thing is clear: Greenberg's prophetic poetry in these pages is a discourse unto itself whose poetics deserves study in its own right. But the meaning of the book's lyric moment and its relationship to earlier responses to catastrophe may now be summarized.

Reduced to schematic simplicity, the lyric sections of *Streets of the River* begin and end at two discernable points. For the poet, it is a movement from guilt, demoralization, and incapacity to an acceptance of loss and a recovery of poetic function. With regard to the image of the slaughtered, it is a movement from disfigurement, abandonment, and the shame of unburied nakedness to a purified radiance and to a restored relationship with the living. It is, however, easier to demarcate the distance traversed than to identify the agent of these changes and understand the conditions that make them possible. The poetry itself may promote the idea—in line with the myth of prophecy—that the power of regeneration was given to the poet, revealed by virtue of his prophetic office. Our own interpretive conventions may urge us to see this as the unfolding of a natural psychological process, the integration of loss through stages of denial, mourning, and acceptance. Yet if our study of the nuances of this process has proved anything, it is that the recovery is something effected, created, accomplished. There is a factor of will beyond psychology and inspiration. This factor is the

poetic imagination in its aspect of power, in its aspiration to trans-
mute the actuality of the world. It is the *thaumaturgic* function of
poetic mind. Thaumaturgy in Greenberg's poetry does not mean
sudden miraculous transformations but rather applying to reality
multifarious tactics of denaturement and recoupment: networks
of motifs (bird, moon, water and precipitation) conducted through
many alterations of state; such master symbols as niggun used to
link disparate phenomena and distances; the manipulation of the
forms of consciousness (nightmare, nostalgia, reverie, vision, revelation). In the strategic application of various techniques to the
project of regeneration, Greenberg's poetry resembles nothing so
much as the work of the Rabbis of the midrash. Although his poetry is not exegetical, as a programmatic attempt at a recovery of
meaning Greenberg's poetry is not less resourceful. For both en-
terprises, the possibility of success relies on the fact that the catastrophe has left something crucial undestroyed: in the case of the
Rabbis it was the inviolability of Scripture and its potential for exegesis and intertextuality; in the case of Greenberg it is the inviolability of the mythopoeic imagination and the maneuvers made
possible by it. Admittedly, there is no small difference between
collective exegesis and individual mythopoesis, yet both presume
the persistence, after destruction, of discourse and textuality as a
ground in which the seeds of recovery can be sown.

The end toward which Greenberg's thaumaturgic energies are
exerted is the purification of images. As if treated to a succession
of chemical baths, the image of unburied corpses is brought through
various stages of recoupment until, cleansed of its shame and defilement, it achieves its own radiance. Once more, the best term
for the function of this final, refined image—as a source of consolation and meaning and as an object of veneration—is *iconic;* and
the elaborated process of refinement is a process of *iconicization.*

The luminous image of the parents, the icon which is the product of this process in Greenberg, is startling in its associations.
Robert Alter has captured this quality well: "The murdered mother,
father, and sister become a kind of Holy Family, undergoing
through martyrdom a celestial Ascension, concentrating in their
transfigured presence all the beauty that was cut off, all the felt

pain of their separation from the surviving son." The Christian associations are inescapable. Beatitude and beatification are the proper names for the configuration Alter rightly describes.[11] What, then, is the meaning of Greenberg's seeming invocation of Christian categories? The transfiguration and adoration of particular individuals from among the martyred dead are, to be sure, an extreme step, yet one which is in fact an extension of a tendency we have come across often before in the classical sources: the necessary resort to personification in the representation of catastrophe in order to give dramatic definition to the experience of loss. The particular kinds of suffering registered in Lamentations would not be imaginable without the figures of Zion and the *gever*. In the midrash the innumerable vignettes about particular victims, both common and noble, are part of the Rabbis' strategy for bringing the biblical text to life.

Yet nowhere is the line between representation and veneration crossed except in the Crusade chronicles and piyyutim. Although never a question of family members, there is an apotheosis, achieved by the manner of death, of individual saintly scholars. Their souls are transfigured and cloaked in heavenly radiance, and from their position of achieved rest in Eden they function as figures of grace, to whom, through the doctrine of *zekhut avot*, less worthy generations could look for succor. Using the iconographic figures of the martyrs of 1096 to establish Greenberg's Holy Family as normative may seem like a curious procedure in view of the fact that many have questioned the "Jewishness" of these medieval ritual suicides. In *The Last Trial*, however, Shalom Spiegel comes to the conclusion that, though unprecedented and unsanctioned, the suicides were not a borrowing from Christianity but the actualization of an impulse prior to both religions.[12] Something of the same sort takes place in Greenberg. Although Christological symbols are not unknown in twentieth-century Hebrew and Yiddish verse, and although Greenberg can hardly be thought of as reluctant to shock his readers, these images seem to belong more to a personal mythology formed out of extreme need than to a religious system appealed to for symbols.

At the center of the family portrait is the figure of the adored son. The restored radiance of father and mother is directed toward one recipient alone. Their love functions exclusively to resuscitate the poet's impaired prophetic faculty and to sustain him in his office. The consummation of each lyric cycle is the reappropriation of a vocation rather than the rehabilitation of the martyrs. Like Bialik's great precursor poem, the theme of the people never overshadows the theme of the poet. Yet the dramatization of the poet is much less like Bialik than like Whitman. The persona of the poet and the sovereignty of his self permeate the great expanses of *Streets of the River* and establish themselves in every interstice. Greenberg's holy megalomania is the most perdurable experience in the book. His poetry is the ultimate fact of his world. And because it survived, so have the foundations of hope.

·6·

THE APPELFELD

WORLD

Greenberg and Appelfeld are the two great writers of the Holocaust in Hebrew literature, yet their imaginative worlds are vastly different, so different in fact as to challenge the usefulness of notions of a shared language or poetics of a Holocaust literature. Temperament aside, the difference between Greenberg and Appelfeld comes down to a basic divergence in biographical circumstance: the situation of the bystander to catastrophe as against the situation of the survivor of catastrophe. Describing Greenberg as a bystander should indicate that the term implies nothing of aloofness. Who could have been more engaged than Greenberg? His poetry foresaw, preached, grieved, broke down, lamented, memorialized. Yet all these modes of engagement reflect the same truth about the nature of engagement itself: implied is an experiencing self and an event that stands apart from it. Although the event may engulf the self and the self may incorporate the event or integrate aspects of it, the apartness remains as a distance to be crossed. Greenberg was a major poet before the Holocaust, and even if afterward the poetry had been transformed beyond recognition—

which was far from the case—that transformation would still be the result of an encounter between a preexistent body of verse and a cataclysmic event.

For Appelfeld as survivor, the Holocaust was the founding event of the self. It is the event which forms him, creating a world with its own conditions and its own laws. The survivor lives inside it. There is no distance to be overcome, and also no possibility of leaving. It was necessary to reach outside for something which the world of catastrophe lacked entirely: a language and a poetics. For Appelfeld there was no preexistent literary language or literary career; his adoption of Hebrew and the fictive techniques of Kafka and Agnon has the force of a borrowing naturalized for his own purposes. Similarly, the place of Jewishness in the works of the two writers: Greenberg's poetry was grounded in (among other things) the great mythic structures of Judaism; when he faced the Holocaust it was in terms of these categories that a response was fashioned. For Appelfeld an awareness of Judaism as a religious and textual system came after the fact. Although Jewishness, in the sense of Jewish birth, is one of the constitutive conditions of his world, theological and mythic structures are irrelevant or, at most, a ghostly residue.

Appelfeld was born in 1932 in Chernowitz to a German-speaking assimilated Jewish family. The war years coincided with his boyhood between the ages of eight and fourteen. He was a prisoner in camps and escaped, and knew the insides of monasteries as temporary refuges. Most of these years were spent in flight and in hiding in the forest of the Carpathians. Toward the end of the war Appelfeld served as a mess boy for Russian units, and eventually found his way to the DP transit camps on the Italian coast, and from there to Palestine in 1946. In an important sense, Appelfeld's rescue was a failure. As an orphan survivor, the boy was educated within the institutions of Youth Aliyah and the youth movements; the ideological indoctrination these adolescents received encouraged them to disassociate themselves from the past: to forget it entirely and to make themselves over as Jews and as men in the image of the sabra. That Appelfeld resisted these pressures—at what cost one can only begin to calculate—was evinced by the fact that in 1962, after military service and a university literature degree, he published his first collection of short stories, whose theme was the subject he was supposed to have put out of mind. That the stories were written in Hebrew is itself something of a wonder. Although raised in German, Appelfeld was cut off from it in the years of hiding, during which he absorbed smatterings of Russian, Yiddish, and Czech. When he arrived in Palestine he essentially had no developed language; the acquisition of Hebrew was entirely an act of will. In the decade of the sixties Appelfeld produced five collections, containing in all some one hundred stories, with another hundred remaining uncollected. In the seventies the novella became his format of choice, and it is two instances of this recent work, *Badenheim 1939* and *Age of Wonders*, which were the first books of Appelfeld's to be published in English translation.[1] The switch to the novella raises involved formal and thematic issues; the focus of this chapter will remain on the corpus of the hundred stories published between 1962 and 1971.

The significance of Appelfeld's short fiction for Hebrew literature and for the literature of catastrophe generally can be epitomized by the following formula: Appelfeld's stories succeed in creating the aura of a credible fictional world. Although this can be said of a number of writers—fewer than we think, really—when it is the reality of the Holocaust that must be made credible, then such an achievement is rare if not singular. By fictional world I do not mean the system of relation and difference set up by any text, but rather "world" in the extensive sense of the epic lineage of the novel form. The fact that the Appelfeld world is made of many short texts indicates that it exists at an even further remove from epic totality than the novel. It is the ghost of that totality, or rather its daemonic mirror image, that makes this multiplicity of discrete fictional gestures, ranging in setting from the forest and villages and monasteries to the Italian coast to small shopkeepers and their society in Jerusalem and Tel Aviv, all part of a recognizable and undisplaceable world; this is a world, moreover, given coherence not just by a shared atmospherics but by the rule of certain laws which are as fixed as nature's. Because these laws derive from the Holocaust, the human actions they authorized are almost always unattractive: accusations, evasions, and betrayals being the chief among them. The agents of these actions in Appelfeld's stories are presented in such a way that the distance of judgment that would ordinarily intervene between character and reader is neutralized. This is the credible quality of Appelfeld's fictional world, credible not just in the sense of believable but more in the sense of acceptable. The fact that we accept the plausibility of these characters with neither censure nor sentimentality means that the boundaries of our experience as readers are stretched, or at least become a bit more permeable. Although identification with the Appelfeld world can hardly be spoken of, there is indeed a quality of connection that the texts make possible. Finally, in stressing the aura of a credible fictional world, I borrow with caution a term from parapsychology that designates an invisible field of force that surrounds the body and, like the whorls of a fingerprint, carries a pattern unique to each person. The reference in Appelfeld is to a quality of strangeness in the texture of the stories produced by the repetition of many small motifs, the recurrence of cognate roots, and the employment of a peculiar literary language that amounts to an idiolect.

Indeed, the question of technique, *how* Appelfeld achieves these effects, raises important issues for criticism. How *is* the illusion of world created in the fictional text, especially in post-novelistic forms? How *is* credibility established in the representation of ignoble behavior? These are questions that require sustained inquiry. In the case of Appelfeld it is clear that much of his success stems from an extremely fundamental choice about what *not* to represent. Everything having to do with what the French call the concentrationary universe—the transports, the camps, the *Einsatzgruppen,* the fascination with the Nazis and the paraphernalia of evil, that is to say, the entire stock-in-trade of conventional Holocaust literature—all this is left out. Before, after, parallel to—yes; anything but the thing itself. After, especially, as if to say that a catastrophe can be known only through its survivors and its survivals. Like Renaissance perspective paintings, the lines of sight in Appelfeld's fictions all recede to one organizing point, which is an origin assumed and necessary but never visible. But unlike the ideal ge-

ometry of the Renaissance, the origin here is a point of negative
transcendence, a kind of black hole that sucks in representation
the closer one approaches. Appelfeld's is a method of radical metonymy, a necessary stance of adjacency and obliqueness. In this
choice there is also no small measure of cunning. Appelfeld assumes a kind of literary competence on our part, a familiarity with
the particulars of the concentrationary universe as supplied by
documentary materials and films and by the more vulgar practi-
tioners of the fiction of atrocity and even of the pornography of
atrocity. Depending upon our knowledge of what is at the center,
Appelfeld can avoid the impossible task of attempting to deal with
it and, instead, can stake out a position along the margins, where
the literary imagination has the chance of maneuvering.

What this means in practice can be seen in the several thematic
nodes around which the Appelfeld world organizes itself. Each node
is a particular time relative to the war and is characterized by a
special set of conditions that define experience. In the short stories this time-experience continuum is divided into four principal
segments. The first segment is set in the indefinite past and evokes
the ancestral order of Jewish life in eastern Europe as a time of
disintegration and incipient apocalypse. These tales are largely
collected in *Kefor ʿal haʾarets* (Frost on the Earth) (1965). The second is roughly parallel in time to the war; it treats of metamorphoses of identity and of the tenuousness of repression. The
characters are Jews who have sought to be absorbed into the peasant life of gentile villages and Jewish children raised in convents
and monastaries: *Bekomat hakarkaʿ* (On the Ground Floor) (1968).
The third segment is the Liberation: the first emergence from the
camps, bunkers, and forests and the first months of rehabilitation
in the Italian transit camps: *ʿAshan* (Smoke) (1962) and *Bagaʾ haporeh* (In the Fertile Valley) (1963). The fourth and largest segment is set in Jerusalem and Tel Aviv of the sixties and deals with
the unwanted persistence of the past in the lives of East European
survivors from the petite-bourgeoisie and the underworld, with a
glance at German Jews from the professional classes: *Adenei hanahar* (Foundations of the River) (1971).[2] (Appelfeld's more recent
fiction, the novellas of the seventies, has gone back to the period

of the eve of the Holocaust in assimilated, German-speaking Jewry, and then ahead to the late forties, the years of adolescence and adaptation in Palestine.)

Appelfeld's development as a writer has involved the progressive appropriation of new segments of the time-experience continuum. His mind works through and explores the conditions of existence determined by each circumstance, and then moves on. This progress, however, is not chronological. The publication dates of the major work or works for each segment do not correspond to a chronological arrangement. (This is a generalized structure; there are stories here and there that would seem to belong more properly to other collections.) The sequence according to the time of writing would be in terms of the ordering above: 3, 1, 2, 4. Liberation, ancestral past, metamorphoses of identity, new life in Israel. Appelfeld works by stages, but this lack of correlation tells us that his is not the way of chronology but of the subjective logic of memory. To follow his work in his order, therefore, is to learn that logic and to track memory as it unburdens itself of feeling, unfreezes as it were, and simultaneously arms itself with the structures of expression.

"Aviv kar" (Cold Spring) in *Smoke* (pp. 49–60), belongs to the second segment of the continuum. The story opens as the delayed news of the Liberation reaches a group of Jews who have survived the war by holding up in an underground bunker in the forests. There are five of them: an adult woman, Tseitl; an adult male, Reb Isaac; an older boy, Berl; and two children, Hershl and the unnamed narrator. When the bunker is first opened they do not know what to do. Reb Isaac goes bounding off across the fields, shouting a woman's name, "Sonia! Sonia!", and never returns. The others huddle in the recesses of the bunker until the melting snows of the new spring flood their home and force them out. As they wander about aimlessly, the peasants point them out as Jews who are searching for their relatives. A monastery rebuffs their request for refuge. Berl breaks away from the group, only later to be found wounded. In caring for him the group experiences something of the exalted solidarity it once had in the bunker. A peasant woman takes them in for the night, but the price is the sexual possessing of Berl; they move on without him the next day, shamed but incapable of protesting. The three who are left—Tseitl, Hershl, and the narrator—are ushered into the presence of a Gentile holy man, a magus, who reveals in conjured images the faces of those relations who have died in the war. Seeing the truth, Tseitl, who throughout has striven to enforce the fiction of a surrogate family in which she played the role of mother, loses her grip. The story ends with her nostalgic utterance: "All I ask is to be together again as we were in the bunker with Reb Isaac and Berl with us; then I'd be ready to march from one end of the world to the other" (p. 58).

The meaning of "Cold Spring" is generated by the opposed movement of two ineluctable and simultaneous processes: the return to normalcy in the gentile countryside signaled by the Liberation, and the disintegration and dismemberment of the ersatz family after the emergence from the bunker. Appelfeld is not one of those writers for whom the very signature of the cosmos has been rewritten by the Holocaust. In the order of gentile time, life goes on. Many of Appelfeld's stories are founded on a topos of the changes of seasons from winter to spring, signifying the world's forgetfulness; this is the eternal return of nature, from which the gentile peasants are hardly differentiated. The world's wounds scab over and heal, but the Jews inhabit a different order of time, whose movement is as inevitable but whose direction is opposite. The community of the bunker is made up of individuals who are each the last survivor of a family; how their families perished and how they survived are the sort of uneasy questions that, in Appelfeld, are always left to the reader's competent imagination. In the bunker they have constituted a substitute family with the roles of mother and father and children, and they have worked to sustain each other in their survival underground. Like gas molecules escaping from an unstopped bottle, the artificial family begins to disband the moment the bunker's door is unsealed. The Liberation is the beginning of the end. The functioning illusion of family had been predicated upon the suspension of memory. With the Liberation comes the return of speech and consciousness; the reactivation of memory, the *real* catastrophe in this text, means that the illusion of restored or reconstituted family must give way to the knowledge of previous loss and ultimate aloneness. When Berl falls ill and is tended by the others, there is an imagined moment of grace, a return to the solidarity of the bunker; but the moment fades before the reality of loss, making possible only the denial and derangement of nostalgia for the bunker. This is as good an example as any of Appelfeld's strategy. Nostalgia for the bunker: a small sadness, a modest redemption, but one which, in suggesting unspeakable matters, opens up a receding vista of loss.

There is an affecting moment in "Cold Spring" when the group comes to a fork in the road and has to choose between the way to Radicz and to Tolcz. Hershl cries out: "Radicz? No Radicz for me. They'll never see my face again!" (p. 56). The sudden association has the effect of the firing of isolated synapses. It is one of the two or three moments in the story, before the concluding revelation, when a connection is made to the past. What happened in Radicz? Was it during the war years or before? We know only that it is a source of pain, whether shame for something he did or hatred for something done to him. Hershl's fleeting association is a sign of the first stirrings of memory after the functional amnesia of the years of hiding. The feelings evoked form one of the major themes in Appelfeld's fiction: the ineluctable relationship between remembering and suffering. Suffering has two faces. Loss is the subject of "Cold Spring," loss of loved ones, whether family or those who have become like family. Shame and accusation are the darker side of suffering; this is the subject of another story from the Liberation period, "Bagovah hakar" (The Cold Heights) in *In the Fertile Valley* (pp. 135–153).

The story is set in a former fortress and monastery perched on an isolated promontory on the Italian coast, which has been mobilized as a temporary recovery station for a group of survivors. Now that the discipline and vigilance of concealment and escape are no longer necessary, they collapse into the pain that until now could not be indulged. Ravenous hunger struggles with nausea and shrunken intestines; mute and sedated, the survivors take to bed, each huddled in the ordeal of his own pain. Bone knitting bone, the process of convalescence slowly proceeds. Wounds heal, bits of speech return, sensations of beauty and pleasure are rediscovered, and practical plans for the future begin to be discussed. Like the return of spring to the gentile countryside in "Cold Spring," the progress of physical healing is matched by a countervailing process of darker import. A man and his niece, Spillman and Liuba, who had survived by joining a gentile troupe of traveling clowns, hold themselves aloof from the general clamor of plan-making. The silence is suddenly broken by a terrible shriek of pain by Spillman. Swiftly he drags Liuba along the veranda by her hair and hurls her over the cliff. The act explodes the busy hopefulness that had begun to establish itself. There are demands for Spillman's imprisonment, indictments of Liuba for fornicating with the gentile circus troupers, and defenses of her purity and immaculate lineage. These violent forces had been there all along; yet "until then everything had been pent up behind a barrier which only Spillman's tough body could smash" (p. 147).

Spillman regains control of himself, Liuba recovers, and the group pulls itself together in preparation for departure. But the costs have been great and irreversible. Uncle and niece have become wasted in spirit and vitality, and the other survivors know that they must now go about reconstructing their lives with no expectation of solidarity. The consequences of remembering, it is implied, cannot be otherwise. To survive is to have done terrible things or at least to suspect others of having done them. When memory comes, it decimates, because, for the survivor, the only contents of memory can be shame and accusation, real or imagined. Now, the return of memory is not inescapable. The way out is never to let it surface or to force it back underground by clinging tenaciously to a state of present-mindedness. This is not the ideal here-and-now of contemporary psychologies—the unimpeded availability to emotion—but the opposite: the present as a medium of incessant short-term calculation aimed at keeping emotion at bay. In Appelfeld this stance is expressed in the commercial ethos of the minor entrepreneurs, small merchants, and loan sharks who populate Jerusalem and Tel Aviv of the later stories.

The disingenuous origins of this ethos are the subject of such stories from the time of the Liberation as "'Al yad haḥof" (Along the Shore) in *Smoke* (pp. 163–180), *In the Fertile Valley* (pp. 116–134), which begins:

Immediately after the war, a world of opportunities opened up; the trains rushed to the ports, to the blue gates which now opened toward the world. A few succeeded in boarding ships; the rest remained here, onshore, near the small huts left by the army, near the waves. A bustle of activity ensued; there were even those who removed their clothes and offered them up for sale; the more enterprising set up stands.

Berl sets out a suitcase and does a brisk trade in nylons and army clothes. Together with Fishl he gives himself over to the frenzy of petty transactions and grander schemes for emigration and business deals. Ostensibly, Berl and Fishl have avoided the burnt-out fate of Spillman and Liuba by suppressing the forces of inner subversion and deflecting them into the untiring energies of enterprise. Yet despite themselves there remains something that binds them to the past. The requisite for success in the newly opened world of opportunities is mobility. A man must be ready to travel quickly and travel light to seize his chance, and Berl has an encumbrance to get rid of before the world is his. Her name is Gitl; she had been nine years old when Berl had found her in the snow and brought her into the bunker. He had abandoned her twice in the past. Once, in the forest, he had gone back to get her. At the end of the war she had found him. Dazed and feeble, she clings to him, and he to her, appearing to the others "like lovers doomed to friendship by a supreme decree" (*Smoke,* p. 171). But as the frenzy of expectations mounts, the renewed bond loosens. Berl and Fishl cannot resist the call to set out for the South and the opportunities that await them there. To gain freedom of movement they hand over Gitl to a convent, earnestly assuring her and themselves that she will be in good hands and will learn French there. Outwitting the debilitating forces of memory, Berl and Fishl make their escape; yet the costs are clear, and they extend beyond those suffered by Gitl. For Berl the repetition of his betrayal means that he has abandoned himself to a world so devoid of trust that the circle of betraying and being betrayed can never be broken. By eluding memory he has fallen into the clutches of the past.

Does Berl, after all, have a choice? The alternatives are the madness of Tseitl, the lobotomized gaze of Spillman, the repeated victimizing of Gitl; and even these can hardly be said to be choices as much as outcomes. This is the great and simple secret of the Appelfeld world: there is no freedom. With one or two exceptions in the later stories, the lives of survivors bend to the shape imposed by iron laws of destiny. This shape is inevitably the same: a journey of evasion which is forced back to the ground of truth, as if repossessed by a gravitational force which can never be broken. At the apogee of denial at the center of most of the stories, there hovers a moment of grace in which the characters repose into a belief in the restoration of what has been lost or at least a hope for cessation of the process of disintegration and denudement. In "Cold Spring" this is the moment of Berl's unexplained wound, which makes him dependent upon the ministrations of others and briefly allows the group to reexperience itself as a family. In "Cold Heights" it is the moment before Spillman's eruption, when the survivors are busy making plans for the future and hoping to keep together as a group. In "Along the Shore" it is the interval of reunion with Gitl, when even Berl believes that he will never again abandon her. These moments always pass, yet there is no apparent causality; no one does anything to tip the balance. There is no need for explanations. The moment of grace has merely been a reprieve, an interruption in the unfolding of a process that admits of no ultimate alteration.

In a world shaped by predetermined forces, heroic action is hardly thinkable. Nor does Appelfeld allow even the existential dignity of the symbolic protest of the condemned man. This is a dour vision in any climate; in a national literature forged by the Bialik of "In the City of Slaughter" and carried on by the writer-warriors of the Palmah generation, it amounts to a kind of sedition.[3] Deeply shamed by the supposed reality behind the slogan "like sheep to the slaughter," the leaders of the young state sought to deflect attention away from the morally compromised survivor and to highlight counter-examples of uprising and resistance. The Day of Holocaust and Bravery *(Yom hasho'ah vehagevurah)*, established in the 1950s, left no doubt in practice which of the two was the privileged term. Now Appelfeld would have obliged this national sentiment if he had made us feel the ugliness of what, on the part of his characters, are indeed ugly acts. But he declines to do so. Nor does his refusal take the opposite tack so common in contemporary Western literature: the glorification of the survivor as the heroic figure of the new world of persecution and absurdity, or more radically, the aestheticization of evil through an entry into a Genêt-like world of redemption through transgression.

Appelfeld's is a middle course, yet one that never leads to the blandness of clinical presentation. It is a question not of neutrality but of neutralization. The writing works to defuse the norms of judgment that govern the representation of survival in Hebrew literature and to establish in their place a stance of understanding. Understanding is not forgiveness, which implies a cordon of purity from across which remission is offered. To understand means to accept that such is the nature of things, that to survive in a world in which what happened happened means to have done certain things and to be a certain way. Appelfeld's goal is our knowledge of that world; he wants us to accept the reality of it against instincts of evasion every bit as strong as his characters'. To the extent to which Appelfeld succeeds in rendering this given and determined world fictionally plausible, to that extent he manages to purchase our acceptance of his characters' humanity. And this is the paradox: this humanity is attained precisely because they have no freedom.

In Appelfeld's project of rendering his world fictionally plausible, there would seem to be an inherent limitation. If this is a world of implacable laws, how can it be interesting? The answer is that although the ultimate reality is fixed, the proximate means of evasion are manifold. The conditions and climes, the stages of life and of history, the differences of class and temperament are variegated; although the points of departure and arrival are always the same, the voyage of bad faith is different each time. It is this space in between, so briefly given and so hedged in from both sides, that is the zone of these characters' humanity—what is left of their freedom—and they people it densely and variously. Appelfeld's world is monochromatic; but the intensity of contrasts he forces us to discover within his limited part of the spectrum has the effect—indeed the presumption—of suggesting that the part be taken for the whole.

Instead of taking its characters forward in time from the forests and the transit camps, Appelfeld's fiction of the early sixties—as collected in *Frost on the Earth* (1965)—moves backwards. The themes are taken from the life of East European Jewry in a world that ostensibly knows nothing of the destruction to come: the pilgrimage of a group of Hasidim to their rebbe; the memoirs of a skeptical rabbinical court beadle; the declining of power of the last in a family of shtadlanim; the confessions of a businessman stuck for the winter in a distant trading post; the weariness of commercial travelers and Zionist lecturers in their rounds of distant villages; the failed preparations of a town to emigrate to America. One might expect that Appelfeld is probing for origins, searching for structures of consciousness and behavior that would explain what came later. In fact the opposite is true. Instead of attempting to reconstruct the past, Appelfeld intentionally and systematically commits the fallacy of projecting onto the past a knowledge of later events. It is as if the ancestral order, as a world suffused with despair, entropy, and disintegration, was always already under the star of the Holocaust.[4] Here is the same condemned destiny of human life, the same implacable laws, the same temptation to evasion— though, of course, the strategies of evasion are particular to time and place. This sameness of conditions is a way for Appelfeld to assert that the nature of existence is one, and that it matters little if one writes of survivors, who have gone through the event, or of their predecessors, those who later, at best, may have the chance to become survivors. "There is no earlier and later *(ein mukdam ume'uḥar)*, only the burning present," says one of Appelfeld's narrators, echoing the rabbis' counsel against seeking a sequential order of events in biblical narrative. It is in these tales that Appelfeld most closely approaches the canons of a mythic scripture. Indeterminate journeys, far-away capitals from which laws are issued but which can never be reached, isolated and nameless monologists, powerlessness in the face of encroaching forces—this is an ambience which suggests nothing so much as the wanderings of Israel in the desert as retold by the Kafka of *The Castle*. For the reader of Hebrew literature steeped in Abramowitsch, Berkowitch, and Agnon, Appelfeld's reworking of the long-used thematics of the shtetl has the force of a successful defamiliarization.

"Hagerush" (The Expulsion) (pp. 56–65), one of the most accomplished stories in this series, literalizes evasion in the form of an actual journey, and shows how finely textured the representation of this idea can be. The story concerns a community of Hasidim who are banished from their town and make the long trip to the provincial capital en masse in open wagons. The circumstance of the expulsion edict, the machinations of the gentiles, the failed intercessions and bribes—of all this there is nothing, implying that such information is beside the point. Expulsion is inscribed in the cosmos; as in Appelfeld generally, such a fate is a defining condition of existence rather than a product of history. The truth that is evaded is simply put: their journey is coerced, not elected; what awaits them in the capital is further rejection and dispossession; this is the beginning of a decline which will stop only in destruction and death.

When they first take to the road, the Hasidim are exhilarated; they experience their leaving as a liberation. All these long years their lives have been ground down by the threats and harassments of the gentiles. Nor have they been left in peace by their fellow Jews; the westernizers and half-breeds have persecuted them and ridiculed their faith. The unrelenting press of business and livelihood has dulled their spirituality. Now, as they move through the open fields, they shed their diffidence and abandon themselves to the vast openness of the heavens. The beauty of the countryside seems revealed for the first time, and they give themselves over to intoning the niggunim from whose spiritual strength they have long been cut off. Their progress evokes a nostalgia for the festival pilgrimage journeys to their rebbe's court in happier times.

The women are less exhilarated than agitated. The small-mindedness enforced by years of haggling in the market make them resist the abandonment of the men and stick closer to the details of the journey. In the past they have trod the road to the capital, not for pilgrimages but to transport merchandise; they know how very long the journey is and how dear the price of housing there. It is they who have intimations that this expulsion is not a periodic annoyance but a permanent uprooting, and they are frantic because a hasty departure prevented them from taking leave from the graves of their ancestors. From their everyday intercourse with the gentiles, the women know them better than the men and can less easily shake off their anxieties.

The women's reservations remain unvoiced because articulation is against the principles of the community. They are known as the Mute Hasidim. Their strength lies in their restraint. In the welter of questions and calculations about the journey—how long? how many? where to?—they see the devil working to undermine the stance of faith. They know the art of silence and await the Redeeming Word. When the silence is at last broken, however, it is not by a redemptive utterance. One of their number, Reb Hershl, steps in front of the caravan and shouts: "Halt! Where are the horses taking us?" (p. 59). Although it fails to stop them, Hershl's cry reverberates subversively. It implies that neither they nor a higher providence controls their movements; they are led by their horses. More than violating the silence, Hershl's provocation lies in its explicitly joining a name and a thing. Precisely what name to give to the kind of movement the group is embarked upon is a critical point: journey (*masᶜa*)? wandering (*nedidah*)? expulsion (*gerush*)? The nominative potential of language is what is feared: to speak is to name; to name is to interpret; to interpret is to admit the possibility of alternative interpretations, which welcomes doubt and saps the will of the faithful.

That the question of language and truth is central to the story is underscored by the encounter of the Hasidim with a traveling troupe of mummers. The mummers are Jews who, in exchange for taking a solemn vow to renounce family, property, and their Jewishness, have been given an aptitude for comic imitation and mimicry. The mummers and the Hasidim are presented as each other's double. Both are covenantal communities endowed with special gifts, traveling the countryside detached from home and hearth. Yet for the mummers, their dispossession and their wandering are elected and acknowledged for what they are. If the

Hasidim protect (or evade) a sacred truth by silence, the mummers ridicule corrupt truths by overarticulation. In their stage parody of a rich man's attempts forcibly to marry off his daughters, what is conspicuous about their speech is its loudness and inflection; they speak "so that each word should be heard and each rhyme sounded, and so that this Reb Shmuel on the stage should seem the most miserly of misers, the most fanatical of fanatics . . ." (p. 63). Their language tells too much of the truth; it exaggerates what is already extreme. The plasticity of their expression, its mimicking disguises, its very volubility disclose no truth worth protecting. The Faustian relinquishing of their Jewishness has made their wanderings truly aimless. Unlike the Hasidim they lack even a longing for a lost center—or the illusion of still having one.

While the mummers cheapen reality, the Hasidim are in danger of making it into something much more than it is. The practical men among them seek to enforce the discipline of an operative illusion: their movement is a journey to a goal which will alleviate their plight. Required are moderation of behavior, attentiveness to the road, avoidance of speculation, confident faith on the model of the old pilgrimages. This restraint is opposed and overtaken as the narrative progresses by an apocalyptic and mythicizing tendency. There are the "soaring conjectures" *(hirhurim mafligim)* of those who would interpret their present afflictions as an opportunity "to be tested, as it were *(kivyakhol)*, by the same trials to which the Patriarchs were submitted" (p. 60). Their journey resembles the descent into Egypt; the capital is a necessary Pithom and Ramses to be endured before a greater redemption. The typological restraint represented by the "as it were" is soon abandoned. In the Sabbath observance, which corresponds to the moment of grace in most of the tales, there is a will to project existence onto the plain of already redeemed time. There were those who, "in their desire to exalt the hour, later told that this was a Sabbath as it was first given *(kenetinatah);* even the smell of the sacrifices wafted to their nostrils" (p. 64).

"The innocent would not corroborate this," the text continues immediately afterwards, "because they are wary of any making of comparisons or parables" (p. 64). This perspective of innocence, by which the variegated evasions of others are revealed, is the possession of an orphan from whose point-of-view "The Expulsion" is narrated.[5] Unprecocious, the child's mind is uncluttered by acquired knowledge; not yet knowing what to fear, he is untempted by the need to interpret reality and unpracticed in the art of interpretation. The boy's orphanhood gives him both an independence from human bonds and the special protection of the community. His unique place is lodged "between rumor and astonishment" (*bein hashemu'ah vehapeli'ah*, p. 56), where he can mediate between what people say about events and what he himself observes. (The noninterpretive amazement of the child later becomes the basis for the novella *The Age of Wonders*, 1979.)

The issue is sight versus interpretation, and Appelfeld clearly puts forward the figure of the orphan as standing for the possibility of a fictional discourse which registers rather than construes, observes rather than interprets, and ultimately suppresses the urge toward imaginative transfiguration. It is not farfetched to see in this defense something of the claims Appelfeld would make for his own writing:

[The orphan's] eyes registered each sight, so that when the time would come he would be able to relate them in his own language, though he did not know then that only he would be the faithful witness. The depredation of time had effaced in them, without their knowing it, all expressions of glory. Only he, in his innocent attentiveness, could piece together image to image. Perhaps the practical men even understood that with his wondering gaze, only he could grasp the moment; and they therefore allowed him to move among them so that no detail should escape his eyes. (p. 61)

This self-reflexive meditation is one that Appelfeld seems to allow himself only within the mythic ambience of the ancestral tales. Although much of Appelfeld's fiction may be said to be broadly autobiographical, it is impersonally autobiographical, and there are few passages that reflect on the role of perception and writing. This passage stresses a quality of fateful prescience; there is a shadowy grasping of the orphan's future role not just as survivor but as teller. What is passively and wordlessly witnessed now will at some future time be transposed into language, and not just language but *his own* language. This hindsight/foresight framework presents the experience of the writer as coming in two stages. As a child young enough to be unburdened by grids of interpretation and dull enough to be free of precocious learning, his mind was the perfect blank film upon which images could record themselves—serially, comprehensively, without patterning. Later, after the events, when he gains language—and this is by no means merely a matter of age—he effects the transposition into words and arranges the images in meaningful configurations. Appelfeld's particular conceit is the claim that for him the writerly second stage carries over something of the photographic innocence of the first. His project of neutralizing judgment, his refusal to demonize or sentimentalize, is born out of a desire to be "the faithful witness," the one who eludes the pressure of later historical meanings and attempts to articulate images as they were grasped by the "wondering gaze" of the child.

"We must make a simplistic distinction between those who saw suffering through to the end, exhausted, as it were, and between those who escaped to the forests, disguised themselves as farmers and circus performers, and, so carrying death within them, wandered from place to place," declares the narrator of "The Cold Heights" (*In The Fertile Valley*, pp. 135–153). Appelfeld's work—concentrated in his fourth book of stories, *Bekomat hakarkaʿ*, (On the Ground Floor) (1968)—represents a choice clearly taken. During the actual years of the war, it is the world *parallel to* the organized torture of the concentrationary universe that is explorable terrain. This is the world of Jews who, because of their constitution, their will, and their resourcefulness, succeeded in effacing all signs of their Jewishness, imitating the conduct and manner of the gentiles, and fading into the rural countryside as farmers, itinerant peddlers, and performers. This disguised life offers rich fictional opportunities for the anatomy of the curious type of the non-Jewish Jew or for an obscene picaresque in the manner of Kosinsky's *The Painted Bird*. Yet for Appelfeld it is not the perversity of this situation that interests but its typicality. The peculiar figure of the Jew-turned-gentile serves as an occasion for raising large

questions about the nature of Jewishness, the possibility of becoming an other, the encounter between the self and its double. These
are questions that arise, in part, out of the separate experience of
the Holocaust Kingdom, but just as much out of the mind's quan-
daries in the fables of identity of modernist fiction.

Again, Kafka is the bridge. The thesis story in *On the Ground
Floor* (pp. 55–62) concerns a Jewish man and a Jewish woman who,
pursued into the forest, suddenly discover that in body and gesture they have changed into gentile peasants. The story's title,
"Hahishtanut," translates as "The Transformation" or "The Metamorphosis," and the allusion, perhaps the homage, is unmistakable. Like its precursor, the effect of Appelfeld's text is created by
the interchangeability of disparate orders of things, as this confusion is rendered plausible by the matter-of-factness of natural-
istic detail. Appelfeld's nameless protagonists awake after their
months of flight to find that their skin has coarsened and hair grows
on their hands. They find themselves able to swim, scale rocks, climb
down into caves, fish in the streams. They make for themselves
coats of pelts and tar-sealed boots and converse with the farmers
in the local dialect. As in Kafka, too, the sudden thereness of the
transformation is comically absurd. The text has the quality of time-
lapse photography: the male character is giddy from the rapidity
of the change, as if he were watching his skin toughen and hair
sprout before his very eyes. For the reader it is a parody of evo-
lution, in which the gradually acquired adaptive traits in the long
struggle for survival are compressed into a few moments. Finally,
like Gregor Samsa's fate, the suddenly altered state of Appelfeld's
characters probes a critical ambiguity about the nature of the link
between before and after. Is the metamorphosis a fate visited by
the decree of unspeakable events beyond their control? Or is it a
chosen destiny, the certain consequences of willed evasion, or even
the accelerated culmination of tendencies already latent?

For a while the couple's transformation is a fortunate fall into
the lap of nature. They live a primitive life by a river: bathing and
drying themselves in the sun, learning to cure fish and dry fruits,
reading the signs of the wind and the clouds. In nearly every Appelfeld story, especially the tales of the Liberation and the coun-

tryside, seasonal change serves as both the setting for the action and its clock, and it is always the circuit from early spring through summer. It is the metronome, set at different tempos, which is always ticking in the background of the text. Nowhere are the workings of this master trope as conspicuous as in "The Metamorphosis." The unalterable movement of nature through the seasonal cycle parallels the implacability of the laws which govern the destinies of the refugees and survivors. The parallel, however, is only a mimicking. Nature has its perennial rebirths, and the peasants, though at times hardly differentiated from the earth, have shelter enough to survive the dying flux of the seasons. The Jews, however, move along another track. The beneficent warm months, which suggest the arrival of safety, turn out to be a false promise, merely a momentary coinciding.

This moment of grace is represented in "The Metamorphosis" as a still point between two movements: the memory of Jewishness has been effaced and the full naturalization into gentileness has not yet taken place. But things change with summer's end. On Sundays she goes with the other women to church to light a candle; when she returns he is drunk. Sometimes he flies into a jealous rage and beats her and she runs away weeping. Other times he weeps, "the way grown gentiles weep beside a stone or a religious statue or when the lord raises his whip over them" (p. 60). When their garden bower freezes over there is no one to take them in. She would have them indenture themselves to the farmers in exchange for shelter; he refuses, convinced that this is a ruse to give vent to her adulterous desires. On the morning of the first snow, he awakes to find her gone, and his frostbitten feet prevent pursuit. Clutching his knife, as the story ends, he "realizes that now everything is ice: the garments, the river, even he. But when the spring thaw comes, he will bring her back and tie her down (veya'akod otah) here" (p. 62).

This use of a rare word that can summon up only the Akedah in Genesis 23 is a subtle effect. The purpose is less to urge a closely observed comparison between the two contexts than to strike a concluding semantic chord of dissonant complexity. The man's blood-thirsty desire has nothing of Jewishness about it, certainly none of the high faith of Abraham and Isaac. It is the gentile brutality that has taken him over. Yet Appelfeld's insistence on the root ʿakod for this most non-Jewish of urges suggests the impossibility of the separations the story would at first seem to propose. The effacement of Jewishness is a state which can be approached but never arrived at absolutely. There remains an unwished-for yet irreducible residue of consciousness which subverts the consummation. The Jew has forgotten enough to acquire the gentile's earthy brutishness but not enough to be allowed (or to trust in) the primitive shelter of gentile society. The restraints on human nature have been removed, and so have the protections. The frozen legs, savage thoughts, and Jewish words—these are the markers of the story's final image of arrested metamorphosis.

What would happen if the transformation in fact succeeded? Appelfeld locates the nameless hero of "Habriḥah" (The Escape), *On the Ground Floor* (pp. 5–20) at a considerably advanced point along the path to gentileness. When the enemy rounded up the Jews of his region, he happened to be on the road. He bought himself a fur coat and a horse and set about assuming the identity of an intinerant gentile peddler. Within a month's time the ruse had been brought off to perfection. The features of his face rearranged themselves; he strode with the gait of a man familiar with the forest trails; his body exuded the smell of farmers; he learned to bless and to curse at the right times and to comport himself in the proper manner with landowners and priests. Within the year he was established in the countryside, not an isolate shunning human habitation, but a relied-upon supplier of small necessaries, a man respected and called by name. As in "The Metamorphosis," the transformation takes place with an almost miraculous effortlessness, and this astonishing change in individual identity finds an ironic correspondence in the fate of the Jews of the region as a community. Just as the peddler has succeeded quickly and cleanly in replacing the Jewishness within him, so the countryside as a whole, once the Jews have been removed, has easily managed to forget their existence. Grass grows over the Jews' houses; their valuables "soon find their place in the farmers' houses, loose their Jewish color, and bloom on the commodes" (p. 7). A few Jewish words are left in the local speech; more than that, nothing at all.

The displaced candlesticks and wine goblets, though in themselves inert, represent the trace that is inevitably left by any change, no matter how seemingly total. Although the peddler's manner never faltered in his transaction with gentiles, when alone in the woods he sometimes becomes afraid and finds himself murmuring broken verses from the prayer book. "His Jewishness," observes the narrator, "lay beside him like the fallen leaves beside the trees in the fall. It decomposed beside him and within him" (p. 7). Although the tenor of this image chiefly underscores the separableness and dispensability of the former identity, the vehicle permits other implications. The leaves, now shed, were once organically part of the trees, which will again put forth leaves; and even what has been discarded rots not just externally but within as well, a cankerous presence. Soon the text reveals that the eradicated Jewish community has also left traces that are not just inanimate objects. Rustling sounds in the forest betray the presence of several other Jews who, like the peddler, survived by accident, but, unlike him, have remained visibly Jewish and therefore must hide. The discovery of these mortified creatures is the fulcrum of the story; the peddler's response to them tests the nature of his transformation.

Self or other? At first he views them with fascination and disgust. Cringing, rag-tag, they crawl through the high grass of summer, steering clear of the villages. They appear to him like grotesquely magnified insects flushed from their lairs. He regards them as a hunter regards an unworthy prey which he could cut down with one swoop if he so troubled himself. Soon the Jews' presence in the forest becomes something more than an annoyance. He feels his life invaded and infested; if he fails to reveal his identity to them, he fears "they will swarm over him like desperate summer roaches, storm him with the last of their anger, and bite into his alien flesh" (p. 11). The peddler's fears neatly recapitulate the hysterias and demonologies that traditionally flourish in the absence of real contact with Jews. It is not until such an encounter that his alienness is disturbed.

The irritants come in the form of two boys and an old man,

whose presence is given away by the audible strains of their sing-song *ḥumash un taytsh*. They are stuck in the high grass because their feet froze in the winter and they cannot move far; it was their immobility which saved them when the area was combed for un-apprehended Jews. The plaintiveness of their Jewish voices has stirred something inside the peddler, and when they inquire, he tells them the story of his own accidental escape. The two boys are struck with amazement. The figure who stands before them is gentile in every detail; "how is it possible," they naively wonder, "for a man to change so much?" (p. 18). The old man is less cred-ulous and converses with the peddler with the cautiousness of a man used to the wiles of the world. The invitation to tell his story, the boys' astonishment, and the old man's suspiciousness combine for the first time to tamper with the complete externalization of self the peddler has achieved. The sensation of having his mem-ory pricked involves beholding a self prior to his present one and, like the boys, wondering at the vastness of the change. "He was caught now in his own enigma" (p. 18).

As the sun sets the Jews draw off to themselves to pray, and the peddler is left standing by himself like an accused man *(kineʿesham)*. Struggling to say something to them in Yiddish, he comes up with the foreign words that are now all the language he has. Though he offers them clothing and a horse and urges them to begin trading in the villages, they have become afraid of him and slip away in the darkness. Their rejection is a judgment: he may or may not once have been Jewish but now he is one of *them*. The peddler, who began by feeling superior to and separate from these despicable and puny creatures, ends by finding himself "impris-oned by their gaze" (p. 17). They have unmanned him by making him aware of his alienness. Yet paradoxically and tragically, the metamorphosis has been too successful; he has crossed over, and there is no way to come back. The encounter with the Jews has robbed him of his obliviousness and left him stranded in the mid-dle, a survivor just beginning to realize the costs of his survival.

It is worth emphasizing that the agents of the peddler's undo-ing are Jews. While one might have expected some unrecon-structed bit of behavior to give away the disguise, the peasants and the farmers in all the stories on this theme entertain no suspicions, and there is not one scene of discovery. By making these unmaskings come from the stirrings of memory in the self or from the encounter with the other-as-Jew, Appelfeld is fashioning conundrums of identity and staging Jewish dramas that remain unconditionally internal. But he is doing something less than that as well. What he is keeping out is as significant as what he is keeping in. Excluded is the face of the enemy: peasants, farmers, landowner, local collaborators, and most of all, Nazis. This absence is the rule not just in these tales of the forest and countryside but up and down the line in all of Appelfeld's stories. The representation of gentile existence is undertaken only in the case of Jews who have entered into a gentile identity. This exclusion is the result, in part, of Appelfeld's rigorous aesthetic discipline, which calls for the avoidance of melodrama and gross effects. One senses in Appelfeld a moral stance as well. The fascination with evil is a highly appetitive faculty, and Appelfeld knows that the reader would prefer to have it fed than to be forced to concentrate on the threadbare and pitiable ordeals of the victims of evil, especially survivors. To represent the figure of the enemy in the medium of narrative prose fiction, moreover, means to understand and humanize it, and this is a project which leads in its own direction and carries its own responsibilities.

Removed from the context of the Holocaust, Appelfeld's choice is striking for its continuity with the precedents of the Hebrew literary imagination. The poets of Lamentations, the Rabbis of the midrash, and the payyetanim of the Crusader massacres are joined in keeping the enemy in the background lest the destruction fail to be grasped as an issue of the covenant between God and Israel. Bialik kept the perpetrators of the Kishinev pogrom out of his poem in order to check evasion of responsibility for Jewish self-defense. Elusive of theological and ideological goals, Appelfeld cannot be said to have such programmatic motives; and the metaphysics of his fictional world makes no provision for a commanding, covenant-forming God. Nevertheless, the choice is the same, and so the effect. The force of Appelfeld's fiction is centripetal, drawing our consciousness inward toward the Jewish people, toward the lives of survivors, toward the human heart. It is a writing of self-confrontation which offers no outlets.

Appelfeld's strongest stories are largely contemporaneous with the time of their writing. These are the tales of new life in *Adenei hanahar* (Foundations of the River [1971]—perhaps a play on *Streets of the River*). Set in Jerusalem and Tel Aviv of the 1960s, they concern survivors who have reestablished lives as merchants, restaurant proprietors, and loansharks. It is just because this milieu seems so unpromising as fictional material that Appelfeld is able to exert the maximum control over his medium. In the earlier stories the narrative voice had to work against the grain of the narrative situations. Appelfeld's understated and minimalist mode of telling was in tension with feelings and events that were inherently overwhelming and melodramatic. This was a tension creatively exploited but uneasily maintained; the polarity was sometimes schematic and jarring. With the bunkers, forests, and DP camps behind them by fifteen or twenty years, and now settled in to occupations roughly continuous with their lives before the war, Appelfeld's people present a reality which is tractably drab. Although this ordinariness is only evasion in another guise—the sign of a past more deeply buried—the layers and the surface provide an opportunity for more subtle texturing and for a narrative language that need be less on guard. Appelfeld's Hebrew style changes as well. Lush, difficult, and outré, the language of the early collections is a style whose artificiality contributes to the aura of strangeness in those tales. During the sixties Appelfeld's Hebrew undergoes a process of naturalization. It becomes more like standard literary Hebrew and less like—in the tradition of Gnessin—a replication in Hebrew of European literary diction. The style is still recognizably Appelfeld's; like his characters, it is far from assimilated into the new milieu, but it is at least more at home there.

Appelfeld's retreat from strangeness is hardly a failure of nerve. Just the opposite. While he restricted his fiction to faraway settings and spoke in a difficult tongue about deformed creatures, his work could be respected as occupying a separate, perhaps sacred, niche within Hebrew literature. The later stories, with their new setting and new style, presume to claim a place within the mainland of the national literature and to leave behind the status of venerated anomoly. The positive heroes of the Palmah writers and the symbolic antiheroes of the younger writers who eclipsed them were drawn alike from the founders and sons of the New Yishuv. Kibbutz members, soldiers, teachers, writers—their lives took place within the institutional realities of the young state and were judged variously in reference to the faltering ideals of the socialist Zionist tradition. Appelfeld's shopkeepers and loansharks stretch the scope of classes and types deserving of the attention of serious literary art. The main force of this move, however, is to take up for sympathic study a population for whom the Zionist revolution and the founding of the State remain facts of consummate irrelevance. This indifference is not the result of ideological counterstatement or political illiteracy; the stories do not touch this level of consciousness. Rather, in the existence of the survivors the transforming event has happened long ago. That their lives were rehabilitated in the Land of Israel, whose creation as a modern state was thought by its founders to alter the framework of Jewish history, does not seem to touch them. They could be living just as well—probably much better—in New York or Buenos Aires. They remain unredeemed, their only deliverance coming, perhaps, from Appelfeld's writing about them. Nor can these characters be dismissed as a perverse selection, a collection of hard cases. The challenge of these stories to the values of Hebrew literature lies precisely in a normative claim: the State and all that it represents are, at some level, powerless in the face of other, prior realities.

There is, in fact, only one of these stories in which the State figures thematically. "Bronda," the first story in *Foundations of the River* (pp. 12–16), is set in Jerusalem on Independence Day in one of the years when the city was the scene of great military parades after the Six-Day War. Jerusalem in the story is alive with the swirl of gay crowds, bright dresses, and musical instruments, as old and young join in a day of festive acclamation. The mood is summarized by a children's choir's singing the song "Yerushalayim shel ma'alah" (Jerusalem the Heavenly). The title of the song, which is a fictional variant of the then-popular lyric "Jerusalem the

Golden," implies the existence of a fallen double, a Jerusalem neither heavenly nor golden, which becomes the true setting for the
narrative. For the inhabitants of this other Jerusalem the celebration is a day to stay away and stay inside. "How forlorn were the
cafés! People huddled by the espresso machine, drawn into themselves, as if the secret of their impermanence had been revealed
to them" (p. 11). Among the gloomy company is Kandl, the loanshark, who is doubly dejected because of the death on the previous day of his lover, a blind woman named Bronda, to whom in
the past he would repair for comfort on days like this.

The kind of comfort Kandl used to receive from Bronda was of
a perverse kind. He needs to be comforted because his life of late
has not been going well. Trained in the black market of occupied
Germany, Kandl has transferred his profession of moneylending
with interest—with its methods of risk and intimidation—to life in
Israel. But he has become a superannuated figure in the new environment; most merchants now use the banks, and those who owe
him money feel little need to settle their accounts. He is caught
between the world's contempt for him and his universal distrust
of the world, emblemized by the savings sewn into the sleeves of
his never-removed coat. What Bronda offered him was an explanation for his bad luck. She believed that his afflictions are a punishment for sins committed during the war, evasions and betrayals
about which only he can know. Kandl is a man who has lived without God, she claimed, and until he seeks atonement he will have
no rest. He, in turn, disdained her accusations and her talk about
God and repentence. Try as he might, he could remember of his
early life only that he was born in Lodz, hidden by a gentile woman
during the war, and afterwards had escaped to Germany, where
he began his activities. Of parents, brothers, and sisters—nothing.
Yet despite his protestations, Kandl cannot get free of the conviction that there is something rotten inside him, and each of Bronda's curses cuts him deeply. His memory is so deeply frozen by
what he saw and what he did in those years that to thaw it would
be to risk a pain much greater than what he endures now. Kandl
and Bronda are bound together like sinner and confessor, with
the difference that he can never name his sin and she can never

supply absolution. He is like the figures of Lamentations, who bear the crushing conviction of sin without the knowledge of specific transgressions. He is unlike them in that he has no convenantal faith with which to console himself. He has only Bronda, and when she dies on the eve of Indepedence Day, the bond is severed. While the nation celebrates independence as freedom, Kandl experiences independence as abandonment and as the beginning of his end.

The bond between two survivors is the principal social unit in the Appelfeld world. In the fables of identity, like "The Escape," the bond exists between the Jew-become-gentile and a more visibly identified Jewish double. In most of the stories the bond is between two people, often unrelated by family, whose relationship was forged by the cooperation necessary for survival during the war—and sometimes by the betrayals as well. Like most things in the Appelfeld world, this relationship is less elected than given; the two people are forcibly and permanently "bonded together" by the necessity of events. In the narrative space of the stories that necessity has already become psychological and spiritual. Appelfeld never shows us the crucible of brute, physical necessity in which the bond was formed. In the tales of the forest and the gentile countryside the originating events are only in the recent past (the pursuit of the couple in "The Metamorphosis," for example). The stories in *Foundations of the River* study the fate of the bond after fifteen or twenty years. What emerges strikingly from this examination is, after so much time and such different circumstances, how little has changed: the nature of the bond remains stamped by its origins in need and suspicion. The need now has become a need for companionship with someone who has been through the same ordeals, who knows what things were like, who shares the past; and concomitantly there is a need for protection, unspoken and conspiratorial, from the contingencies of the world. Now, what unfortunately works against the functional success of this companionship is the fact that mutual suspicion was as integral to the beginnings of the bond as mutual support. The necessary habit of constant distrust of one's surroundings was internalized forever;

and danger could be expected not only from the enemy but from internal betrayals as well.

The bond, then, is actually an equilibrium between the pushes and pulls of two contradictory—and, each in their way, absolute—forces: the need for the protection of others and the distrust of others. The fragileness of this balance is the subject of one of Appelfeld's most affecting stories, "Ḥilufei mishmarot" (Changing the Watch) in *Foundations of the River* (pp. 54–59). The bond in this case is between Simha and Baruch, partners in a store who also share a room together. So often are they in each other's company that the residents of their pension call them "the couple." Yet despite this constant companionship each man maintains a separate business life of small private deals; they are forever borrowing and lending—with interest—between each other, and each is convinced that it is the fixed intention of the other to outsmart him. "Twenty years of hidden struggle. Yet the struggle had always balanced out. Over the years they had exchanged coins, gold, dollars, and pounds, and even these exchanges balanced out" (pp. 56–57).

The tipping of the balance finally comes one Yom Kippur when their private ritual of observance is interrupted. Each year on that day they would lay in a store of vodka and tinned foods, close the shutters, get into pajamas, and sleep through the night and the day, arising occasionally to nibble and drink. Their ritual seems to be both a symbolic reenactment of an ordeal of concealment during the war, perhaps years in a bunker, as well as a strategy for avoiding the questions of sin, atonement, and judgment insisted on by the awesome holy day. And it is of course, too, a withdrawal from the world into the security of their own bond. This year, with all the preparations made, Simha fails to come home, and as Baruch lies in the dark, he becomes seized by the painful conviction that his partner, who had borrowed a sum of money from him earlier in the week, has bilked and betrayed him. Toward the end of the day Simha does return and explains that the borrowed money had been for doctors and that his absence was due to a convulsion which had immobilized him all day. The explanations, however, put nothing back together again. The knot has been doubly undone: internally the malevolence of distrust has broken free of its restraints; from the outside, death, so long kept at bay, has also broken through. Though they would outwit it, Yom Kippur has rendered its judgment.

The functional survival of the bond has much to do with the vicissitudes of memory. Staying together depends on a delicate homeostasis between recollection and forgetfulness. An example is the survivors of a town called Soloczin in "Ha'akhsanya'" (The Inn) (pp. 35–39). The few left assemble on holidays in the cellar restaurant of Shimon Singer, where Singer's wife, his second, whom he married after the war and not a native of Soloczin, serves them the dishes of the town she has learned to cook from her husband. Beyond the tastes of Soloczin and the very fact that they are natives of the town, they can remember very little else, not even the names they went by there nor their families and their lineages. Singer himself is a partial exception because he is visited by unexpected moments of recollection. On occasion he will lead them in the singing of a suddenly recaptured niggun special to Soloczin, or be able to describe the upper and lower towns, or recall to one amazed member of the group that as the genius son of the town rabbi he used to be called the *Yanuka*. The survivors of Soloczin are drawn to Singer because of these powers, and as they sit around his table on Sukkot, Hannukah, and Passover they resemble nothing so much as Hasidim at a rebbe's court, brought together not by religious enthusiasm but by the promise of memory.

While memory remains a promise, the bonds of confraternity hold. At Hannukah, the midpoint of the year's cycle, the men of Soloczin enjoy the Appelfeldian moment of grace: "A spirit stirred in their eyes as if in their blind gropings they had sensed intimations" (p. 37). When the intimations deepen into surges of memory, what is brought up from the past is not nostalgia for pleasant melodies and dishes. Characteristically we are not given the content of these recollections and are left to imagine rivalries, betrayals, and losses as the plausible explanations for the behavior that follows. For by Passover they are at each others' throats. The card games erupt in quarrels; Singer has begun to suspect his wife of unspecified infidelities; the Yanuka is tormented for the unsuitability of the woman he has become engaged to marry; and they cease believing in the power of Singer's memory. By Sukkot and the winter the group has disbanded entirely; the last survivors of Soloczin, after all they have lost, have now lost even each other. "They had now drawn deep," the story concludes, "into their infinite forgetfulness" (p. 39). The opening of memory had been only momentary, but it had been enough to snap the bond and to drive them so deeply into repression as to preclude even the consolations of their guarded companionability.

The message is clear: to remember means to jeopardize the arrangements of one's life. Appelfeld's Jerusalem and Tel Aviv are populated by men who have put their lives back together again after the war, merchants and shopkeepers who have made a go of it and who live lives of moderate habits and measured amusements. Although they are not happy in a conventional sense—they are withdrawn and bear a vague feeling of unworthiness and guilt— they have nevertheless done well for themselves and have control of their lives. Yet the constitution of the Appelfeld world does not permit its subjects to persevere in their evasions, no matter how long established and scrupulously maintained. Something inevitably happens to provoke the past into reasserting itself, not with the sweeping force of a purgation, but with just enough pressure to bring down the foundations of the newly constructed life. The uninvited reassertion of the past can be so sudden and so catastrophic that Appelfeld resorts to the technique of the comic absurd to represent this moment. It comes about in "Aḥar haḥatunah" (After the Wedding) (pp. 141–147) when the story's nameless protagonist seeks to break out of his loneliness by marrying. His bride, Lisia, is an orphan who has wandered through many lands and has just now had the fact of her Jewishness revealed to her by distant relations. "The charm of her strangeness touched my forgetfulness. I fell in love," says the protagonist (p. 143). Befitting a man marrying in his middle years, he has planned a quiet, private ceremony. But immediately after the ḥupah he looks around and discovers an immense throng of abandoned celebrants, a group of fiddlers and singers, including a large contingent brought from America by one rich man.

They are all, it turns out, survivors of the town of Rotzov, and according to them, he is the Rotzover, the son and heir to their deceased spiritual leader, the Rabbi of Rotzov; and now the remnant of Rotzov has assembled from around the world to celebrate the marriage of their leader. Does *he* know that he is the Rotzover? At some level of consciousness the fact of his identity is known to him, but that is all. Rotzov itself and all it means lies in the oblivion over which he has constructed his new life. Passive and stunned, he is handed around from person to person and reminded of names and faces; he remembers no one. They, for their part, feel let down and are certain that he is dissimulating. In "After the Wedding" the betrayal that lurks in the past has to do not with moral transgressions of the war years but with a later abandonment of the leadership of a community. It is, circularly, this defection that has caused the loneliness and shame which this character seeks to escape by falling in love. But his marrying only triggers the exposure of his evasion. He is a man whose secret has been revealed, yet it is a secret which he has long since ceased being able to comprehend.

Even Appelfeld's law has its exceptions. From this bleak, determined world, which is constantly recapturing its escaped prisoners, there is only one way out. It is a path that seems barred to men and opened only to women because they bear a different relationship to memory. The issue is not just the willingness and the capacity to face the past but the question of which past and of the *depth* of the past: how much of personal history can memory be stretched to include? Appelfeld's men have devoted their best efforts to clinging to a precariously established new life; the past they labor to keep at bay is one-dimensional: the war years and the entailed range of experience between personal loss and personal turpitude. For the women, the past is much less constricted, and this makes the difference. There are several female characters in *Foundations of the River* who possess this breadth of memory; they are important figures, because in this fictional domain they offer the only models of what it means not only to survive but to succeed in living.

Regina, in the story of that name (pp. 27–31), is the center of one of Appelfeld's surrogate families. There is her husband Zeitchik, who has a small restaurant, and his two waiters, his nephews Misha and Murba; they all went through the war together and continued on together in Israel. All of them are in decline: Regina is an invalid who more and more has had to take to her bed; the two waiters have grown sullen and dispirited under Zeitchik's petty tyranny; and Zeitchik himself is so devoted to Regina that his desperation has grown as her condition worsens. Yet from among them all Regina is an exception. Her decline is only physical; she remains interested in life, vital as a source of strength to the others.

The source of Regina's spiritual invulnerability can be discovered by comparing the divergent ways in which she and Zeitchik (the names are significant) remember the past. Here are his memories:

When he first met Regina she was pretty as a frightened wildflower. They were already dulled and emptied out, with neither language nor love. Misha used to say, like you find everywhere. Murba did not behave well toward her. The evil winds of war, which had blasted everyone, had not skipped her. She had changed along with them, but already then he could see that she could not be humbled as other women. Who then could distinguish between pure and impure, between those who had their ancestors within them and those who go through this life without ancestors, lifeless? (p. 29)

Zeitchik's rambling, fragmentary associations are as close as any Appelfeld character gets to a direct description of the experience of the war. Nevertheless, even these allusions are enough to evoke a time of universal degradation, dispossession, and cruelty. Although these forces worked on and affected Regina as well, she retained a fundamental dignity that could not be effaced. The basis of her perseverance is linked to her being one of those who have "their ancestors *(avot)* within them." *Avot* can mean fathers, parents, patriarchs, or ancestors, and having the *avot* within one implies possessing inner resources that derive from an incorporation within the self of the vitality and values of one's family and people. Zeitchik and the others share the fate of those not so endowed.

Zeitchik's recollections dramatize the limitations of his consciousness. His mind does not go back to before the war; he was "dulled and emptied out" in such a way that those earlier human bonds and experiences were lost to him. His life—his non-life, in fact—dates from the war, and the only truly living content in his life lies outside of himself, in the person of Regina. What she remembers as she approaches her death gives an indication of what else is possible:

> Her memory became progressively more lucid. Many events flitted through her mind, faraway places and long-passed years. Her recall of names and places was astonishing, and Zeitchik, whose memory was as feeble as an ant's, stood beside her the way that peasants stand tongue-tied beside the post office. These were in fact delirious visions. Her ancestors would appear to her. She would talk with them. Laughing, she would ask questions and answer them. She knew that soon the train would come to a halt; the cars would bang against each other and she would return to the place that she had been cut off from long ago, without Zeitchik, without Murba, without Misha. All this went through her mind without pain. A kind of pity stirred in her for Zeitchik, who had changed without his transformation (*shehishtanah belo' shehishtanuto*) bringing him tranquility. (p. 30)

For others of Appelfeld's women remembering is less serene but still life-giving. The capacity for true mourning is what distinguishes Rosa in "Shemesh shel ḥoref" (Winter Sun) (pp. 149–157). A waitress in a restaurant, her inner dignity attracts the love of a well-off merchant, a bachelor of middle years, whose emotional life has been frozen since the war. The scene that consummates their love is an all-night vigil in the salon of her pension. Rosa shows him photographs of her lost family and for hours tells him about them, crying and telling. Although he himself can remember nothing, he is drawn to her capacity for memory and emotion as if to a source of his own salvation. The surrender to her love means the collapse of the carefully constructed mercantile ethos that until now has structured his life.

Strength of memory is not just a personal endowment but also a cultural fact. In "The Merchant Bartfuss" (pp. 43–51) it is linked to the differences between East and West. Bartfuss is the scion of an upper-middle-class acculturated Austrian Jewish family who has reconstructed his life in Israel; he has put his excellent commercial instincts to work in building a large and successful retail operation. But like many of Appelfeld's men, he bears a symbolic wound of unspecified origin that seems to result from the shame of something done during the war; gradually he looses interest in the business and, sick and infirm, withdraws to his house. To take care of him the store dispatches Bronka, an ugly, Yiddish-speaking, middle-aged woman. She is the daughter of a *shohet;* she lost her brother and sisters in the war; and she had been left some time ago by her husband. Though at first Bartfuss is repelled by her appearance and *ostjud* manner, over time there ensues a reversal of power and desirability. She is a kind woman with unstinting vitality, and to the waning merchant her presence is nearly restorative. Even her Yiddish, a language repugnant to him, comes to seem charmingly musical. "Compared to her speech, his Viennese German sounded artificial and hypocritical" (p. 46). Most of all, the blows and losses she has suffered do not show on her; she manages to live buoyantly in the rhythms of life. The secret of Bronka's indominability lies in her remaining in touch, in her heart and her imagination, with her dead family, with their world, the world of her childhood. In the stories she abundantly tells about life in her village, it is apparent that in some sense her existence is still grounded there. The strength of her prewar Jewishness, a matrix of family bonds and religious faith, has much to do with the quality of her later life. "And if her present life does not match what her father would have wished—well, it is only a temporary passage. In the future she will return to herself" (p. 46).

In the portraits of Regina, Rosa, and Bronka, Appelfeld is clearly making a statement about the capacity of some women to sustain great love and great pain and thus to escape the need for evasion. As a mode of response to catastrophe, the example is not limited to women, nor to individuals. Appelfeld is implying that a national culture is doomed to be subverted from within unless it can do two things: acknowledge and mourn fully and without shame or judgment what was lost, and at the same time maintain a living and affirmative conversation with the cultural world of those who were destroyed. This is a difficult confrontation indeed, and the great majority of Appelfeld's characters do not fear it without reason, but their fates demonstrate how much more frightening are the consequences of declining the encounter.

Reconnecting with the strength of a cultural or family tradition through mourning and memory remains only an imagined possibility. For Appelfeld the writer, like almost all of his characters, it is unavailable altogether. The stories of the sixties resist recalling a personal past; at most they invoke the heavily mythicized ancestral order. When in the seventies Appelfeld returns to the period of childhood before the war in *The Age of Wonders* it is not the Jewish tradition that is explored but the culture of assimilated Austrian Jewry. To the great tradition of response to catastrophe in Hebrew literature, of which Bialik and Greenberg are the exemplars in the modern period, Appelfeld is an outsider. If he is at all the bearer of a tradition in pre-Holocaust literature, it is the elected patrimony of Kafka's modernism. Appelfeld's stance is reflected in his exquisitely restrained Hebrew style. Given the supercharged associative texture of the Hebrew language, Appelfeld's literary idiom is remarkable in its absence of Judaic allusion. Although the reader will sometimes come across a term that suddenly releases an abundance of subtexts, this explosion of meaning only calls attention to its defamiliarized surroundings. If such native writers as A. B. Yehoshua labor to fashion a detraditionalized Hebrew prose, they struggle to arrive at what is, quite naturally, Appelfeld's point of departure.

The greatest writer of the Holocaust in Hebrew, then, stands apart from Hebrew literary history. This has more to do with the cultural circumstances of Appelfeld's early life than with tendentious statements that are hastily made about modes of writing necessitated by the radical experience of the Holocaust. Explanations, in the end, are less important than achievements. Appelfeld's fiction is a moment of impressive discontinuity in Hebrew literature. Like other strong writers, he initiates his own tradition.

·7·

THE UNEASY

BURDEN

There is no exaggerating the importance of the Eichmann trial in Israeli culture. In the shift in the early sixties away from the statism of Ben Gurion to a civic culture that saw Israel as less than a radical break with the immediate Jewish past, the changing attitude toward the Holocaust was crucial. In this reorientation the trial was not only a chronological marker but also itself an efficient cause. Daily for seven months (between March and September 1961), in the largest auditorium in Jerusalem, before tiers of local and international press, the destruction of European Jewry was systematically anatomized. Few revelations issued from the trial; the information given in testimony was on record in previously published memoirs and research, in archives and museums. The trial, nevertheless, had the force of an electrifying discovery. Of the tens of thousands of documents pertaining to the Holocaust, Haim Gouri writes: "When this material was taken up by the prosecution and made part of the bill of indictment, when these documents broke out of the silence of the archives, it was as if they were now speaking for the first time . . . and that their latent potential had been suddenly actualized. The process released the

enormous energy that comes with the realization 'Now I understand!' "[1] This is the sort of moment drama aspires to achieve, and the Eichmann trial can be understood in this vein. With its mixture of carefully staged judicial rituals and spontaneous eruptions of pathos and rage, the trial resembled nothing so much as, *mutatis mutandi*, a massive passion play in which the members of an entire community played parts. At the center of the drama stood a series of acts of narrative telling, in the first person by the witnesses and in the third person by the prosecutor; it was the strength of these narratives, their powerful authenticity, that transformed information into experience. With the exception of *Streets of the River*, the Eichmann trial was the most important "text" produced by Israeli culture in the twenty years after the Holocaust.

If the trial was a text, Haim Gouri was one of its most important readers and interpreters. Gouri reported on the trial several times a week in the pages of *Lamerhav*, the newspaper of the left-labor party Ahdut Ha‘avodah. His columns were later collected in *Mul ta' hazekhukhit* (The Glass Booth) (1962). The interest of his chronicle lies in part in Gouri's own profile as a writer. Born in Tel Aviv in 1923, Gouri served in the Haganah from 1942 onward, including a mission to the DP camps after the war, and fought in the War of Independence; primarily a poet, Gouri's verse reflects on the themes of war and death, adolescence and memory. Gouri, then, is situated at the center of consciousness of the Palmah generation writers, with their secular humanist values, their indictment of the Diaspora, and their vision of Israel as a radical departure from Jewish history. His undertaking of a day-by-day chronicle of the Eichmann trial was tantamount, therefore, to a sustained confrontation with just that event which, for his generation, had been the most difficult, the most compromising, the most repulsive. Gouri's openness in this encounter is remarkable. While writing from a rootedness in the values of his generation, he attempts to assume the stance of an unbiased observer who allows the facts to emerge and shape themselves into their own story. The story that does emerge rebounds upon the writer and changes him. Gouri's achievement in the workmanlike digesting, sorting, and presenting of the matter of the trial is substantial; the subjective theme of the writer's reassessment of his own values and those of his generation's, though secondary to the undertaking, is the more interesting.

A major change in attitude concerns the image of the victims and the survivors. The revulsion toward the civilization of East European Jewry was counteracted at the trial by the testimony of such historians as Salo Baron, who unfolded a rich fabric of political, cultural, and religious creativity. If the result was not quite the classic idyll of the lost past on the model we have seen in earlier Hebrew sources, the new perception constituted at least a neutralization of judgment and an openness to explore further recent Diaspora history. The imputed submissiveness of the slaughtered victims was a shame much more difficult to exorcise. Early in the trial a witness, Morris Fleischman, relates how, as an act of public humiliation, he and the chief rabbi of Vienna were ordered to go down on their hands and knees and wash the sidewalks, and how the rabbi—dressed in a *talit*—endured this as an act of God. Gouri's immediate response is disgust: "I had no desire to listen to this broken, decrepit man go on and on about his afflictions. . . . I would prefer being present at the Nahal (the army pioneer corps) ceremonies taking place today at the stadium and seeing attractive and strong young people. But Morris Fleischman's testimony grabs me by the throat with incredible force and says to me: 'Sit down and listen to every last word!' " (p. 33). Gouri does persevere, and in time the pained accusation "How could they go like sheep to the slaughter?" is dissolved by a growing awareness of the complexities surrounding the issue of resistance. For many, he learns, there simply never was the chance; for others the desire to live was exploited by the Germans: a thin thread of hope was constantly dangled before ghetto and camp inmates. This was a world of total control and absolute force in which individual action could at the most aspire to symbolic gestures. Even the possibility of such gestures was undermined by the dulling effect of constant fear. And then there was the hope that soon the war might end.

Dealing with the figures of those who did in fact manage to survive was more difficult still. It is in the nature of trials that only the living can testify, and, therefore, aside from written documents and expert witnesses, it was only from the mouths of survivors that the story of the Holocaust could be told. Given the associations of venality and corruption that hitherto surrounded the image of the survivor in Israeli literature, the Jerusalem trial was a curious occurrence. Rather than remaining shadowy stereotypes, the survivors were given the chance to present themselves in their own voices, in a public forum, over and over again for months. This was, needless to say, a powerful catharsis for the witnesses themselves and, collectively, for the large population of survivors in Israel. In a way which parallels the effects of Appelfeld's later stories, it was as if a repressed sector of society were allowed to take center stage. For Gouri, the encounter with the person rather than the type was also consequential. As witness followed witness, the sense was created of the Holocaust as a vast world unto itself with its own internal laws. To apply outside standards of judgment came to seem irrelevant.

Instead of being suspended, the question of judgment in the end doubles back upon the questioner. In light of the powerlessness of European Jewry, the possibilities of effectual action could be lodged only with those parties who did not operate under the same constraints: the British, the other Allies, and—the Yishuv itself. During the trial Gouri wrenchingly experiences the sudden reversal of the moral transaction. The questions which were once put by the Yishuv to the victims now "return like a boomerang to smash us in the face: Why didn't you expose the facts? Why didn't you scream them out? Why didn't you demonstrate? Why didn't you fast? Why didn't you drive the world to distraction? What can we answer to the question: Did you do all you could have done to help?" (p. 108). Gouri's thoughts belong to that order of questions for which historically researched answers—if they exist at all—are beside the point. The bystander's accusing himelf of complacency and avoidance is in its own way just as unreal as accusing the victim of ignoble complicity in his own fate. These stirrings of guilt, though in themselves unuseful, are nonetheless a sign of a deeper and more consequential movement of the spirit. For a process of genuine encounter with the destruction to begin, the cordon of superiority separating the bystander from the victim must fall.

There are even moments during the trial when all the boundaries are in danger of being washed away. Gouri's daily communion with catastrophe imprints in his mind this one memory alone and erases all others; at times he is lost in the world of the Holocaust, on the brink of an engulfment that would cancel his own identity. The concluding achievement of *The Glass Booth* lies in Gouri's pulling up short before this self-effacement and in his succeeding in recovering a sense of his own role in reporting the trial. Although what was lost to the survivors cannot be restored to them and although the sins of omission against the dead cannot be undone, one real positive act does remain. Speaking of the witnesses, Gouri asks:

> Could we have given these men more than we gave them? We gave them what their murderers stole from them: the right to tell their story in the first person singular. . . . The truth [of the trial] lay in the uniqueness of each testimony. No witness duplicated the words of those who preceded him. . . . Each of the prosecution witnesses was, therefore, the hero of an act of rescue [hatsalah]. I refer to the rescue of the testimonies of these unfortunate people from the danger of being perceived as all alike, all shrouded in the same immense anonymity. (pp. 242, 241)

Like most acts of creative survival in earlier Hebrew literature, Gouri shows an understanding of the fact that at a certain point—after breakdown and bereavement—attention must be shifted to what can still be recovered from the destruction. And like the Rabbis, Gouri performs a kind of midrash upon the key term "rescue," *hatsalah*. In the years after the war, hatsalah connoted the efforts of the Yishuv through its emissaries to transfer the survivors to Eretz Yisrael, where they would be rehabilitated and redeemed, and where they could forget the past. In Gouri's usage, rescue becomes restraint from imposing the amnesia of this kind of redemption; this means an attempt to create conditions under which the story of the past can be told and in which the role of the bystander will be less to act than to listen.

Gouri goes far in fulfilling his own prescriptions. He observes and listens, and is changed by what he sees and hears. His willingness to question some of the fundamental assumptions of his generation prepared the ground for a potentially deeper and more sustained encounter with the Holocaust than had hitherto been undertaken in Israeli literary art. *The Glass Booth*, however, is prevented from itself realizing that goal by its generic limitations. Even the best reportage, such as Gouri's is, is subject to the exigencies of quick portraiture, lucid summary, and extensive coverage. Gouri's writing is a discursive account of the beginnings of a critical turning point in Israeli consciousness; to find the results of a deeper reckoning with the meaning of the Holocaust, one has to examine forms of creativity such as art and theology that are not subject to the immediacy of journalism. In the years since the Eichmann trial, the record of literary art in taking up the tasks Gouri set before it has been equivocal. Appelfeld, who began to publish in the years just preceding the trial, is the great exception; no other writer has succeeded in creating so sustained and credible an imaginative world. Besides Appelfeld, Israeli literature has produced a number of isolated works which, together, explore in a fragmentary yet significant way the issues raised by the Holocaust. These works divide themselves into two groups, each of which treads its own path: novels by native Israeli writers and poem cycles by survivors.

By isolated works I mean that the four important novels on this theme—*The Brigade* by Hanoch Bartov, *Not of This Time, Not of This Place* by Yehuda Aimichai, *Adam Resurrected* by Yoram Kaniuk, and *The Chocolate Deal* by Gouri himself—are each a one-time departure from its author's usual literary production. To say this is not to make a judgment. To the contrary: the fact that each of these writers interrupted a previously established body of work devoted largely to personal and Israeli concerns in order to write a novel about the Holocaust testifies to the power of the "rediscovery" of the Holocaust in the sixties. The status of these novels as "interruptions" further prompts the question of their links to the rest of their authors' works: Given the radically different nature of the Holocaust as a subject, how different was the literary molding given it?[2]

At once the most conventional and the most psychologically perceptive of these novels is Bartov's *The Brigade (Pitsᶜei bagrut,* 1965).[3] This is an autobiographical novel of the coming-of-age of a nineteen-year-old member of the Jewish Brigade, the Palestinian units which fought with the British army at the close of World

War II. *The Brigade* is conventional in its faithfully carrying over
of the techniques of the Palmah generation novel: the identification of character with ideological stance, the building of a narrative around a group of fighting men, the rendering of the interior
thoughts of a protagonist who does not fit the norm. Against this
received structure, the otherness of the Holocaust does not make
substantial inroads. And it is precisely Bartov's consciousness of
this failure—his making it a thematic element of the narrative—
that gives the novel its interest. *The Brigade* is the first serious inquiry in Israeli literature into the emotions of shame and revulsion toward the survivors of the Holocaust.

Bartov's soldiers have come to fight in Europe for only one purpose:

Not for Roosevelt's freedoms or the British Empire or Stalin. We're here
to take revenge. One wild Jewish vengeance. Just once to be like the Tar-
tars. Like the Ukrainians. Like the Germans. All of us—spoiled, sensitive
farmers, students, humanists, workers—all of us will move in on one city
and burn it street by street, house by house, German by German. Why
should we be the only ones to remember Auschwitz? Let them remember
the one city that we'll raze. (pp. 46–47)

These fantasies of retribution are in little danger of being fulfilled. The thirst for vengeance functions chiefly to call attention
to the emotion against which it is a defense: the impotence of the
Yishuv in the face of the destruction of European Jewry. The Zionist settlement in Palestine, which had staked its identity on its
ability to assume an active role in Jewish history, had been reduced to the stance of a passive bystander at this critical moment
in Jewish life. Bartov's soldiers have made a direct translation of
their frustration and shame into the search for revenge. On the
sides of their vehicles they paint the slogan *DIE JUDEN KOM-
MEN!* so that as they pass through occupied territory all will understand that they are "fighters in a glorious Jewish legion, in history's first Star of David conquest" (p. 71). For the murderers,
vengeance, for the survivors, rescue. In their search for the "surviving remnant," the brigade views itself as an army of redemption. It will save these broken Jews, rehabilitate them, and hurry
their immigration to a free homeland.

In the end, reality trivializes these powerful aspirations. The Jewish units are allowed to see action only in the final weeks of the Italian campaign, and then never quite at the front; the young narrator, Elisha Kruk, is hospitalized with measels and is not even granted this chance. The worst enemy of the men turns out to be the ennui of enforced idleness; the glorious news that the war has ended comes in the middle of a time-killing poker game. As for vengeance against the Germans, there is virtually no chance for satisfaction. The Jewish soldiers are reduced to petty—and in the end, humiliating—gestures of reprisal. As a caravan of prisoners-of-war passes by, the Jews errupt in an orgy of rage whose only outlet can be the lobbing of cans of tinned food at the defenseless Germans. On another occasion they insult and abuse minor civilian officials, and in two instances women are molested.

Bartov makes the dramatic kernel of his novel the debates among the soldiers about the ethics of revenge occasioned by the first and less serious of these attacks on civilian women. If the women molested were Nazis, the question is put, is their abuse justified as an act of revenge? One position holds that to commit such acts is to forfeit one's honor as a Jewish soldier and to become no better than the Germans. It is the contrary position, however, which Bratov allows to be argued with rhetorical zeal. The argument hinges on the psychological consequences of failing to perform acts of revenge. If the Jewish corps returns home without having exacted vengeance, its failure will never be forgotten. "The one small fist is still clenched in a spasm. It will never open up, this fist. It will stay clenched, its fingernails piercing its own flesh, its blood frozen, the memory of vengeance never unleashed blackening it with gangrene" (p. 117). The fist is never allowed to strike, nor is it consumed by this apocalyptic self-infection. Though not fatal, the experience of impotence is what remains most indelible twenty years later at the time of the narration. The members of the brigade unit are required by the British to stand in a parade formation while the two molested women pass up and down to identify their attackers. "Over the years," says the narrator, "that identification parade has become what is now a searing shame" (p. 128).

In their rescue mission, the brigade members swear themselves to "Dedication, loyalty and love for the remnants of the sword and the camps" (p. 57). Elisha Kruk's several encounters with the survivors in person severely test his duty. His reaction each time is threefold. He is at first transfixed by the pathetic otherness of the recently released camp inmates: their unearthly misshapenness, their dazed affectlessness. As soon as one of these creatures actually steps forth to approach Elisha, fascination turns into terror of being touched. He averts his eyes, turns away, ready to do anything to avoid contact. He is prevented from turning away altogether by the shame that next he feels for his instinctive revulsion: How could he be so repulsed by those he has sworn to love? Elisha tries to join in with the survivors' and soldiers' joyous celebrations of the Liberation, but neither drink nor song can lessen his alienness. He believes he has found a way out when he discovers a distant relation among the survivors. The personal connection embodied by this quick young man with an untrammeled spirit breaks down Elisha's resistance, opens his heart, and elicits a desire to serve him in any way in his power. Urged to talk about his experience during the war, however, the young man matter-of-factly reveals that his survival was due to his work in the *Sonderkomando,* the detail of inmates who worked in the crematoria. Immediately, Elisha is "filled with revulsion at the thought of being connected with him" and is overtaken by the desire "to disappear, melt out of existence" (p. 161).

Elisha never succeeds in moving out of the system of his own pain. He does break out of his passivity when in the concluding scene in the novel he interrupts a rape and at gun point forces several of his own comrades to back down. But his protest is not a stand. He acts less out of a commitment to ideals than out of a residual softness in his soul that prevents him from fully playing the avenger. This delicacy of scruple and faintness of heart are associated in his mind with the character of Diaspora Jews; the equivocal self-knowledge with which the book ends is the realization that this unreconstructed and unwished for vestige of exile will forever be a part of him.

The shame of adolescent gropings, the shame of frustrated revenge, the shame of contact with survivors—these are doubtlessly

genuine afflictions. Yet when juxtaposed to what was endured in
the Holocaust one would expect these ordeals to recede in importance, or at least be placed in perspective. Unfortunately, a sense
of proportion is never unambiguously established in *The Brigade*.
Although there is an element of retrospective irony, the dramatic
action makes self-involvement the dominant and vivid experience
in the work. The Jews who died at the hands of the Nazis and
those who survived do not succeed in penetrating this imaginative
sphere. They are the occasion for the drama but not its subject.

Yehuda Amichai boldly deals with the challenge of allowing the
Holocaust to enter Israeli experience by granting it half of his fictional kingdom. His novel *Not of This Time, Not of This Place* (*Lo'
me'akhshav, lo' mika'n*, 1963) is, in fact, split down the middle.[4]
Amichai takes his protagonist, an archeologist named Joel, who is
facing a crisis of meaning in his mid-thirties, and breaks his experience over a summer into two simultaneous tracks. Half of the
chapters, narrated in the third person and set in Jerusalem, follow
the course of Joel's summer-long love affair with a non-Jewish
American doctor named Patricia. In the alternating chapters, narrated in the first person and set during the same summer, Joel
undertakes a journey of memory and revenge to the town of
Weinburg in Germany, where he spent his childhood. (Amichai
was born in Wurzburg, Germany, in 1924 and brought to Israel
at the age of twelve.) Amichai is Israel's leading poet of the fifties
and sixties, and his antic tampering with novelistic conventions
displays the freedom of a poet taking a holiday in a genre not his
own. The splitting of both consciousness and experience is indeed
a canny move; it neatly reflects the dividedness *and* coexistence in
the Israeli psyche of the erotics of personal existence in the present and the haunting nightmare of collective memory. *Not of This
Time, Not of This Place* succeeds best at the overarching level of this
original archetectonic conception and at the closest level of poetic
diction, expressed in Amichai's genius for startling metaphoric
yokings. In between, in the more novelistic business of the novel,
however, the work is confused. Amichai's difficulties in establishing character, in shaping the flow of events, and, generally, in
keeping his long text from breaking down into brilliant imagistic

fragments are evidence not only of a struggle with the demands of the genre but also the unsusceptibility of the two themes to integration.

The crisis that moves Joel in these two directions is, in part, the classic malaise of the successful man in midlife who is suddenly aware of his end and who is forced to reexamine his life, "like a general who reappraises his forces on the basis of new intelligence about the enemy's movements" (p. 4). The crisis is also specific to the Israeli generation to which Joel belongs, the Palmah generation, whose youth was appropriated by the nation for the public tasks of the hour; experiments with love, identity, and education had to be renounced or deferred. "We belong to a generation," Joel rues, "that acted before it matured, and now our youth is belatedly catching up with us" (p. 210). For the wife of his Palmah years, his companion for so long, Joel is left with the emotion of loyalty rather than love. The compensation for that sacrifice had been the joys of comradeship and the consolations of a shared destiny. Now, however, with the common task discharged, the bonds of solidarity have been dissolved, leaving neither the consolations of youth nor of each other. In one of his characteristically stunning conceits, Amichai conveys the harsh effects of time upon friendship and group:

Where are they, all those who had been swept up by the wave of his generation, full of the joy of life, arms waving, crying out to one another? They had been like the heads of swimmers in the sea. Heads rising out of breakers. Now the wave had smashed against the shore, and everyone was on his own, looking out for his personal salvation or attending to his individual joys, and the roar of the breakers deafened and further isolated them. (p. 320)

The ostensible purpose of Joel's sojourn in Germany is to exact vengeance. His friends and students are convinced that resentment for the destruction of his childhood world is poisoning his adult life, and that unless he purges himself of his hatred he will end by betraying his good wife. The desire for vengeance centers around the extermination of Ruth, his childhood companion, the daughter of the town's rabbi. Ruth is an embodiment of absolute innocence and victimization, which stands for the Holocaust as a whole. As Joel moves through the cityscape of his childhood, he sees apparitions of Ruth everywhere. Civic officials, public monuments, private homes from the time of the destruction all seem to bristle with guilt for the murder of her innocence. Yet the vengeance Joel had hoped to exact in Weinberg is never described, nor is it even imaginable. He soon discovers that he lacks the requisite for vengeful action: the capacity for sustained hatred; that kind of hatred is an emotion he fails at learning. Unlike Bartov's soldiers, Amichai's hero comes in time to understand that the passion for revenge is, in fact, not an ultimate emotion but rather an avoidance of deeper feelings of loss. The visit to Weinberg becomes reevaluated in midpassage as a journey of memory rather than vengeance. He goes about the city attempting to reconstruct the passion of the last days of Ruth's life; he gives the few surviving Jews who returned to the city a chance to tell their stories; he ministers to his aunt in an old-age home in the last moments of her life; he opens his mind—whose susceptibility resembles more a poet's like Amichai's than an archeologist's—to the swirls of images evoked by the overlapping touchstones of his childhood and the Nazi carnage that took place later.

Meanwhile, in Jerusalem, the experience of the Joel who remains at home is as much a journey as that of the Joel who goes abroad. Not only does the descent into the kingdom of Eros parallel the exploration of the kingdom of Thanatos but it is the more perilous. The consummation of his love for Patricia demands the progressive divestiture of all the integuments of personal and national identity. That Patricia is American and Christian is not an occasion for a meeting of cultural differences but a condition of otherness necessary to the leaving behind of culture altogether. The two of them aspire to a purity of encounter in which "they would forget all boundaries; they would not remember their countries and their languages" (p. 65). Joel leaves his wife, puts aside his career and his colleagues and friends, eludes the consciousness and duties of his Israeliness, and, with Patricia, enters a timeless space of sexuality. There is nothing pornographic about their union. Amichai's rendering of Eros rests on a technique of defamiliarization; his language leads away from the body to the world of concrete objects and landscapes whose conjunctions are used to suggest rather than describe the meeting of man and woman. The external field of reference for Joel's and Patricia's affair is the stones and light and quarters of Jerusalem. Because Amichai's knowledge of his city is so deeply intimate he succeeds, as Robert Alter has suggested, in portraying Joel's intimate knowledge of Patricia in a way that cannot be matched by the German sections of the novel.[5]

Both plots culminate in a return to childhood, but the experience in each case is different. As Joel and Patricia let go of the overlayerings of culture and duty they descend back into a time of trust and joy. Yet once they have achieved the primitive sexual innocence of childhood (infancy, really), there is nowhere for them to go. Because it is the demands of socialization that they have renounced, there can be no return to society. Amichai has Joel die an accidental death—a land mine left from an old war; his end is less an absurd contingency than a statement about what can be the only outcome, and perhaps the next logical station in Joel's journey. Joel's experience in the German sections is more a reentry into history, his own and his people's, than a shedding of it. The break in Joel's early life between Europe and Palestine and the appropriation of his youth for war and nation building, have robbed him of the connection with childhood that every man needs at a certain point in his life in order to go forward. The special problem for Amichai's character is that his childhood world has not only been lost—a universal occurence—but murdered. The mourning for its death has been too long deferred, and the consequences have been malignant.

There are both strengths and weaknesses in Amichai's fusing of the issues of childhood and Holocaust. Consonant with the resort to models of personhood in the literature of destruction generally, the intimate memories of himself and Ruth make the larger catastrophe graspable. Personalization, however, carries the risk of trivialization. The Nazis chiefly become the murders of *his* childhood, and the loss of childhood tantamount to the destruction of a world.

In his comic novel *Adam Resurrected* (*Adam ben kelev*, 1969) Yoram Kaniuk studiously avoids lyric self-involvement.[6] The novel, set in

Israel in a private mental hospital for survivors of the Holocaust, is composed of portrayals of the comic-tragic madness of a group of patients. Whereas Amichai's hero is a recognizable persona of the poet-novelist himself, Kaniuk seeks to disappear into the alien world of the survivors. He remains visible, however, in his style; the satirical procedures he brings to the subject of the Holocaust are not invented *ad hoc* but carried over from such earlier works as *The Acrophile* and *Himmo, King of Jerusalem.* Kaniuk is drawn to the creation of characters with enormous endowments of vitality and imagination, whose delusions of grandeur and fantastic obsessions contrast sharply with their actual unimportance in the world, or simply characters whose peculiar manias make them rare species. *Adam Resurrected* contains a German-Jewish matron who has been vouchsafed a desert vision of the apocalypse; a patient who writes automatic script in Egyptian hieroglyphics; a survivor who has never been to America but believes that he is Miles Davis; a young man so traumatized by the war that he has become a dog.

What keeps *Adam Resurrected* from bad taste is a genuine pathos that underlies the comic grotesquerie. Like Appelfeld, Kaniuk never suggests stigma or judgment. However bizarre the deformities of his characters, they are always understood as imposed by the past and as essentially reasonable responses to insane, unspeakable conditions. Kaniuk is out to make a point: for the Holocaust to become accessible to the literary imagination, there is a hushed, mystified piety surrounding the subject which must be broken through. Humor, for Kaniuk, is both the instrument for delivering the initial shock and a technique for rendering the alien familiar; the gap between grandiose delusions and infernal realities constitutes, he might argue, a universal of human understanding and, therefore, a way in through the back when the front approach is barred. The ambitions of Kaniuk's undertaking are matched only by the risks. *Adam Resurrected* is an uneven novel, full of hits and misses. Although he has a genius for inventing comic characters and situations, Kaniuk often lacks the discipline to control the ramifying energies released by their collisions. Kaniuk finds it hard to resist adding another character, another incident, another thematic repetition. The imaginative congestion that results is due not only to Kaniuk's overexerting himself to create the impression of a tour-de-force, but also to the fact that he himself is so fascinated by exorbitance and mania that he is less than the perfect narrative broker between delusion and reality.

The premise of the plot, at least, displays a nice allegorical madness. The central symbol is the desert mental hospital, Mrs. Seizling's Institute for Rehabilitation and Therapy. The institute is the product of a partnership between the money and know-how of a wealthy American widow and the religious vision of a refugee woman who believes that God will soon again reveal Himself in the desert and that the mental healing of the surviving victims of the Holocaust is the key to hastening that event. Though in the service of visionary ends, the institution is built to be the embodiment of a determined Western rationalism. Architecturally, the building is clinically sterile and unforgivingly functional, giving the impression that it had "been designed by a computer to have no connection whatsoever with the human past, any human location, any human feeling" (p. 27). The psychiatric staff is the best money can buy, and they apply to their patients the latest therapeutic techniques with confidence in medical science's necessary advance. Mrs. Seizling's institute is clearly meant by Kaniuk to stand for the state of Israel. The hybrid product of Eastern visionary religiosity and Western technology and capital, the state is a graceless modern structure set down artificially in the elementally arid and hostile wilderness. The state further presumes to offer a healing refuge for the survivors of European Jewry. As a place where previous Jewish history has been forgotten, it can help those tormented by memories to forget also; its normalcy and modernity will be balm to troubled souls.

The principal refutation of this claim to rehabilitation is the resurrected but unreconstructed Adam of the novel's title. Of all of Kaniuk's madmen, Adam Stein's madness is the most global and baroque, and the most commanding. The largeness of his presence urges us to take him, like his name, as standing for much more than himself. Before the war Adam was the most famous clown in Germany, a master of disguises, the owner of his own circus. When he stood in the selection line in the concentration

camp, he was recognized by the camp commandant and allowed
to save himself in exchange for playing his fiddle to entertain the
Jews, among them his own wife, as they marched to the showers.
In the evenings it was the commandant he had to amuse by acting
like a dog and fighting with the pet German shepherd over bones
and scraps. In a Germany prospering and forgetting after the war,
Adam waxes rich and esteemed, but refuses to perform. When in
1958 he discovers the existence in Israel of a daughter he thought
had perished in the camps, the guilt-free life he had managed to
live all these years collapses. When he arrives in Israel to find his
daughter, who had died in the meantime, the demons of his past
are released in him, and Adam becomes a patient in Mrs. Seizling's institute. His madness takes the form of an incessant oscil-
lation between the extremes of human nature: between acts of
kindness and homicidal rages, between Olympian intellectuality and
regressions to quivering animality. "Adam," the narrator summa-
rizes, "is a man of instant transformations: from soap to distinguished citizen, from distinguished citizen to a strangler of an old
woman, to a dog, to a rapist. From the genius of the circus to a
swindler, from swindler to a madman in love . . ." (p. 160).

The question of whether madness of this kind can be cured is
given two different answers in *Adam Resurrected*. When it comes to
a personality as magisterial as Adam's and events as unspeakable
as the Holocaust, the derangement that results resists the technol-
ogies of medicine and psychology; Adam shakes off therapies like
Lilliputian arrows. The only solution is to excise the sources of exuberance and destructiveness; finally Adam is lobotomized and ends
his days in vegetal contentment. The less drastic and more prom-
ising "cure" in the novel is accomplished through nonscientific
measures. The hardest case in the sanitarium is the boy-dog. This
is a child of indeterminate age whose war-related experiences have
induced an extreme autism or schizophrenia. The break with reality
has been so absolute that the child does not believe he is a dog,
but in the imaginative terms Kaniuk has established, he has in fact
become a dog: whimpering, growling, and pawing at the end of a
chain. The figure of the dog obsesses Kaniuk throughout *Adam
Resurrected* in part because of the English anagram GOD/DOG, and

in part because of the idea of domesticated bestiality; the dog represents that strain of subhumanity which has an infinite capacity for submissive loyalty to masters. This is a condition whose real meaning cannot be understood by psychologists but only by someone who has been there himself, who at one time has himself become a dog. By establishing a bond of understanding which involves his own regressive journey, Adam succeeds over a prolonged period in bringing the child back to the world of human emotions and communication.

The implication is that the normalcy and rationality of Israeli society are insufficient conditions for a meaningful recovery from such deformations of the spirit. The veneer of normalcy is itself deceiving; avoiding becoming a patient in Mrs. Seizling's institute is not necessarily a sign of rehabilitation. "During the day," says one of the characters, "we may be complaining, yawning, making money, building houses . . . but at night we are insomniacs in our spacious houses . . . , at night we dream nightmares and shriek, for Satan has tattooed our forearms with blue numbers" (p. 51). If there is such a thing as a cure, the novel implies, it can come only out of a deep knowledge of that nightmare and shriek, not out of the lull of normalcy. To know and to understand do not mean the simple extending of empathy but the acknowledgment that within one's self resides the potential for descending to the depths of animality, that is, to become a dog; and that is an admission not without its subversive risks.

The trouble with *Adam Resurrected* is that in the end Kaniuk does not make us feel the desirability of being cured. Kaniuk is possessed by the cliché of Western literature that lunacy is insight, and what is more, that it is high fun. While their variegated delusions are indeed zany and fascinating, their eventual cured state is not so interesting by half; and this saps the motivation to undertake the deep and dangerous understanding necessary for the task. For Kaniuk, only madness fascinates. He is himself an inmate, and his novel fails to convince us that life on the outside is much worth living.

Outsized craziness is the stock-in-trade of Kaniuk's fiction generally, and the significant, though limited, successes of *Adam Res-*

urrected are due to his having brought the subject of the Holocaust inside his own workshop. So too with Bartov and Amichai. Bartov's exploration of the phenomenon of shame is an episode in a career-long chronicle of the struggles of his generation; for Amichai the destroyed European past is absorbed into an evolving autobiographical myth of the poet and his origins. In contrast, the treatment of the Holocaust in Haim Gouri's short novel *The Chocolate Deal* (*'Iskat hashokolad,* 1965) stands distinctly on its own.[7] The story, which concerns two survivors in the months following the Liberation, gets told in a way that seems entirely immanent to the theme. The text is composed wholly of the consciousness of these two men without any apparent linkage to a frame of reference representing Gouri and his generation. Like Appelfeld's fiction, in other words, *The Chocolate Deal* seems to be *of* the Holocaust world rather than a work that reaches out to it from another system. The novel is an impressive invention for a writer who has no personal experience of the destruction, but not a surprise to anyone familiar with Gouri's reporting of the Eichmann trial. It is as if the large and manifold realizations experienced during the trial and discursively recounted had been allowed to settle and then been distilled into one brief but taut fictional experiment.[8]

The thematic ground Gouri covers is the moral and existential ambiguities of survival. Rubi Krauss and Mordi Neuberg are the last of each other's relatives and friends when they discover each other in a large German city right after the war. Immediately Rubi wants to put his life back together again; he generates a series of schemes which involve parlaying family connections and the indebtedness to him of a gentile doctor into a fantastic killing on the black market. Like Appelfeld's petty entrepreneurs selling stockings on the Italian shore, Rubi is all activity and mobility unburdened by shame and self-reflexive memory; like Appelfeld, too, information about how he survived is absent from the text. He finds a woman to relieve his sense of loneliness and to reestablish his manhood, and it does not bother him that the woman turns out to be a former mistress who in the meantime had been a camp follower of the Nazis. For all his activity and enterprise, however, it is doubtful whether he accomplishes anything; his scheme to corner the market in Allied surplus chocolate—a Kaniukian bit of madness, indeed—seems in the end to be taking place only in his pathetic appetitive imaginings.

The story of Mordi's survival, in contrast, is supplied in the text. In the years before the war he was pursuing a doctorate on troubadour poetry in France; at the initiative of his gentile professor a hiding place was found for Mordi in the cellar of a provincial monastery. For this gesture the professor was tortured and broken by the Gestapo. We know Mordi's story only from his own consciousness; unlike Rubi, Mordi is flooded by memory. He recalls not only his own suffering and that of others but also of those, like the professor, who have suffered for him. In the six months after the war he has failed to find a single person whom he recognizes, and the knowledge that he, alone of all his friends, survived—and not even by his own efforts—overwhelms him with guilt. "I don't do a thing. I float, set upon wandering waters, . . . crossing another region I was thrown out of, unnecessarily, at the expense of others, those who had futures, whose brows were iron to split things and whose nails knew how to take hold" (p. 65). When Rubi briefly abandons him for a woman, the growing sense of the gratuitousness of his life saps Mordi's will to resist the great alienation that envelops him, and he dies an unspecified, symbolic death.

Like most parabolic fiction, Robert Alter has remarked, the two choices represented by Rubi and Mordi are exaggerated in their difference.[9] Yet Gouri's investment of narrative sympathy is so evenly distributed that it is impossible to say that one is favored over the other. There is little sense of an Israeli writer making an assessment of the survivors relative to the values of his own generation. The writing strains to understand rather than to judge. In the end what remains impressive about *The Chocolate Deal* is less the balancing of moral dilemmas than Gouri's resourcefulness in making us believe in the experience of the characters who inhabit them. Gouri's vocation as a poet—this was his first novel after several volumes of verse—helps him more than Amichai in fashioning a unique narrative medium that seems to belong more to the experience of the Holocaust than to the prose fiction of Palmah writers.

Take, for example, these thoughts of Rubi's after their first meeting, as Mordi leads him home to his room in the basement of a convent:

We walk and we walk, and get nowhere, thinks Rubi, his suspicion mounting, and here it's already the rainy season. Leaves are falling. It's chilly. I'm in summer clothes. The police don't like us. And soon neither will the weather. Only the statues feel good at night. (pp. 19–20)

This is a writing that excels in an absolute presentness of perception. Time is experienced as a succession of states of feeling, with no trust from one to the next in any structure guaranteeing a continuity of meaning. The two men are on route to Mordi's lodgings, but Rubi can sustain a belief neither in their walking's having a direction nor in Mordi's in fact having a place to sleep. The only certainty is the coming of cold weather, and although the weather clearly functions as a euphemizing metonomy for the hostility of the world, the feeling remains on the most concrete level. This choppy flow of perceptual bits, moreover, displays a childlike quality. The crucial and the trivial ("I'm in summer clothes. The police don't like us.") exist side-by-side on the same plane of expression. The simultaneous or serial experiencing of vulnerability, need, and fear in the relations between these two grown men is sustained throughout. If it weren't for the striking figurative possibilities of this primitive discourse, it would bore us. When Rubi's thoughts finish with "only the statues feel good at night," for example, it has the effect of at once epitomizing his situation and initiating an open series of associations: artifice/experience, monumentality/insignificance, security/homelessness and so on. Although the resonances are rich and profound, Gouri keeps the image anchored within the perceptual range he has established for his characters. It is an impressive performance.

Between the writer who is a survivor and the writer who is not there remains, in the end, a gap; this is expressed less in the limits of what can be achieved artistically than in the relation of the work of art to the literary career. No matter how accomplished, Gouri's novel *The Chocolate Deal* and those of Bartov, Amichai, and Kaniuk remain isolated efforts. Each of these writers has made a one-time sojourn in the Holocaust kingdom and then returned to the concerns that characterized his career as a whole. For the survivor, in contrast, the catastrophic past is always *there*, and if he does not continually write about it (only Appelfeld takes the Holocaust as his whole literary vocation), he does not have to work it up. When the survivor writes about the Holocaust it has the effect of an evasion interrupted or curtailed rather than an experience encountered or investigated; and when he writes of other things, the Holocaust seems to hover as an ontological condition, whether explicitly alluded to in the work or supplied by the reader's often privileged knowledge of the writer's biography.

This is particularly true of two poets, Abba Kovner and Dan Pagis. Neither of them is entirely or primarily a Holocaust poet, yet the fact that they are both survivors *and* poets contributes to their success when they do write on the subject. Works of narrative prose fiction, seized as one-time opportunities for saying all that an author wants to get said about the Holocaust, are prey to an epic intention that the ordinary novel cannot bear. *Not of This Time, Not of This Place* and *Adam Resurrected* are seriously overwritten works, and *The Chocolate Deal* suffers from too polarized a moral vision. The alternative in fiction is the multi-volume works of Naomi Frankel and Yonat and Alexander Sened, and their methods of programmatic historical reconstruction. In poetry both Kovner and Pagis also have epic intentions; they do not simply write discrete lyric poems. Yet, not only do they return to the subject of the Holocaust at various times, but as poets their medium permits and encourages them to speak of large things with slender means.

Abba Kovner is a unique figure in Israeli literature. Born in 1918, Kovner was active before the war in the left Zionist youth movement Hashomer Hatsair in Poland. During the Holocaust, he was a commander of resistance in the Vilna ghetto, and after escaping the city, a leader of partisan groups in the forest around Vilna, and later a leader of the Briḥah movement to Palestine. He settled on Kibbutz Ein Hahoresh and served as an officer in the Givati brigade in the War of Independence, about which he wrote a fictional trilogy, *Panim el panim* (Face to Face) (1953–1956). Because

Kovner's poetry, like his biography, has bridged the moments of the Holocaust and the struggle for independence, he has spoken within Hebrew letters as a persona grata, with the special authority of both a survivor *and* a Palmah fighter, all the more so because his identity as a survivor was that of a fighter as well.

"Hamafte'ah tsalal" (The Key Sank) (1950 and 1965), like a number of Kovner's compositions, displays an epic form.[10] The twelve brief chapters of the poem of some fifty pages encompass the entry of the Nazis into an East European city, the sealing off of the Jews into a ghetto enclosure, the formation of resistance units, the escape of a lone partisan, the beginnings of the liquidation of the city. What permits Kovner to deal with such a broad sweep of events successfully is a combination of reductive procedures. From "In the City of Slaughter" Kovner has adopted Bialik's technique of radical metonymizing in the representation of catastrophe. The poet avoids the pathos of the relations between victim and victimizer by relaying almost all of the dramatic action through a series of inanimate metonymical counters: the river, the fence, the wall. The fence, for example, functions as a depersonalized stand-in for the Nazis as they go about preparing the Jews for liquidation; but the fence is also grotesquely reanimated and made a witness, like the river, of the atrocities committed in its view. Kovner always employs a perceptual origin for viewing events which is oblique, deflationary, and unsentimental. In the opening of the poem, the bombing of the city, which is an anticipation of what is to follow, and the Jews' dazed reaction to it, are presented from the dual points-of-view of a crow circling the city and a goat standing impassively on the roof of a house. Kovner also employs a dramatic and imagistic minimalism that owes something to both modernist verse and the newsreel techniques of film. "The Key Sank" consists of a series of compressed and truncated poetic gestures, staccato in tempo and atonal in musical quality; the poet relies upon the reader's willingness to construct the frames of reference that connect these gestures and, like Appelfeld, upon the reader's competent knowledge of the terrible events that supply the contexts. This is a scene of confrontatioin between the Nazi commander and the city's Jews:

He laughed at the Thousand
All the Thousand wept.

He screamed at the Thousand
The Thousand smiled.

He became silent—
The Thousand knelt down.

(p. 134)

There are no personal or proper names throughout the text; Kovner operates with a series of depersonalizing fixed epithets: the Jewish community is "the Thousand," in contrast to the partisan who escapes, who is called "the one"; the Nazi is simply "he." This nominative one-dimensionality contributes to the comic-strip character of the scene as a whole, which consists of a series of actions stripped of the least nuance or shading of meaning. These actions are grouped in three pairs (laughter/weeping, screaming/smiling, silence/kneeling), and and the text requires us to imagine a dramatic situation in which each action in the pair would be a plausible response to the other and in which the sequence of the three pairs would become part of an intelligible narrative. Kovner succeeds in suggesting much more of the ominousness of this encounter this way than if he actually supplied such words as "mortification" and "groveling."

It is not only techniques of expression that Kovner carries over from Bialik. His indictment of the Jewish victims bears the same sardonic unforgivingness as his precursor's. The Jewish community, conceived of as an undifferentiated mass called the Thousand, faces its rapidly deteriorating situation with bovine insensibility. Animal similes abound: The trepidation of daily life in the Exile has been domesticated like a house cat (p. 142); the Jews who file out to inspect the fence built around them are compared to a procession of ants (p. 143). The ridicule of millennial faith is also familiar. The glistening dew on the ghetto fence is refracted in the imagination of the faithful into the horns of the redemptive ram dispatched by God in the Akeda story (p. 138). (Kovner plays on the parodic rhyme *tayil,* "barbed wire" / *ayil,* "ram.") Just at the midpoint of "The Key Sank," however, there is an event that breaks the Bialik-like wrath. A single voice disentangles itself from the mass and takes stock of the situation. Without hysterics or false hope, the speaker—who is called "the one" as opposed to the Thousand—sees clearly the end that is being planned for the Jews. Since to remain would be to share that fate, he attempts to escape across the river. Against anticipated charges of cowardice, he avers that if there are survivors others can bear witness, say Kaddish, and expire from mourning.

With his successful escape, "The Key Sank" switches its poetic debt, both in theme and in prosody, from Bialik to Alterman. The identity of the partisan becomes fused with the figure of the wanderer (the *helekh*) in Alterman's poetry of the thirties and the figure of the vengeful husband in *Joy of the Poor;* the clipped, metallic rhythm of the first half of the poem gives way to the regular rhythms of the balladic line. The partisan has passed from the world of East European Jewry with its timorous anxieties and lamentations into the new ethos of the vagabond fighter. Renouncing the consolations of home, family, and love, the wanderer embraces the life of the road and accepts the aloneness that goes with it. (He is alone with God, Who, like him, is naked and bereft.) His escape, however, is not a defection. He is committed to return to his people, although he knows that he will come back not as a glorious redeemer but as a mole burrowing beneath the enemies' positions. The way back, paradoxically, is only through wandering, and through life underground. "Like the mole who feels / How the paths seeks out his eyes, / Blindly I drank in the course of events" (p. 172).

"The Key Sank" is the complete Zionist poem on the Holocaust: It encompasses both the decline and destruction of the European Exile as well as the rejection of and escape from it. In the meantime one hides, resists, and fights, but after the catastrophe, and despite it, there remains a separate Jewish reality (though it does not lie within the poem itself) to escape *to.* The figure of the partisan, as it emerges in Kovner's poetry, mediates between the abject image of the victim-survivor and the proud (and evasive) image of the sabra-bystander. Unlike his native Israeli compatriot, the partisan has lived the Exile, and witnessed the destruction; he has not been given the opportunity for evasion. The fact of the partisan's speaking in the first person in "The Key Sank," and the fact of Kovner's own well-known participation in the War, combine to create an autobiographical myth of great authority in Hebrew letters. It is a myth of great acceptability, as well, because it operates within the Bialik-Alterman literary-political fusion, extending it to the Holocaust but not essentially tampering with it.

The Holocaust poetry of Dan Pagis (b. 1930), similarly based on an autobiographical myth, is utterly different. The autobiographical figure in Pagis is unassimilable and irrelevant to Jewish national existence, just as the lives of Appelfeld's survivors are in Jerusalem but not of it. The contrast is even more salient: Pagis' Hebrew style is at once more classically Judaic and colloquially Israeli than Appelfeld's. Yet this specificity of national and cultural reference in language only ironically underscores the estrangement of the self from participation in nation and culture in life.

In life. . . . Much of Pagis' poetry is devoted to a subtle exploration of the alternatives to life. To survive your death does not mean to live. The status of the survivor is liminal and ambiguous. He is already dead, yet existent. His fate is this-worldly immortality. In the following poem Pagis establishes a mythic conception of this state of being.

AUTOBIOGRAPHY

I died with the first blow and was buried
among the rocks of the field.
The raven taught my parents
what to do with me.

If my family is famous,
not a little of the credit goes to me.
My brother invented murder,
my parents invented grief,
I invented silence.

Afterwards the well-known events took place.
Our inventions were perfected. One thing led to another,

orders were given. There were those who murdered in their own
  way,
grieved in their own way.

I won't mention names
out of consideration for the reader,
since at first the details horrify
though finally they're a bore:

you can die once, twice, even seven times,
but you can't die a thousand times.
I can.
My underground cells reach everywhere
When Cain began to multiply on the face of the earth,
I began to multiply in the belly of the earth,
and my strength has long been greater than his.
His legions desert him and go over to me,
and even this is only half a revenge.[11]

Often in his poetry Pagis ventriloquizes through a persona. In this
case the title makes the relationship of the speaker to the poet
special. Although after a few lines we identify the speaker as the
biblical Abel, there is a sufficient interval of uncertainty in the first
reading to create the expectation that the body of the poem will
be an autobiographical statement in the poet's own name. The
identification of Abel does not entirely take this away. Pagis begins
Abel's story at the point at which the Bible concludes it—with death.
The persistence of a speaking subject forces us to imagine the
conditions in which speech continues to be possible. Even the fact
of speech is put in question. Although Abel is the member of the
family who invented silence, and even perfected it, it is he who
speaks the poem, making the poem discourse of a very peculiar
sort.

The inventions of his brother and parents, murder and grief,
constitute the substance of life above ground. The perfection and
proliferation of these institutions over time are spoken of in a tone
of extreme banality, as if to say that this, the manifest history of
humanity, that which we imagine to be all there is, is not what is
important. The real life is beneath the surface of life; over the ages

Abel has been establishing his dark kingdom underground. If Cain has multiplied in clamorous and familiar ways, Abel has increased with silent tenacity, like the spreading cells of a cancerous infection or a virulent ideology. It is in the nature of Cain to strengthen Abel; each innocent victim of historical strife becomes a defector to Abel's spectral subterranean domain.

Between these two camps the reader is not allowed to remain neutral. When we first read the lines "you can die once, twice, even seven times, / but you can't die a thousand times," we hear this utterance as a commonplace observation on the shared nature of things, taking the "you" as "one." Yet when the speaker says in the next line, "I can," the effect is to turn the "you" into "you the reader, as opposed to me." There is, now, no condition which the speaker and the reader can share. He is completely other; and we become not simply the readers of a poem but citizens of the surface world for which the only modes of being are murder or grief. Once you become a victim yourself, you go over to him.

"Karon ḥatum" (Sealed Transport) is the most accomplished short poem cycle on the Holocaust in Hebrew verse.[12] Pagis continues here to explore the liminal state of survivorhood and to employ a confessional mode of first-person discourse. But the materials for his personal shift from the primal family (though it briefly appears here as well)[13] to the common stock of Jewish doctrines about the nature of God. The metaphor for the survival of the victim is less the fungal, subterranean growth of "Autobiography" than a phantom, a disembodied wraith, which darts in and about the corners of existence.

The very origin of survival in these poems is as a mistake, a banal administrative error. The phantom figure makes his appearance in "Hamisdar" (The Roll Call), which describes the frustration of a conscientious concentration camp officer when he discovers that he is short one prisoner at the morning lineup. Abruptly the poem continues and concludes:

> only I
> am not there, am not there, am a mistake,
> turn off my eyes, quickly, erase my shadow.

> I shall not want. The sun will be all right
> without me: here forever. (pp. 23/25)

The speaker rushes to take advantage of this unexpected and random slip in procedure; he quickly erases all signs of his corporeality. His exaltation at the prospect of escape is expressed in the stammering repetitions. His anticipation of deliverance is rendered in the ambiguity of the Hebrew *Po ehsar,* literally, "I won't be missing (. . . in the roll call)," but which also—as Stephen Mitchell wisely translates it, "I shall not want,"—evokes Psalm 23 and the confidence that God will shepherd his faithful servant. This exuberance collapses in the final, dangling phrase of the poem: "here forever." The speaker abruptly realizes that the price of survival is remaining in this spectral state for eternity. The prisoners will soon be murdered and released from their ordeal; his will go on forever.

The next poem in the cycle seems to be spoken after the fact:

TESTIMONY

> No no: they definitely were
> human beings: uniforms, boots.
> How to explain? They were created
> in the image.
>
> I was a shade.
> A different creator made me.
> And he in his mercy left nothing of me that would die.
> And I fled to him, floated up weightless, blue,
> forgiving—I would even say: apologizing—
> smoke to omnipotent smoke
> that has no face or image.

> (pp. 24/25)

The witness is giving testimony at an undefined procedure, a kind of war crimes trial, whose task is to assign guilt for the events that have occurred. (In the next poem, " 'Edut aheret" [Another Testimony], God and his collaborators, the angels, are indicted for collusion in the primal crime of the creation of man.)[14] Hence, in " 'Edut" (Testimony), the witness is unsophisticated; his speech is conversational and unpolished, halting, as he searches for the right word ("How to explain?" "I would even say . . ."). Yet the theological terms he uses and the statements he makes are anything but ingenuous. In repudiating the commonplace about Nazis' being animals, the witness proposes a dualistic Gnostic scheme as a plausible explanation. Since it was the murderers alone who remained whole and unblemished, then it must be they who are the true corporeal reflection of the creator-God of Genesis ("And God created man in His image"). The speaker was fashioned by another god for whom the body is an inessential aspect of creation. When relieved of his body, the speaker was returned to his pristine state and could gratefully rejoin the source of his being. The weightless ascent of smoke to *its* source parodies the weightless ascent of the immortal soul to the biblical God. The two (demiurge and God) are further joined by Pagis' deft appropriation of the phrase "has no face [literally, body] or image" *(ein lo guf udemut)*, from the *Yigdal,* a synagogue hymn that versifies Maimonides' Thirteen Principles of Faith. In the traditional credo this principle warns against imagining in human terms a God Who is pure spirit and will; but the absence of body and image can apply equally to a creator whose essence is smoke. Pagis' intent is less to parody than to present, with wit, a serious parallel. The poet charts a kind of anti-matter universe: the victims and victim-survivors of the Holocaust inhabit an existence with its own theology and ontology which parallels the created world but is built out of nothingness rather than essence. The conventionally created world of essence has become the possession of the "uniforms" and the "boots."

Yet, although the survivor's being is a possession of the shadow world, he must nevertheless reenter, somehow, the ordinary world as we know it. The precise moment of reentry is brilliantly imagined by Pagis in one of the closing poems of "Sealed Transport," which literalizes the doctrine of resurrection and combines it with conventions of science fiction and espionage fiction.

INSTRUCTIONS FOR CROSSING THE BORDER

Imaginary man, go. Here is your passport.
You are not allowed to remember.
You have to match the description:

your eyes are already blue.
Don't escape with the sparks
inside the smokestack:
you are a man, you sit in the train.
Sit comfortably.
You've got a decent coat now,
a repaired body, a new name
ready in your throat.
Go. You are not allowed to forget.

(pp. 26/27)

Nameless authorities issue these instructions; perhaps they are the servants of the smoke god. The exact moment is the culmination of a process whereby a body has been fabricated for one of the wraith figures. It is not what was formerly his body; it is not even a human body, rather an artificial creation simulated to answer to a set of specifications. His name and identity have been invented to allow him to pass for a man, and he inhabits his new state uncomfortably. Like most double agents, he is coerced into undertaking his mission, his escape route barred ("Don't escape with the sparks / inside the smokestack"). Although the ultimate purpose of the mission is not given, he is clearly being infiltrated into an alien country, where, moving in constant fear of exposure, he will pose as a native.

Pagis' image of the survivor as an invented man, torn between contradictory instructions to forget and to remember, is one of the strongest moments in Hebrew literature. Although the works of fiction and poetry on the Holocaust written in the decade following the Eichmann trial are not numerous or consistently successful, they are studded with such moments of luminous artifice. They supplement the monumental achievements of Greenberg and Appelfeld, making these two masters less austere in their isolation. In remaining true to the experience of the Holocaust, these works have had the effect of undoing the meaning that was hurriedly stamped on the Holocaust in Israeli culture in the years after the war. Literary art has succeeded in stimulating a deeper encounter with the event and thereby put a brake on its premature absorption into a preexisting framework of meaning. There can be nothing more important than this authentic encounter at a time when the Holocaust is variously exploited and appropriated on all sides for its use as a potent political symbol.

The time for interpretation and mythmaking will come. Looking at the course of responses to catastrophe in Hebrew literature as a whole, one is struck by two things: how disconnected the literature of the Holocaust is from the classical traditions and how little time has passed since the events of the war. It took the Rabbis of the midrash generations before they undertook to interpret the Destruction. The literature of the Holocaust in Hebrew is still very much in the making, although a point will soon be reached when the authority of the survivor's voice will cease to play the role it has until now.

The meaning of events is not inscribed in them waiting to be deciphered; meaning is a human construct to be chosen and made. Whether the Holocaust will remain starkly set off by itself or whether it will be drawn into Jewish historical memory is just this sort of choice. To be sure, no age can copy the solutions of another, and the role of tradition in our world can amount to no more than that of a resource in the seeking of a way. Yet the resources of tradition, the spiritual and artistic ingenuity and power of the classical responses to catastrophe, have hardly begun to be explored. In rejecting the decadent and powerless society of the shtetl, Zionism threw out the high culture of Judaism as well. The long estrangement between the contemporary Zionist enterprise and the full Jewish past is ready to be lessened. The encounter is just beginning.

NOTES

1. THE RHETORIC OF LAMENTATIONS

1. "Sumerian Lamentation," S. N. Kramer, tr., in James B. Pritchard, ed., *Ancient Near Eastern Texts Relating to the Old Testament*, 3d ed. (Princeton: Princeton University Press, 1969), pp. 611–619.

2. My assumption in these pages is threefold: (1) although the chapters of Lamentations are probably the work of different authors, (2) each chapter displays a discernable unity and can be treated as a coherent whole produced by a principal author, and (3) the design of the whole book is the result of an informed redactional intention.

3. All translations are from *The Five Megilloth and Jonah* (Philadelphia: Jewish Publication Society of America, 1969).

4. Chayim Cohen, "The 'Widowed' City," in *The Gaster Festschrift, Journal of the Ancient Near East Society of Columbia University*, 1973, 5:75–81.

5. The controversy is conveniently summarized by Delbert R. Hillers in *The Anchor Bible: Lamentations* (Garden City: Doubleday, 1972), pp. 61–65.

6. Hillers, pp. 64, 73. See also Robert Gordis' concept of "fluid personality" in *The Song of Songs and Lamentations* (New York: Ktav, 1974), pp. 172–174.

7. Translations are from *The Prophets* (Philadelphia: Jewish Publication Society of America, 1978). For an important treatment of the rhetorical dimension of Second Isaiah, see Yehoshua Gitay, *Prophecy and Persuasion, A Study of Isaiah 40–48* (Bonn, 1981).

8. A summary of the historical background is given by Alexander A. Di Lella in *The Achor Bible: The Book of Daniel* (Garden City: Doubleday, 1978), pp. 38–42. Translations are from this edition.

2. MIDRASH AND THE DESTRUCTION

1. For a summary of the historical situation surrounding the Destruction and the Bar Kochba Rebellion, see Salo W. Baron, *A Social and Religious History of the Jews*, 2d ed. (New York: Columbia University Press, 1952), 2:89–128. For a comparison of the religious responses, see Jacob Neusner, "Judaism in a Time of Crisis: Four Responses to the Destruction of the Second Temple," *Judaism* (1972), 21(3):313–327. On this general subject, see Shaye J. D. Cohen, "The Destruction: From Scripture to Midrash," *Prooftexts* (January 1982), 2(1):18–39.

2. Though material concerning the Destruction is scattered in variant forms over the whole canvas of rabbinic literature during the first eight centuries of the Common Era, fortunately there exists a single midrash collection, Lamentations Rabbah, which brings together most of the traditions bearing on the Destruction in the form of an exegetical commentary on the biblical text. Lamentations Rabbah was compiled in Palestine, most likely in the fifth century—though the traditions it records may go back much farther in time—and it is counted among the four early Amoraic midrashim. Although a certain amount of the materials is also found in the Babylonian Talmud, it seems clear to most scholars that the versions contained in Lamentations Rabbah are prior. Passages are quoted here from the British Museum manuscript as edited by Solomon Buber, *Midrasch Echa Rabbati* (Vilna, 1899), and page references are given according to this edition. In translating passages I have been aided by the English version of the standard printed version of the midrash in the Soncino *Midrash Rabbah*.

3. See David M. Stern, "Interpreting in Parables: The Mashal in Midrash, With Special Reference to Lamentations Rabba," Ph.D. Dissertation, Harvard University, 1980; and "Rhetoric and Midrash: The Case of the Mashal," *Prooftexts* (September 1981), 1(3):261–291.

3. MEDIEVAL CONSUMMATIONS

1. Some of these formulations derive from the thinking of Gerson D. Cohen put forward in his seminal essay "Messianic Postures of Ashkenazim and Sepharadim," in Max Kreutzberger, ed., *Studies of the Leo Baeck Institute*, pp. 115–158 (New York: Ungar, 1967), and in various scholarly lectures which have not yet appeared in print.

2. Salo W. Baron, *A Social and Religious History of the Jews* (New York: Columbia University Press, 1958), 4:89.

3. Shlomo Eidelberg, ed., *The Jews and the Crusades: The Hebrew Chronicles of the First and Second Crusades*, Shlomo Eidelberg, tr. (Madison: University of Wisconsin Press, 1977), p. 110. The Hebrew text of the chronicles as well as that of the piyyutim may be found in A. M. Habermann, *Sefer gezerot Ashkenaz veTsarfat* (Jerusalem, 1945). See also Robert Chazan, "The First-Crusade Chronicles," *Revue des Etudes Juives* (1974), 133:237–254, and "The Hebrew First Crusade Chronicles: Further Reflections," *Association for Jewish Studies Review* (1978), 3:79–89.

4. Eidelberg, p. 114.

5. *Sefer yosifon*, vol. 1, David Flusser, ed. (Jerusalem, 1978), pp. 311–319, 425–431.

6. See Ivan G. Marcus, "From Politics to Martyrdom: Shifting Paradigms in the Hebrew Narratives of the 1096 Crusade Riots," *Prooftexts* (January 1982), 2(1):40–52.

7. The great exposition of this theme is Shalom Spiegel's *The Last Trial*, Judah Goldin, tr. (New York: Schocken, 1967). See also the Akedah piyyut *Adonai tsaddik yivḥan*, Habermann, p. 111.

8. See Proverbs 3.12, Job chs. 33ff. George Foot Moore, *Judaism in the First Centuries of the Christian Era*, (New York: Schocken, 1971), 1:546–552; and E. E. Urbach, *Ḥazal, pirkei emunot vedeʿot* (The Sages: Their Concepts and Beliefs) (Jerusalem, 1971), pp. 393–396.

9. Habermann, p. 31.

10. Habermann, pp. 105–106.

11. Habermann, pp. 69–71. All but the central three stanzas are translated in T. Carmi, *The Penguin Book of Hebrew Verse* (New York: Penguin, 1981), pp. 374–375.

12. An additional consummation theme involves an equivalence between the martyrdoms and the giving of the Torah at Sinai and the days of preparation preceding it. The massacres took place late in the month of Sivan and early Iyyar around the time of Shavuʿot.

13. Baron, pp. 147–149.

14. See my "The Song at the Sea and the Question of Doubling in Midrash," *Prooftexts* (1981), 1(2):185ff.

15. Y. M. Elbogen, *Hatefilah biyisraʾel (Der Jüdische Gottesdienst)*, Yehoshua Amir, tr., Y. Heinemann et al., eds. (Tel Aviv, 1972), p. 74, passim.

16. Rabbi Abraham, *Adabrah betsar ruḥi;* Habermann, p. 62.

17. Y. Halprin, ed., *Sefer Yeven Metsulah* (Tel Aviv, 1966).

18. See Jacob Katz's important article, "Between 1096 and 1648" [Hebrew], *Sefer yovel leʾYithak Baer* (Fritz Baer Jubilee Volume) (Jerusalem, 1961), pp. 318–337.

19. See above, chapter 2.

20. Y. H. Yerushalmi, *Zakhor: Jewish History and Jewish Memory* (Seattle: University of Washington Press, 1982), pp. 49–52; see also Robert Chazan.

4. THE RUSSIAN POGROMS AND THE SUBVERSION OF THE MARTYROLOGICAL IDEAL

1. See my "Guenzburg, Lilienblum, and the Shape of Haskalah Autobiography," *AJS Review* (1979), 4:71–111.

2. See Dan Miron, "The Background of the Dilemmas of Hebrew Literature at the Beginning of the Twentieth Century" [Hebrew] in *Sefer hayovel le-Shimʾon Halkin* (Simon Halkin Jubilee Volume) (Jerusalem, 1975), pp. 419–487.

3. Richard Pipes, paper delivered at a conference, "Perspectives on the Pogroms of 1881 and Their Aftermath," Harvard Center for Jewish Studies, December 14, 1980.

4. Salo W. Baron, *The Russian Jew Under the Tsars and the Soviets* (New York: Macmillan, 1964), pp. 51–56.

5. Baron, p. 87.

6. Pipes, lecture.

7. "My Sister Ruhamah" was first published in *Migdanot*, a supplement to *Hamelits* (1882), vol. 20.

8. Israel Klauser, "The Pogroms in Russia at the beginning of the 1880s in Poetry and Prose," *He'avar* (1962), 9:7–15.

9. Hayyim Jonah Gurland, *Lekorot hagezerot ʿal yisraʾel* (Sources for the History of the Persecutions of Israel) (Przemysl, 1887–92).

10. Adolf Neubauer, ed., *Hebäische Berichte über die Judenverfolgunge während der Kreuzzüge* (Berlin, 1892).

11. *Divrei yemei yisraʾel*, 8 vols. (Warsaw, 1890–1902).

12. Solomon Buber, *Midrasch Echa Rabbati* (Vilna, 1899).

13. *Kol kitvei Mendele Mokher Sefarim* (Tel Aviv, 1958), p. 384.

14. *Ibid.*, p. 384.

15. *Ibid.*, pp. 444–448.

16. *Ibid.*, p. 444.

17. *Ibid.*, p. 446.

18. Saul Tchernichowsky, *Shirim*, 2 vols. (Tel Aviv, 1966), 2:523–550. References will be to pages in this edition. The poem was begun in Odessa in the late 1890s and finished in Heidelberg in 1900. It should be noted how long before Kishinev, with which "Baruch of Mainz" is often associated, the poem was actually written. For the rather complicated publishing history of the poem, which involved problems with the censor, see Joseph Klausner, *Shaʾul Tshernikhovski, haʾadam vehameshorer* (Saul Tchernichowsky, The Man and the Poet) (Jerusalem, 1947), pp. 86–91.

19. A. B. Habermann, *Gezerot Askenaz veZarfat* (Jerusalem, 1945), pp. 37–38.

20. See Yosef Haefrati, *Haʾidilyah shel Tshernikhovski* (The Idyll in Tchernichowsky) (Merhavyah and Tel Aviv, 1971).

21. See the piyyut "Kelalah veshamta" in Habermann, pp. 105–106.

22. Klausner reports that in addition to the curses, the most admired and anthologized section of the poem was the description of the coming of night in the idyll.

23. Translated in Nahum N. Glatzer, ed., *The Language of Faith* (New York; Schochen, 1967), p. 194.

24. Baron, *The Russian Jew under the Tsars*, pp. 67–69.

25. For an exhaustive historical survey of this territory with publication details of the poems mentioned here, see A. R. Malakhi, "The Kishinev Pogroms as Reflected in Hebrew and Yiddish Poetry" [Hebrew] in Getzel Kressel, ed., *ʿAl ʾadmat Besarabiah* (On Bessarabian Soil), 3 vols. (Jerusalem, 1963), 3:1–98.

26. "In the City of Slaughter" was published with the title "Massaʾ Nemirov" ("The Prophecy of Nemirov") in Ben Zion Katz, ed., *Hazeman* (1904), vol. 3. The title, which refers to 1648, was used to satisfy the censor's demand for nontopicality. The poem was published as "In the City of Slaughter" in pamphlet form in 1905–1906 together with two other poems. The pamphlet was titled *Mishirei hazaʿam* (Songs of Wrath) and included the restoration of several censored lines. The Yiddish version ("In a shkhite shtot"), in which the poem gained wide diffusion, was done by Bialik himself in 1906 upon Peretz's failure to render a translation that satisfied Bialik. The Yiddish version is not a translation so much as a new version with its own artistic integrity.

27. Some of the testimonies that Bialik took down have been published by Israel

Halpern, ed., *Sefer hagevurah: antologyah historit-sifrutit* (The Book of Heroism: A Historical-Literary Anthology), 3 vols. (Tel Aviv; Am Oved, 1951), 3:4–14. This project, whose first sections were published in 1941, records documents pertaining to Jewish self-defense amidst persecution from Massada to World War I. It was the first book issued by the publishing house Am Oved, and it is an extraordinary example of a Zionist attempt to create a counter-mythology to traditional martyrology.

28. *The Complete Poetic Works of Hayyim Nahman Bialik*, Israel Efros, ed. (New York: Histadruth Ivrith of America 1948), 1:129–143.

29. The only critic fully to address the rhetorical situation in the poem is Menakhem Perry in *Hamivneh hasimanti shel shirei Bialik* (Semantic Dynamics in Bialik's Poetry) (Tel Aviv, 1977), pp. 147–154. Perry rightly identifies God as the speaker and shows how this reversal of the reader's expectations is related to similar phenomena of inversion throughout Bialik's work. His emphasis on God-as-speaker, however, is exaggerated. He makes a rhetorical strategy into the overriding theme of the poem and disregards the more important subject of the poet-prophet. Still, much of Perry's general conception of Bialik's poems as texts that subvert the reader's expectations is appropriate to "In the City of Slaughter," especially as regards the use of the popular pogrom literature.

30. The critic was probably Nahum Syrkin. See Malakhi, pp. 70–72 and p. 79, on David Frishman's criticism.

31. Jules Harlow, ed., *Mahzor for Rosh Hashanah and Yom Kippur* (New York: 1972), pp. 556–559. Also, Chaim Stern, ed., *Gates of Repentance: The New Union Prayerhood for the Days of Awe* (New York: Central Conference of American Rabbis, 1978), pp. 429–442. On the absorption of these texts into a tradition, see the important essay of David Roskies, "The Pogrom Poem and the Literature of Destruction," *Notre Dame English Journal* (1979), 11:89–113.

PART III. INTRODUCTION

1. For a sampling see the anthology edited by Natan Gross et al., *Hasho'ah bashirah ha'ivrit: mivhar* (The Holocaust in Hebrew Verse, A Selection) (Tel Aviv, 1974).

Hanna Yaoz, *Sipporet hasho'ah be'ivrit* (Holocaust Fiction in Hebrew) (Tel Aviv, 1980).

2. The case of the major poet Amir Gilboa (b. 1917), who is often associated with the Palmah generation, should be mentioned here. Scattered throughout Gilboa's work are several original and strong poems (*Yitshak* and *Penei Yehoshu'a*, especially) which proceed from the slaughter of Gilboa's immediate family to a larger sense of loss and impotence. See Robert Alter, "A Poet of the Holocaust," *Commentary*, November 1973, pp. 60–61.

3. For the postwar Buczaz material, see Sidra DeKoven Ezrahi, "Agnon Before and After," *Prooftexts: A Journal of Jewish Literary History*, 3(1):78–94. Other stories of Agnon's include "'Im kenisat hayom" and "Layla min haleilot."

4. My thanks to Ilan Avisar, whose graduate paper (Comparative Literature, Indiana University) surveys the treatment of the Holocaust in six Israeli plays.

5. Charles S. Liebman and Eliezer Don-Yehiya, *Civil Religion in Israel: Traditional Religion and Political Culture in the Jewish State* (Berkeley: University of California Press, 1983), ch. 4.

5. URI ZVI GREENBERG IN *STREETS OF THE RIVER*

1. See especially the poem "Hazkarat neshamot" in *Anakreʾon ʿal kotev haʿitsavon* (Tel Aviv, 1928), p. 49, and the manifesto *Kelapei tishʿim vetishʿah* (Tel Aviv, 1928), p. 26.

2. In *Hagavrut haʿolah* (Tel Aviv, 1927), p. 26.

3. For a description of the general features of German Expressionism, see Walter H. Sokel, *The Writer in Extremis* (Palo Alto: Stanford University Press, 1959), especially chs. 1 and 2. On the poetics of Greenberg's verse, see Benjamin Hrushovski, *Ritmus haraḥvus—halakhah umaʿaseh beshirato haʾekspresiyonistit shel Uri Tsvi Greenberg* (The Theory and Practice of Rhythm in the Expressionist Poetry of U. Z. Greenberg) (Tel Aviv, 1978).

4. Jerusalem and Tel Aviv, 1954, 2d ed. All translations are mine. All page references are to this edition.

5. Examples are 94–95, 103–104, 158–159, 236–237.

6. See Arnold Band, "The 'Rehabilitation' of Uri Zevi Greenberg," *Prooftexts* 1(3):316–326.

7. This poem was one of the first from *Streets of the River* to be published in a periodical (*Haʾarets*, August 8, 1945), and it was one of the first pieces of Greenberg's writing to appear after the public silence of the war years. For the publishing history of the individual poems of *Streets of the River,* see the important volume by Yohanan Arnon, ed., *Uri Tsvi Greenberg, bibliografiyah shel mifʿalo hasifruti umah shenikhtav ʿalav* (Uri Zevi Greenberg: A Bibliography of his Literary Work and Criticism on It, 1912–1978) (Tel Aviv, 1980).

8. Prose translation by T. Carmi in his *The Penquin Book of Hebrew Verse* (New York: Penguin, 1981), p. 529.

9. See the sensitive analysis of the poem that immediately follows, "Silence's Martyrs" (*Kedoshei dumiyah,* p. 216), by Robert Alter in "A Poet of the Holocaust," *Commentary,* November 1973, pp. 62–63. Alter was the first to identify and appreciate the lyric component of *Streets of the River.*

10. On the figure of the Temple organ, see Gideon Katznelson, "A Key to the Poetry of Uri Zvi Greenberg" [Hebrew] in Yehuda Friedlander, ed., *Uri Tsevi Greenberg: mivhar maʾamarei bikoret ʿal yetsirato* (Tel Aviv, 1974), pp. 137–146.

11. Alter, p. 62.

12. Shalom Spiegel, *The Last Trial,* Judah Goldin, tr. (New York: Schocken, 1967), pp. 86–120.

6. THE APPELFELD WORLD

1. *Badenhaim 1939* (Boston: Godine, 1980) and *The Age of Wonders* (Boston: Godine, 1981).

2. *ʿAshan* (Jerusalem, 1962), *Bagaʾ haporeh* (Jerusalem and Tel Aviv, 1963), *Kefor ʿal haʾarets* (Givatayim-Ramat Gan, 1965), *Bekomat hakarkaʿ* (Tel Aviv, 1968), *Adenei hanahar* (Tel Aviv, 1971). Translations are my own.

3. See Appelfeld's remarks about his changing attitudes toward Bialik's writings in *Masot beguf rish'on* (Essays in the First Person) (Jerusalem, 1979), pp. 87–92. On Agnon's *A Guest for the Night,* pp. 101–108.

4. The idea of primordial catastrophe *(shevirat hakelim)* is echoed here. In public lectures Appelfeld has remarked upon the great influence on him of Jewish mysticism as discovered through the writings of Gershom Scholem.

5. The only other writer in the stories is the sometimes narrator of "Cold Heights" *(In the Fertile Valley*, pp. 135–153).

7. THE UNEASY BURDEN

1. Haim Gouri, *Mul ta' hazekhukhit* (The Glass Booth) (Tel Aviv, 1962), p. 243.

2. Two additional fictional projects are worth mentioning: Naomi Frankel's trilogy *Sha'ul ve-Yohanah* (Shaul and Johanna), 1956–1967, and Yonat and Alexander Sened's two-volume *Bein hametim uvein haḥayyim* (Between the Living and the Dead), 1971. Both works are meticulously researched historical novels of epic proportions. Frankel's trilogy is set in Germany in the decade before the Holocaust and attempts to represent the interplay of historical forces in both Jewish and gentile society that led to the later catastrophe. The Seneds' focus is less historical process than psychological realism. They take a group of students in a Jewish gymnasium in a Polish city and trace their psychological, moral, and spiritual responses to the rise in antisemitism in the late thirties and the ordeals of ghetto and uprising during the war. For a perceptive account of these works see Gershon Shaked, *Ein makom aher* (No Other Place: On Literature and Society) (Tel Aviv, 1983), pp. 78–113.

3. Chaim Bartov, *The Brigade*, David S. Segal, tr. (Philadelphia: Jewish Publication Society, 1968).

4. Yehuda Amichai, *Not of This Time, Not of This Place*, Shlomo Katz, tr. (New York: Harper and Row, 1968).

5. Robert Alter, *After the Tradition* (New York: Dutton, 1969), pp. 167–168.

6. Yoram Kaniuk, *Adam Resurrected*, Seymour Simckes, tr. (New York: Harper and Row, 1971).

7. Haim Gouri, *The Chocolate Deal*, Seymour Simckes, tr. (New York: Holt, Rinehart, and Winston, 1968).

8. Of all the works discussed here, this novel seems like the best candidate for being included in a discussion of Holocaust fiction as a displaced literary idiom, separate from previous national literary histories. See Sidra DeKoven Ezrahi, *By Words Alone: The Holocaust in Literature* (Chicago: University of Chicago Press, 1980), especially chs. 3 and 4.

9. Alter, p. 172.

10. The poem appears in *Mikol ha'ahavot* (Merhavya, 1965), pp. 127–178. Kovner's other major poetic work on the Holocaust is *Aḥoti ketanah* (Merhavya, 1967), which deals with the encounter between Judaism and Christianity through the story of a Jewish girl hidden in a convent.

11. Dan Pagis, *Points of Departure*, Stephen Mitchell, tr. (Philadelphia: Jewish Publication Society, 1981), p. 3.

12. The cycle, except for one poem, is translated in *Points of Departure*. The whole appears in *Gilgul* (Ramat Gan, 1970), pp. 21–27. In the page references here the Hebrew is given first, then the translation in italics.

13. "Written in Pencil in the Sealed Railway Car," p. 22/23.

14. This is the poem omitted in the translation. See *Gilgul*, p. 25.

INDEX